本书为教育部人文社会科学研究规划基金项目（17YJA740050）的研究成果

本书获厦门理工学院学术专著出版基金及厦门理工学院外国语学院资助

A CCAT-BASED MULTI-MODAL STUDY ON
TRANSLATION PROCESS

CCAT平台下翻译过程的多模态研究

王朝晖　余　军◎著

厦门大学出版社　国家一级出版社
XIAMEN UNIVERSITY PRESS　全国百佳图书出版单位

图书在版编目（CIP）数据

CCAT 平台下翻译过程的多模态研究 ＝ A CCAT-BASED
MULTI-MODAL STUDY ON TRANSLATION PROCESS／王朝晖，
余军著. -- 厦门：厦门大学出版社，2023.10
　　ISBN 978-7-5615-9093-5

　　Ⅰ．①C… Ⅱ．①王… ②余… Ⅲ．①一对一翻译（机
器翻译)-语料库-研究 Ⅳ．①H085.3

中国版本图书馆CIP数据核字(2023)第156262号

出 版 人	郑文礼
责任编辑	王扬帆　苏颖萍
美术编辑	张雨秋
技术编辑	许克华

出版发行　*厦门大学出版社*

社　　　址	厦门市软件园二期望海路 39 号
邮政编码	361008
总　　　机	0592-2181111　0592-2181406(传真)
营销中心	0592-2184458　0592-2181365
网　　　址	http://www.xmupress.com
邮　　　箱	xmup@xmupress.com
印　　　刷	厦门市明亮彩印有限公司

开本	720 mm×1 020 mm　1/16
印张	19
插页	2
字数	390 千字
版次	2023 年 10 月第 1 版
印次	2023 年 10 月第 1 次印刷
定价	78.00 元

本书如有印装质量问题请直接寄承印厂调换

厦门大学出版社
微信二维码

厦门大学出版社
微博二维码

前　言

　　翻译作为人类文化交流的重要桥梁,具有深厚的文化底蕴。最初,翻译研究的对象只局限于翻译文本,然而,随着研究的深入和对翻译过程的重视,研究者开始将目光投向翻译过程本身,这无疑扩展了翻译研究的领域。不仅如此,从静态的翻译文本到动态的认知活动,翻译研究在某种意义上实现了质的跨越。而这种变化,不仅象征着翻译研究正朝着更为科学化和实证化的方向稳步迈进,更是为翻译研究开辟了一片更广阔的天地。

　　在翻译过程的实证研究中,研究工具和方法论是首要影响因素。当前,国内外的研究多为实验性研究和动态描述法,数据收集则主要通过有声思维法(thinking-aloud protocols,简称 TAPs)实施。近年来,一些学者开始运用眼动仪、脑电等神经科学工具对翻译过程进行研究,但最受欢迎的研究方法仍是三元数据分析模式,即 TAPs 与 Translog(键盘记录,一个翻译过程记录工具)相结合,以及译文评估的分析模式;然而,键盘记录无法全面揭示翻译过程的全貌。如何获取大规模的数据是另一重要问题。迄今,国内外的研究者们用于实验的对象数量一般不超过 10 人,而且实验次数也往往只有一两次,数据获取相对复杂,规模也较小。此外,目前大部分对翻译过程的研究都集中在传统的翻译模式上,而对于语言服务行业中常见的人机协作翻译过程的相关研究相对较少。

　　本书基于自创的 CCAT(语料库及计算机辅助的翻译)技术应用理论,以翻译过程为研究对象,融入 AI(人工智能)技术,构建语料库与 CAT(计算机辅助翻译)相结合的 CCAT 平台,在 CCAT 平台下对翻译过程进行深入研究。采用了一种比 Translog 记录更全面的屏幕记录法,将翻译过程数据整合成包含文本、视频的多模态双语语料库。通过构建翻译过程的多模态研究模式,分析了多模态实证语料,深入探讨了人工智能背景下翻译过程的微观环节和认知特征,有助于促进翻译过程心理认知研究的发展。基于翻译过程的认知特征,探索 CCAT 平台下的翻译实践及教学模式,以期持续提高翻译训练的效率,促进翻译教学水平的提高。

在研究过程中,应用了基于人工智能的自然语言处理技术。CCAT 在线翻译平台的研发引入了多项创新功能。该平台下的多模态研究方法,将翻译过程的研究从以文本为主(TAPs 法需要将音频转写为文本)的单一模态拓展到包括文本和视频等多模态,实现了更大规模的翻译过程研究。

随着人工智能技术的崛起和不断成熟,翻译过程的研究将进入一个全新的阶段。在这个阶段中,AI 技术的融入将为翻译过程的研究提供更多的可能性,让研究者们能够从更多的角度和层面来审视翻译过程,从而使得翻译过程的研究更加全面和立体。

在本书成稿之际,我们要感谢所有关心、支持本书出版过程的机构和个人。本书获厦门理工学院学术专著出版基金资助,同时,厦门理工学院外国语学院也为本书的出版提供了资助,在此一并致谢! 感谢魏志成教授在学术上给予我们的激励和帮助!

希望本书能引起更多人对于人工智能背景下翻译过程研究的关注。由于水平有限,不当之处在所难免,诚挚地希望广大读者批评指正。

王朝晖　余　军

2023 年 6 月于厦门

目　录

第 1 章　绪论

1.1　引言

翻译过程研究(translation process research,简称 TPR)作为翻译研究的一个重要领域,主要关注翻译过程中的认知机制和心理机制。自 20 世纪 60 年代以来,翻译过程研究得到了迅速发展,研究方法和研究对象范围不断拓宽。

随着人工智能技术与机器翻译的快速发展,特别是神经网络与深度学习的广泛应用,人工智能翻译(即神经网络机器翻译)的性能得到了长足提高,人机协作的翻译模式日益成为主流,但迄今对人机协作的翻译过程本身的理解和研究仍远远不够。

有鉴于此,本研究自主构建了融入语料库技术、人工智能翻译以及 CAT 技术的 CCAT 在线翻译平台,通过录屏技术捕捉学习者翻译过程中的各类信息,构建包含译文文本、翻译过程视频的多模态双语语料库,充分挖掘人工智能背景下学习者在翻译过程中的认知、情感、行为等多层面信息,探索该翻译过程中的规律与特征,以期更全面地深入理解翻译过程的本质。

作为一种新的翻译范式,CCAT 平台下展开的翻译活动,在许多方面有别于传统的翻译行为,而 CCAT 平台下翻译过程的多模态分析模式,有助于深入了解翻译过程的微观环节,对于促进翻译过程的认知研究具有一定意义和价值,主要体现在以下几个方面:

(1)丰富翻译过程研究的方法论。多模态研究方法的引入,有助于突破传统翻译过程研究的局限,为翻译过程研究提供新的视角和方法。

(2)深化对翻译过程的认识。通过构建多模态语料库,本研究能够全面展现翻译过程的复杂性,有助于揭示翻译过程中的认知、情感、行为等多层面现象,从而深化对翻译过程的认识。

（3）提升翻译实践的效率。本研究关注学习者在 CCAT 在线翻译平台上的操作行为和策略选择，有助于了解学习者在实际翻译过程中的需求和困境，为翻译平台的优化提供有益建议，从而提升翻译实践的效率。

（4）促进翻译教学的发展。本研究关注学习者的翻译过程，有助于揭示翻译教学中的问题和挑战，为翻译教学提供有益启示。

1.2 翻译过程研究现状

翻译过程研究是翻译学的一个新兴研究领域。对翻译过程的关注，最早起源于翻译学家 Holmes(1973)《翻译学的名称与性质》一文。

根据郑冰寒(2012)的研究，西方对翻译过程的实证研究经历了探索期(1982—1989)、发展期(1990—1999)、成熟期(2000—2006)等几个阶段：在探索期，研究内容主要为翻译单位、翻译策略等基本问题；在发展期，数据获取以有声思维法(TAPs)为主，但扩大了变量范围，从翻译单位、翻译策略等基本变量拓展到被试的自我形象、翻译态度、任务常规性等变量；在成熟期，以结合键盘记录(Translog)和 TAPs 的三元数据分析模式为主要方法。近年来，翻译过程的研究方法已经跨学科，开始利用神经科学技术进行研究，其中包括眼动仪和脑电图等。

以上分期主要是以研究方法为依据。刘艳春、胡显耀(2022:75)则从理论模式的角度考察了国外翻译过程研究 30 年的发展，将其分为三个发展阶段：20 世纪 70—90 年代的信息加工模型(Nida & Taber,1969;Bell,1991)，90 年代以来的翻译能力模型和翻译认知模型，以及近年来的具身认知模型。

国内学者对翻译过程的研究晚于西方学者，相关研究主要包括认知语言学、认知心理视角(宋志平,程力,2006;刘绍龙,2007;王怀贞,2008;谭业升,2012;王寅,2017;邓志辉,2011;邓志辉,2012)、口笔译过程的认知负荷(王一方,郑冰寒,2020;苏雯超等,2021)、翻译能力与翻译教学(马会娟,2013;胡朋志,2016;郭高攀,廖华英,2016;俞敬松等,2020)、隐喻认知加工(王天翼,王寅,2018)、翻译过程中的选择(胡庚申,2008;曹明伦,2021)、译者身份对翻译过程的影响(许多,2018;聂炜,许明武,2022;李翼,2022)、翻译过程中译者的主体性(宋志平,2000;夏锡华,2007;李庆明,刘婷婷,2011)、研究综述(李德超,2005;王娟,2016;王湘玲,王立阳,2022)、眼动追踪(冯佳,王克非,2016;王一方,2017;王均松等,2022)，以及译后编辑的过程考察(卢植,孙娟,2018)等。

总体而言,这一研究正引起国内学者的关注,但成果相对不多。

与其他翻译研究相比,翻译过程的研究一度是较少有人涉足的领域,但翻译学的研究既要描述翻译结果,又不可忽视翻译过程。以翻译教学为例,吉尔(2008:20)认为,"在翻译培训中,无论是学徒模式还是大学培训模式,无论是在现代语言学系还是在翻译学校,基本操作往往都是注重翻译结果……这种操作有三种弊端"。吉尔(2008:20)同时指出"在注重程序的教学中,关注的重点更多的不是译文本身,而是学员翻译的过程"。可见翻译过程是非常重要的。

近十年来,翻译过程研究的重要性日益引起人们的关注。潘文国(2012:91)认为,翻译过程研究是继作者转向、文化转向、译者转向之后翻译研究的第四次转向,即从对译者的关注发展为对译者的翻译过程的关注,是"翻译过程"转向。

翻译过程研究历经三十余年的发展,已在国内外成为显学,但整体而言,仍存在一些问题,简述如下:

(1)语料获取效率较低,数据规模偏小:目前国内外研究者在翻译过程中通常采用 10～20 人的实验对象,数据收集的方法以 TAPs(有声思维法,需将音频转写为文本)为主,或是 TAPs 与 Translog(键盘记录)相结合。这个过程较为复杂且效率较低,而且通常只有一两次实验,因此数据规模相当有限。这种情况在一定程度上影响了翻译过程研究的发展。

(2)认知语料模态单一,缺乏全貌:目前热门的 TAPs＋Translog＋译文评估的三元数据分析模式以文本为主,并不能展示翻译过程的全貌。

(3)研究对象偏向传统,滞后于时代:目前翻译过程研究关注的主要仍是传统的人工翻译模式,语言服务行业中日趋主流的人机协作模式的翻译过程则罕有相关研究,已滞后于时代发展的需要。

因此,利用比 Translog 记录更全面的屏幕录制法,构建多模态双语语料库,将翻译过程研究由文本为主的较为单一的模态,转向包括文本、视频的多模态,开展更大规模的翻译过程研究,尤其是人机协作的翻译过程研究,将成为翻译过程研究的发展趋势之一。

1.3 多模态语料库与翻译过程研究

1.3.1 语料库与翻译过程研究

语料库翻译学与翻译认知研究之间存在诸多共性,二者最终融合并催生了基于语料库的翻译认知研究这一全新的研究领域(胡开宝,李晓倩,2016: 39)。该领域研究一方面有效克服了传统翻译认知研究的局限性,深化了翻译认知研究;另一方面将语料库翻译学的研究领域拓展至翻译过程和翻译认知研究,从而扩大了语料库翻译学研究的疆域(胡开宝,李晓倩,2016:39)。

翻译中的认知情况在一定程度上可以通过表达出现的频次、词型搭配的数量和认知维度的分布情况反映出来;根据研究目标和研究对象的不同,可使用不同的语料库方法和不同标注类型的语料;除使用双语语料库外,可以单独研究译文语料库,也可以和本族语语料库(含当代语料库和历史语料库)进行对比,以确认译者认知策略的创造性(谭业升,2020:27)。

在国内,基于语料库的翻译过程研究,其实证成果并不丰富。在中国知网中,以"语料库"和"翻译过程"为主题进行搜索,获得的实证研究论文数量极少,仅两篇。刘晓东和李德凤(2022)利用自建的汉英双语平行语料库,对比考察交替传译、笔译和字幕翻译三种不同翻译工作方式的翻译认知加工路径模式;叶文兴(2023)运用基于认知语言学的概念隐喻理论,结合语料库的方法,以《红楼梦》两个英译本中对"死亡"隐喻表达的翻译为例,回溯译者对于此类隐喻表达的翻译认知路径。

国内语料库翻译认知研究呈跟风趋势,独创性、协同性和国际能见度匮乏(刘泽权,朱利利,2019:29)。语料库翻译研究目前主要关注语言及其背后的社会－文化动因,认知维度的研究力度不足,未来研究应加强国际或者区域合作,创建共享语料库平台,拓展研究课题,完善语料库辅助的翻译认知过程研究(侯林平等,2019:69)。语料库翻译学和认知翻译学研究面临发展困境,前者陷入研究结论互相矛盾、研究发现难溯其源的境地,后者囿于研究旨趣重理论轻实验、研究内容"空心化"的窘境(王恒兰,孙崇飞,2022:89)。

Tummers 等(2005:233)认为,考虑到其离线性质,语料库并不适合用来证实语言使用背后的心理过程,因为它不能提供认知过程的直接证据,还需要语料库之外的实验证据的支持。

利用屏幕录制的方法,将翻译过程录制下来,并通过将时间轴与译文关联,形成译文文本＋视频的多模态双语语料库,可以弥补这一不足。

1.3.2 翻译过程的多模态研究

翻译过程的多模态研究在当今学术领域中占据着重要地位。与传统的TAPs(有声思维法)相比,语料库法＋屏幕录制法可以更全面、客观、真实和深入地观察翻译过程。

本研究利用自建的 CCAT 在线翻译平台,通过日常翻译练习自动获取译文文本,利用屏幕录制的方式获取视频数据,并通过时间轴实现文本和视频之间的链接。相较于 TAPs,CCAT 在线翻译平台在操作简便性和可扩展性方面具有明显优势,因此具有较大的实用价值,值得在相关领域推广应用。

多模态研究方法在翻译过程中的应用,为翻译教学和实践提供了新的视角。通过对学习者翻译过程的多模态分析,可以更好地了解其在翻译过程中的认知、心理和行为特点,从而为翻译教学、翻译质量评估和翻译工具的开发提供有益的启示。

本研究的实施将有助于提高翻译教学质量,使学生能够在实践中更好地掌握翻译技能。多模态研究方法在翻译过程中的应用,还将为翻译教学的改革提供重要依据,推动翻译教学向更加实用、高效和智能化的方向发展。同时,研究成果也将为翻译行业的发展提供重要参考,推动翻译技术和翻译服务水平的提升。此外,多模态研究方法在翻译过程中的应用,还将有助于揭示翻译过程中存在的问题和挑战,为翻译研究者提供更多的研究思路和方法。

在人工智能时代,多模态研究方法在翻译过程中的应用,将为人机协作翻译模式的发展提供有力支持。通过对翻译过程的多模态分析,研究者可以更好地了解人类译者与人工智能翻译系统之间的互动,从而为优化人机协作翻译模式提供有益建议。

翻译过程的多模态研究具有重要的理论意义和实践价值。通过对翻译过程进行全面、客观、真实和深入的多模态分析,可以更好地了解翻译过程中的各种现象和问题,为翻译教学、翻译实践和翻译技术的发展提供有力支持。

1.4 翻译过程研究的 CCAT 视角

CCAT 是将语料库与 CAT 技术相融合的翻译研究范式(王朝晖,余军,2016)。所谓 CCAT,指的是 corpus and computer-assisted translation(语料库及计算机辅助的翻译),其中计算机辅助部分指 CAT 软件,而 corpus 主要指双语语料库,以专门用途双语语料库为主,也包括网络语料库。

CCAT 平台由参与人员、CAT 软件、语料及在线平台构成,是一个完整的系统。

第一,参与人员。包括译者、译文审查者、译评人、出版商、翻译研究者等等。

第二,CAT 软件。在国内外多款 CAT 软件中,雪人 CAT 是最适合 CCAT 平台的,因为其句子对齐功能强大,软件易用性突出,功能符合 CCAT 需要,且性价比高,支持定制。

第三,语料。包括单语语料库、双语语料库,以及 CAT 软件的翻译记忆库及术语库。语料库研究领域的语料库多用于翻译研究,CAT 领域的翻译记忆库和术语库则侧重于翻译应用。之前学界很少注意到两者的关系,其实两者是相辅相成的,代表同一事物的理论和应用两个方面。双语语料库与翻译记忆库可以轻易便捷地相互转化,CAT 的术语库也可以从双语语料库中提取。

第四,在线平台。在线平台指语料库及翻译记忆库、术语库的网络平台,可以是共享性质的,也可以是收费性质的,视将来的发展而定,可能两种都会存在,只是语料规模不一样。这一在线平台和 CAT 软件是联系 CCAT 系统中译者、译文审查者、译评人、出版商、翻译研究者的纽带。

CCAT 这一理论包括应用和研究两个层次的内涵。应用方面,不论是文学翻译,还是非文学翻译,如果在语料库及 CAT 的共同辅助下进行,在翻译准确性、翻译效率等方面都将有可观的改善;研究方面,不论是语料库翻译学研究,还是 CAT 研究,唯有二者融合,优势互补,方能深入下去,突破瓶颈,开辟一方新的天地。

以上有关 CCAT 的阐述,详见《基于 CAT 及语料库技术的电子商务翻译研究》(王朝晖,余军,2016)一书。

在人工智能时代,机器翻译迅猛发展,质量越来越高,各种人工智能应用也突飞猛进,如 AI 纠错、AI 改写、AI 语音识别、AI 文字识别等等。在这一背景下,我们将 CCAT 的界定扩大为语料库(corpus)＋CAT(computer-assisted translation)①。

作为一种新的翻译范式,CCAT 平台下展开的翻译活动在许多方面有别于传统的翻译行为,值得进行深入研究和探讨。本研究在 CCAT 平台下展开实验,将实验对象的翻译过程以译文文本、译者评注、屏幕录制的形式记录下来,构建多模态双语语料库,对 CCAT 平台下的翻译过程进行基于实证的深入研究,在理论方面具有一定创新。

---

① 书中凡 CAT 皆指 CCAT 中的 CAT 部分,包括机器翻译、其他 AI 应用、Python(一种编程语言)、AIGC(生成式人工智能)和在线翻译平台,以及传统的 CAT 软件,如 Trados、memoQ、雪人翻译软件等。

第 2 章　CCAT 在线翻译平台的研制

2.1　引言

翻译过程的深入探究,必须在真实的语言实践环境中进行。为此,我们以 CCAT 为理论指导,精心设计并开发了 CCAT 在线翻译平台。该平台集成了语料库技术、计算机辅助翻译(CAT)技术以及人工智能翻译等多种先进技术。

语料库技术的应用,使得译者能够便捷地查阅和参考大量的相关翻译实例,这对提升翻译的精确性和效率起到了关键作用。计算机辅助翻译技术则能够自动处理一些烦琐的翻译任务,如术语的一致性检查和重复句子的翻译,从而使译者能够更专注于处理复杂的语义转换问题。人工智能翻译技术是 CCAT 在线翻译平台的一大特色,通过嵌入多种人工智能机器翻译工具,译者可以在翻译过程中参照比较多种机器译文,从而提升翻译效率。

这些技术的融合,使得 CCAT 平台能够精准地复现人机协作模式下译者的翻译过程和翻译环境,提供更为真实、全面的语言实践环境,从而更好地服务于翻译过程的研究。

2.2　研制背景

当前,作为全球共同关注的技术创新焦点之一,人工智能的发展热潮推动了信息技术革命的深化,使技术进步对就业的影响演进到自动化和智能化阶段。人工智能的迅速发展深刻改变着人类社会生活,形成巨大的市场需求(张爱玲等,2018:88)。人机结合,亦即人机协作的翻译模式成为行业趋势。云翻译技术发展迅速,各种翻译平台涌现,如译马网、Tmxmall、LanguageX 等。

图 2-1　CCAT 在线翻译平台首页

随着人工智能翻译的兴起,对翻译教学进行改革、培养具备翻译技术能力的应用型翻译人才的呼吁越来越多。秦颖(2018:55)认为,翻译教学在人工智能的大背景下,需要更多地借助技术手段,培养更高水平的翻译人才,实现人机协同翻译;王湘玲、贾艳芳(2018:86)提出理论与实践层面创新具备译后编辑能力的应用型翻译人才培养研究;等等。

但目前可用于翻译教学的翻译技术平台并不多见,译马网和 Tmxmall 等平台只支持术语库和翻译记忆库,不支持自制语料库的检索查询,不支持多个机译对比,等等,这与我们理想中的 CCAT 平台仍有差距。

2.2.1 人工智能翻译的兴起

机器翻译作为 CCAT 平台的核心组成部分之一,其发展历程以人工智能的应用为分水岭,可以划分为传统机器翻译和人工智能翻译两个阶段。传统机器翻译以统计机器翻译为主要代表,现已被人工智能翻译(即神经网络机器翻译)所取代。

自 2017 年兴起的人工智能翻译,其翻译质量相较于传统机器翻译有了显著提升。以谷歌神经网络机器翻译(Google neural machine translation,简称 GNMT)系统为例,谷歌的研究人员在对维基百科和新闻网站的样本句子进行测定时发现,GNMT 在多个主要语言对的翻译中将翻译误差降低了 58%～87%(Wu, Y., et al.,2016:19)。

相较于传统机器翻译,新一代的人工智能翻译已经有了质的飞跃。因此,以传统机器翻译为基础所做的相关研究,包括译后编辑研究,其部分结论可能已经与当前机器翻译的现状不完全相符,需要进行更新。此外,人工智能翻译的深度学习能力强大,其发展进化速度远超传统机器翻译。因此,有关人工智能翻译的研究也需要与时俱进,及时更新。

但有关机器翻译的研究,从已发表的学术论文(崔启亮,2014;崔启亮,李闻,2015;冯全功、李嘉伟,2016)来看,绝大多数是基于传统的统计机器翻译,使学界对机器翻译形成了质量不高的印象;而近年来神经网络机器翻译的兴起,又令人惊呼机器翻译将要取代人工翻译,但迄今鲜有相关实证研究评估其译文质量。

此外,如果不区分传统的统计机器翻译与新兴的神经网络机器翻译,在引述机器翻译研究观点的时候,可能张冠李戴,如《材料类文摘机助翻译的错误剖析》(孙逸群,2018)一文,例证从时间来看,属于神经网络机器翻译,但其引述的李梅、朱锡明(2013)"一项基于 10 万句对的统计分析结果显示,在机译的句法类错误中,最多的是次序,占 35.8%,且错误率与句子的长度成正比",明显是针对统计机器翻译的。《谷歌翻译汉译英错误类型及纠错方法初探》(包凯,2017)一文(以下简称《初探》)分析了谷歌翻译汉译英的常见错误类型。虽然谷歌于 2016 年公布了神经网络机器翻译引擎,但向公众开放的时间较晚;《初探》的例证获取于 2017 年 3 月之前,从译文质量及错误特征来看,为统计机器翻译。

以下从该文中摘取例证,使用谷歌神经网络机器翻译引擎重新翻译,对比两代机器翻译的质量,并探析神经网络机器翻译的错误类型,希望有助于厘清对机器翻译的认识。

2.2.1.1 神经网络机器翻译与统计机器翻译的对比

神经网络机器翻译较之传统的统计机器翻译,译文的流利度显著提升,可读性较高。两者的基本区别是,对于简单的句子,统计机器翻译也可能出现语法错误,但神经网络机器翻译则较少语法错误,其错误往往出现在原文较为特殊之时,如单词存在歧义、句子存在省略、原文带有文化因素,或者原文句式较为复杂等。

《初探》一文所举例证原文都较为简单,但机器译文却错误频出,这是统计机器翻译的明显特点。

较之统计机器翻译,谷歌神经网络机器翻译质量提升的一个方面体现在其对统计机器翻译普遍存在的各种错误,几乎皆能纠正。以下例 1—例 17 按照《初探》所归纳统计机器翻译错误分类列举,译文 1 均来自该文,为谷歌统计机器翻译,译文 2 为谷歌神经网络机器翻译。

1.缺少主语

【例 1】主题是一个靶子,一旦有偏差,就会导致写作不顺畅。

译文 1: The theme is a target, once there is a deviation, it will lead to writing is not smooth.

译文 2: The theme is a target, and if there is a deviation, it will lead to poor writing.

统计机器翻译属于片段式翻译,片段之间常无法在句子层面融合衔接,译文 1 即是如此,"is"前缺少主语。神经网络机器翻译能更好地处理句法问题,如主谓一致、过去分词、双宾语、补足语、同位语、定语从句、状语从句等问题,缺少句子成分的情况已较为罕见。此处将"写作不流畅"译为"poor writing"并无语法错误,甚至注意到了"if"前面要加"and"。

2.缺少谓语

【例 2】又比如计算机的发明者摩彻利和埃卡特基,让每个人的工作更加方便快捷。

译文 1: Another example is the inventor of the computer Mocher and Eckerty, so that everyone's work more convenient.

译文 2: Another example is the inventor of the computer, Mitchell and Ekatki, to make everyone's work more convenient and faster.

译文 1 中,"so that"后的名词短语缺少谓语动词,而译文 2 采用的是"make+宾语+宾补"结构,无需谓语动词。

【例 3】清华大学的学术成果受到中国公众的关注。

译文 1: Tsinghua University's academic achievements by the Chinese public attention.

译文 2: The academic achievements of Tsinghua University have attracted the attention of the Chinese public.

译文 1 没有谓语动词,译文 2 则句子成分完整,不存在语法错误。

3.句子不全

【例 4】而中国学生却并不了解这些规则。

译文 1: While Chinese students do not understand these rules.

译文 2: Chinese students do not understand these rules.

译文 1 为 while 引导的状语从句,缺少主句。译文 2 略去"而"不译,纠正了这一错误。

【例 5】而华侨痛恨卖国。

译文 1: While overseas Chinese hate the traitorous country.

译文 2: And overseas Chinese hate selling countries.

与上例一样,译文 1 缺少主句;译文 2 将"而"译为"And",避免了译文 1 的错误。

4.动词重复

【例 6】《英语体验写作》看重'体验'二字,它在消除读者的写作恐惧,帮助他们发现英语文章之美之趣上有着神奇的效果。

译文 1: "English experience writing" value 'experience' word, it is to eliminate the reader's writing fear, *to help* them *find* the beauty of English articles *have* a magical effect.

译文 2: "English Experience Writing" values the word "experience", which has a magical effect in eliminating readers' writing fears and helping them discover the beauty of English articles.

译文 1 出现了"help+名词+动词+名词+动词"的错误结构,译文 2 避免了这一错误。

【例 7】相关规定,在指导思想、帮助我履行义务上有着很大作用。

译文 1: Relevant provisions, in the guiding ideology, to *help* me *fulfill* the obligations *have* a great role.

译文 2: Relevant regulations have a great role in guiding thoughts and helping me fulfill my obligations.

同上例,神经网络机器翻译无语法错误。

5.连词重复

【例 8】但是只是大多数而已,有一部分建筑即使是满足了以上的需求,但也会让人感觉到不够舒适。

译文 1: But only most of it, some of the building even if the need to meet the above, *but* it will make people feel uncomfortable.

译文 2: But only the majority, even if some of the buildings meet the above requirements, but also make people feel less comfortable.

原文使用了两个"但",句式较为复杂,谷歌神经网络机器翻译的译文较统计机器翻译有所进步,但仍存在语法错误,如"but also"前面缺少主语,"But only the majority"应独立成句等。相比之下,360 机器翻译的译文更为准确:But only most of them. Some of the buildings, even if they meet the above needs,will make people feel uncomfortable.

【例 9】虽然女孩们是来自农村的,但是慢慢克服了语言的障碍。

译文 1:Although the girls are from the countryside, *but* slowly overcome the language barrier.

译文 2:Although the girls are from the countryside, they have slowly overcome the language barriers.

神经网络机器翻译译文准确,避免了连词重复问题,补充了统计机器译文缺少的主语"they"。

6.短语重复

【例 10】他一方面努力工作,一方面还积极投资。

译文 1:He worked hard on the one hand, *on the one hand* also actively invest.

译文 2:He worked hard on the one hand and actively invested on the other.

译文 1 重复了"on the on hand",神经网络机器翻译则将第二个"一方面"译为"on the other"。

7.主谓不一致

【例 11】《英语体验写作》看重'体验'二字。

译文 1:"English experience writing" *value* '*experience*' *word*.

译文 2:"English Experience Writing" values the word "experience".

译文 1 主谓不一致,译文 2 不仅主谓一致,还纠正了译文 1 中"'experience' word"这一错误词序。

8.短语错误

【例 12】一篇好的科学论文应该注意控制引用部分和全文的比例。

译文 1:A good scientific paper should pay attention to *control* the proportion of cited and full text.

译文 2:A good scientific paper should pay attention to controlling the proportion of the reference part and the full text.

译文 1"control"应为"controlling",神经网络机器翻译对此做了纠正。

【例 13】本来,一位故人的过失,除了带给我们难免的伤痛外,本应该在平静的悲伤气氛中被渐渐遗忘与接受。

译文 1:Originally，an enemy's fault，in addition to *bring* us inevitable pain，*this* should be in a calm sad atmosphere was gradually forgotten and accepted.

译文 2:Originally, the fault of an old man, in addition to bringing us inevitable pains, should have been gradually forgotten and accepted in a calm and sad atmosphere.

译文 1"bring"应为"bringing"。神经网络机器翻译除纠正了这一错误外,对译文 1 存在的其他错误也做了纠正,如将"this"删除。

9.词性误用

【**例 14**】他只看见了她的丑陋,恨不得快点离开。

译文 1:He only saw her *ugly*, anxious to leave quickly.

译文 2:He only saw her ugliness and wanted to leave soon.

译文 1 的"ugly"词性错误,译文 2 正确。

【**例 15**】长官看到了他的庸俗。

译文 1:The governor saw his *vulgar*.

译文 2:The chief saw his vulgarity.

与上例一样,译文 1"vulgar"词性错误,译文 2 准确。

10.百科知识不一致

【**例 16**】比如年少的瓦特对蒸汽机车的改良,使其大大增加了能源的使用率。

译文 1:Such as the young *watt* on the steam locomotive improvement, so that it greatly increased the energy use rate.

译文 2:For example, the improvement of steam locomotives by young Watts has greatly increased the energy usage rate.

译文 1 错误较多,"watt"未大写;译文 2 除"Watts"应改为"Watt"之外,其他均正确。

【**例 17**】在大学的学习生活中普遍存在着一种叫作'刷脸'的技能。

译文 1:In the university's study and life there is a *popular* called "*brush face*" skills.

译文 2:There is a common skill in the study life of the university called "brushing face".

译文 1"a popular"和"brush face"错误,译文 2 的"a common skill"和"brushing face"更佳。

从以上分析来看,谷歌神经网络机器翻译的质量远胜于传统的统计机器翻译,且能避免统计机器翻译在语法方面的错误,但并非完美,而是仍存在各种错误,只是错误类型从传统的语法层次,转向一些新的错误类型。

2.2.1.2 神经网络机器翻译的错误类型分析

与统计机器翻译相比,神经网络机器翻译错误大量减少,质量大幅提升,但仍存在一些典型错误,且出现了一些新的特征。秦颖(2018:54)指出神经网络机器翻译在翻译的语言单位、翻译的文体领域、译文的多样性和创造性、译文的容错性和稳定性等四个角度存在问题,但未详细分类。

下面将以汉译英为例,对神经网络机器翻译存在的典型错误进行分析。

1.漏译问题

统计机器翻译经常出现片段式译文,但漏译较少;而神经网络机器翻译似乎会尽量从原文中整合出语法正确的译文,其不理解或无法融合的原文更易漏译。

【例 18】看完旧照才知 86 版《西游记》拍摄多困难,致敬。

讯飞译文: After looking at the old photos, I realized how difficult it was to shoot the 86 version of *Journey to the West*.

彩云小译: After seeing the old photos, I realized how difficult it was to shoot the 86th edition of *Journey to the west*

以上机器译文漏译了"致敬"。据我们考察,漏译是神经网络机器翻译中经常出现的问题。

2.音译错误

与统计机器翻译不同,神经网络机器翻译在处理开放式词汇时,容易出现错误,如音译错误。

3.术语翻译错误

神经网络机器翻译基于海量双语语料训练而成,但由于双语术语资源相对双语词典及普通双语句子匮乏得多,目前在术语翻译方面仍存在较大问题,错误较多。例如,"厦门悦华酒店"的官方英文为"C&D Hotel Xiamen",但 DeepL、微软、讯飞、有道、小牛等机器翻译都将其误译为"Xiamen Yuehua Hotel"。

4.语篇层次错误

神经网络机器翻译的翻译单位为句子,不能在语篇层面处理译文,因此容易出现语篇层次的错误,如前后指代不明、缺少衔接、重复等。

【例 19】崔琦是香港培正中学毕业的。培正在 1950、1960 年代培养了极多人才。

有道译文：Cui Qi graduated from Pui Ching Middle School in Hong Kong. Peizheng trained a lot of talents in the 1950s and 1960s.

培正中学的英文名称为 Pui Ching Middle School，第二个句子中的"培正"就是培正中学，但是被误译为"Peizheng"。根据上下文，可用"It"指代，或译为"Pui Ching"。该例说明在语篇层面上，神经网络机器翻译不能辨别词语间的指代关系。

5.原文理解错误

神经网络机器翻译对于一词多义存在理解问题，有时无法辨别原文词义，或者无法理解原文背景，导致翻译错误。如普遍将"贾珍/方要抽身进去"误读为"贾珍方/要抽身进去"，故而将"贾珍"张冠李戴为"Jia Zhenfang"。

神经网络机器翻译仍存在一些与统计机器翻译类似的问题，如翻译基于句子而非基于语篇，语义理解能力存在缺陷，涉及文化因素的内容处理不佳，等等，但总体质量大幅提升，其错误类型呈现的新特征值得重视和深入研究。对其评估应大规模取样，应包括多种文体、多种句式、多种句长。如果样本限于某一种文体，或是样本过少，可能都无法对神经网络机器翻译做出恰当的评估和判断。此外，神经网络机器翻译的发展迅猛，各种翻译引擎纷纷登场，形成了百花齐放的局面。不同翻译引擎各具特点，各有优劣，可以相互补充。因此，在对神经网络机器翻译进行评测时，应该同时考虑多个翻译引擎，方能全面了解其真实的现状。

2.2.1.3 人工智能翻译的演变

秦颖（2018:54）曾分析 GNMT 在词汇和短语层面的挑战，举了汉英翻译的一个例子（2017-10-30 测试），句中"钱春弦""伍梓培"这两个人名，GNMT 分别误译为"Qian Chun string"和"Wu Zhipi"。笔者用 GNMT 重译（2020-11-04 测试），译文已经不同，分别为"Qian Chunxian"和"Wu Zipei"，已不存在误译。另外，句中"壳牌集团在华投资总额"的译文，也由"Shell Group in China total investment"改进为"Shell Group's total investment in China"。这说明人工智能翻译技术一直在进化发展，翻译质量日益提高。

综上，我们认为，对于机器翻译，应有一个全新的认识。人工智能翻译的兴起使得机器译文的准确率大为提高，其进化速度极快，未来翻译模式将向人机协同、人机耦合演变，人机协作的应用场合将越来越多。

2.2.2 人机协作的新特征

人工智能翻译质量大幅提升,与传统机器翻译相比,人机协作出现了一些新的特征。下面以汉译英为例,列举人机协作的几个特点:

1. 语法错误大为减少

人工智能翻译的语法错误已经远远少于传统机器翻译,如:

【例 20】这风气如今已不流行,年轻的父母们,都不愿意以那样古怪的名字来称谓自己的孩子。

译文 1: This trend is no longer popular nowadays, and young parents are unwilling to use such strange names to refer to their children.(百度翻译)

译文 2: This trend is no longer popular nowadays, and young parents are reluctant to call their children by such strange names.(讯飞翻译)

译文 3: This trend is out of fashion nowadays, and young parents are reluctant to call their children by such strange names.(小牛翻译)

译文 4: This is no longer popular, and young parents are reluctant to call their children such outlandish names.(有道翻译)

译文 5: This custom is no longer popular, and young parents are reluctant to refer to their children by such odd names.(微软翻译)

从语法角度来看,该例的 5 种译文均不存在错误。但从语篇衔接的角度来看,5 种机器译文用"and"连接两个句子,语法上虽然正确,却不如"as""for"之类表原因的连词表意准确。

2. 顺句驱动省时省力

顺句驱动为同传术语,指尽量减少语言结构调整的范围和程度。人工智能翻译已经能够胜任较为复杂的句式表达,较少出现传统机器翻译常见的片段式译文,因而适用顺句驱动的高效修订方式,如:

【例 21】北京是中国的政治、文化中心。在这里您可以游览万里长城中的一段——八达岭;明、清两代皇室居住的地方——故宫;清朝御花园——颐和园和北海,还可品尝到正宗的北京烤鸭、涮羊肉。

Beijing is the political and cultural center of China. Here you can visit Badaling, a section of the Great Wall; The Palace Museum, the residence of the Ming and Qing dynasties' royal families; *In the imperial gardens of the Qing Dynast-Summer*

Palace and Beihai, you can also taste authentic Peking duck and Instant-boiled mutton.（百度翻译）

以上译文中"In"，以及"Beihai"后使用逗号是错误的，译后编辑只需按照原句语序，顺句驱动，做局部修订，将"In"删除，将逗号改为分号即可。

3.漏译问题更需关注

统计机器翻译经常出现各种语法错误，但漏译较少，而人工智能翻译则较易出现漏译，如：

【例22】赤子之心，纯净真诚，如初的花蕾，未经岁月沉淀。

Pure heart, pure sincerity, buds as before, without years of precipitation.（小牛翻译）

以上机器译文漏译了"赤子"。漏译是人工智能翻译的常见问题，"遇到不能翻译的词，系统仍会采取'不译'的做法"（秦颖，2018:54），译后编辑时需特别予以关注。

4.机译互补提升效率

传统机器翻译时代，谷歌翻译可谓一枝独秀，译后编辑其实主要是针对谷歌译文而言。而在人工智能翻译时代，多种人工智能翻译引擎争相发展，除谷歌翻译外，搜狗翻译、有道翻译、腾讯翻译、360 翻译、小牛翻译等亦各具特色，各有千秋，有的汉译英质量并不逊色于谷歌翻译，甚至有所超越。通过机译互补，可以提升译后编辑效率，如：

【例23】青青园中葵，朝露待日晞。阳春布德泽，万物生光辉。常恐秋节至，焜黄华叶衰。百川东到海，何时复西归？少壮不努力，老大徒伤悲！

译文 1: The sunflowers in the green garden, the morning dew waiting for the sun to shine. In the sunny spring, all things shine brightly. I am often afraid that autumn will come, and the yellow flowers and leaves of Kun will wither. When will all rivers reach the sea from east to west? A young idler, an old beggar.（百度翻译）

译文 2: Sunflower in *Qingqing* Garden, morning dew waiting for the sun. In the spring of *Budeze*, everything shines brightly. I often fear that the autumn festival will come, and the yellow leaves will decline. When will *Baichuan* go east to the sea and return west? Young men don't work hard, *but old men are sad!*（小牛翻译）

【例24】对中医药而言，无论是自然科学"圣殿"中的这次演讲，还是即将颁发到屠呦呦手中的诺奖，自然都提供了极好的"正名"。

译文 1：For traditional Chinese medicine, *whether* this speech in the "Temple" of natural science *or* the Nobel Prize to be awarded to Tu Youyou, it naturally provides an excellent "rectification". (百度翻译)

译文 2：For Chinese medicine, both this speech in the "Temple" of natural science and the Nobel Prize to be awarded to Tu Youyou naturally provide an excellent "rectification". (小牛翻译)

例 23 中,小牛的翻译存在较大问题,但百度翻译则接近原意,可替代小牛翻译;而例 24 中,"无论……还是……"小牛翻译为"both...and"是正确的,可替代百度的错误译文。对于译后编辑而言,这种译文互补具有重要价值,应善加利用。

虽然人工智能翻译仍存在一些与传统机器翻译类似的问题,如翻译基于句子而非基于语篇,语义理解能力存在缺陷,涉及文化因素的内容处理不佳,译文容易出现格式问题,等等,但总体质量大幅提升。

2.3　设计理念

在人工智能背景下,基于 CCAT 理论(王朝晖,余军,2016)和魏志成(2007)倡导的比较翻译教学法,我们依托阿里云服务器,在 Linux 系统中构建了基于 PHP(超文本预处理器)的在线翻译平台。

2.3.1 CCAT 理论

有关 CCAT,详见 1.4 小节。胡开宝、李翼(2016:10)认为,机器翻译与人工翻译之间是"相辅相成、相互促进的关系"。在人工智能时代,这一关系可能将逐渐演变为"机器为主、人工为辅"。人助机译(人工辅助机器翻译)模式的应用将越来越广泛,语料库及机器翻译的作用也越发重要。我们自建的在线翻译平台依据 CCAT 理论,集成了 CAT 的翻译记忆库及机器翻译引擎,并加入了语料库检索、网络查询等功能。该平台因而命名为"CCAT 在线翻译平台"。

2.3.2 比较翻译教学法

比较翻译教学法是系统地从比较翻译学的角度实施翻译教学的方法,旨在通过多译本的比较,引导学生结合自己的译文参与比较评析,从而提高自主学习能力和翻译水平(余军,王朝晖,2010:57)。基于比较翻译教学法,我们使语料库技术在微观翻译教学环节得到充分应用(余军,王朝晖,2010)。在人工智能时代,具有代表性的机器翻译引擎多达十几种,异彩纷呈;比较翻译教学法倡导的多译本比较与其正相契合,可谓恰逢其时。

CCAT 在线翻译平台的设计以"比较"为核心,不仅可获取 5 种机器译文相互参照,还可以呈现语料检索结果供译者参考比较,有助于提升译者的翻译效率和译文质量。对于译者培训以及翻译教学,该平台亦是不可多得的利器。

2.4 平台功能开发

依据 CCAT 理论,我们设计开发了多种机译支持、机译显示设定(即设定为显示或隐藏机译)、机译替换、语料库嵌入、多种机译比较、术语库、添加评注、多种译文比较、项目管理等创新功能。根据翻译过程的三个阶段——译前阶段、译中阶段和译后阶段,各个阶段的功能分类以及其他功能概述如下:

2.4.1 译前阶段

1.术语库上传

平台支持学生上传自制的术语库,术语库格式为 UTF-8 编码的 txt 文件,一行一个术语,原文与译文之间用制表符隔开。与小牛机器翻译平台支持上传的术语库格式一致。除上传术语库文件外,也支持手工逐个录入术语,如图 2-2 所示。

上传的术语分为个人术语和公共术语两类,学生可以上传个人术语,个人术语仅限上传者使用;公共术语则平台全部用户均可使用,但需要管理员审核才可以上传。

在翻译过程中,系统会自动匹配术语,并弹出提示,如图 2-3。

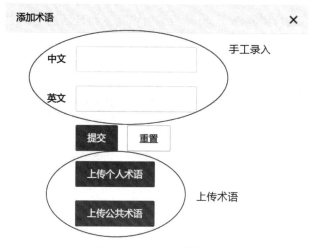

图 2-2　术语上传及录入

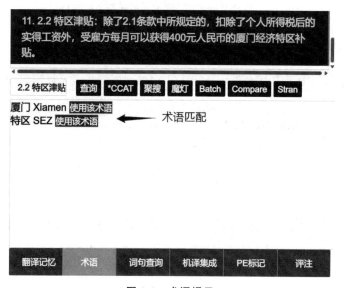

图 2-3　术语提示

2.机译隐藏、显示两种模式设定

平台设计之初,便考虑到翻译训练需要循序渐进。虽然目前在语言服务行业中机器翻译＋译后编辑已成为主流的翻译模式,但并不能一开始就让学生进行译后编辑训练,而要先从人工翻译开始训练,然后逐步过渡到译后编辑。因此,平台需要支持人工翻译和译后编辑两种模式。人工翻译模式下翻译编辑区域不显示机器译文,而译后编辑模式下则显示机器译文。为此,我们设计了机译隐藏、显示两种模式,如图 2-4、图 2-5 所示。

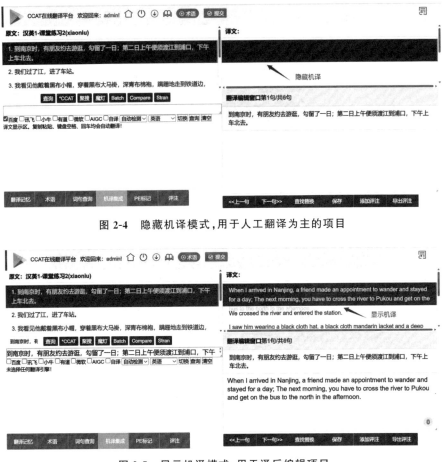

图 2-4　隐藏机译模式,用于人工翻译为主的项目

图 2-5　显示机译模式,用于译后编辑项目

2.4.2 译中阶段

1.支持多种机译,便于机译比较

平台支持小牛、百度、有道、微软、讯飞等主流机器翻译实时显示译文(见图 2-6),并支持 DeepL、谷歌、火山、腾讯等翻译引擎一键查询(见图 2-7)。

图 2-6　多种机译实时显示

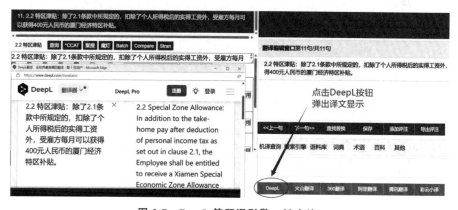

图 2-7　DeepL 等翻译引擎一键查询

2.自译自动显示，避免重复翻译

CAT 工具都具备翻译记忆库功能，译过的句子会自动显示，以避免重复翻译。对于 CCAT 平台而言，除了基本的翻译功能之外，还要为学生提供一个自主学习平台，也就是学生在翻译过程中不可以查看同学已提交的译文，但是练习截止之后,应鼓励其查看、比较同学译文(相关阐述见第 9 章),互评互促。因此,我们将传统的 CAT 工具的翻译记忆功能集成到了 CCAT 平台,以一种可以共享查看的方式呈现,学生在提交译文之后即可查看,但在翻译过程中是无法查看的。因此,需要另一种方式,让学生可以在翻译过程中像使用 CAT 工具一样,译过的句子不用重复翻译。我们为此开发了自译匹配功能,相当于传统 CAT 工具的翻译记忆,如图 2-8。

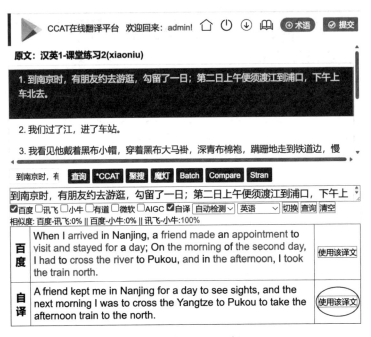

图 2-8　自译匹配示例

有了这个功能,学生译过的句子会自动呈现,只要点击"使用该译文",即可自动填入翻译编辑框,避免重复翻译。

3.嵌入自建大型通用语料库,可一键查询

以一次练习中的"二程"为例,鼠标划过翻译编辑窗口下中文原文的"二程",系统会自动进行网络查询;点击"语料库查询",则会搜索通用语料库。这一创新功能实现了语料库与 CAT 的融合。

如图 2-9 所示,语料库查询结果中出现了"二程"以及"the Cheng Brothers",该英文可作为"二程"的英译。

图 2-9　语料库查询

4.支持搜索引擎、网络词典、在线术语、网络百科等一键查询

除了语料库查询,CCAT 平台还提供了多种搜索引擎、网络词典、在线术语、网络百科等的一键查询。仍以"二程"为例,鼠标划过翻译编辑窗口下中文原文的"二程",该词会显示在下方的查询框;点击"有道词典",则会呈现有道词典中该词的译文(见图 2-10)。

图 2-10　词典查询

其他如搜索引擎、在线术语库、网络百科等的查询方式与此相同。多种搜索资源的汇集极大地便利了学生在翻译过程中的查证操作,提升了翻译效率和翻译质量。

5.评注功能

学生可在翻译过程中添加评注,记录心得、疑问等。评注功能有助于了解学生在翻译过程中的认知思维情况,如图 2-11。

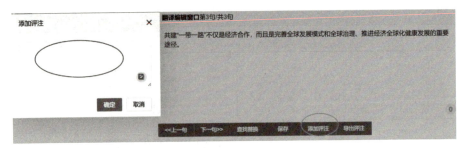

图 2-11　添加评注

2.4.3 译后阶段

1.翻译记忆库支持，可自动显示匹配译文

学生在提交译文之后，即可点击原文句子，查询翻译记忆库中的全部译文（见图 2-12）。管理员可设定翻译记忆库的显示范围，如可设定为仅显示在教学生的译文，往届译文则设为隐藏状态。这一设置主要是便于教师在讲评的时候了解在教学生的情况，在数据统计方面不受往届学生译文的影响。

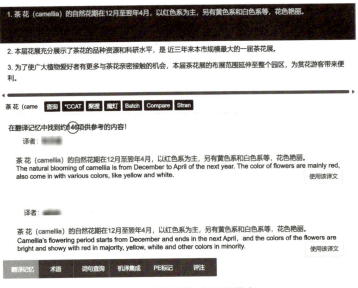

图 2-12　翻译记忆库匹配译文

翻译记忆的查询功能极为方便,学生可借此将自译与参考译文以及其他同学的译文进行比较;教师则可在练习讲评时随时点击查看全体同学的译文。

2.PE（译后编辑）标记功能

该功能可直观显示人工译文或译后编辑译文与机器译文的差异,如图2-13:

图 2-13　人工译文或译后编辑译文与机器译文的差异

3.多种类型的译文比较

在教学中,我们注重引导学生进行多种类型的译文比较,包括自译与其他同学译文的比较、自译与机器译文的比较、自译与参考译文的比较等等。通过多种译文的比较,可以发现不足,取长补短,有助于翻译能力的提升。

学生可点击项目列表中的机译比较按钮及参考译文比较按钮,分别查看自译与机器译文及参考译文的比较情况,如图2-14:

图 2-14　机译比较及参考译文比较查看按钮

两种译文比较的示例请参看第 9 章。

4.项目状态显示

学生在翻译过程中可能会出现漏译或未提交译文的情况。我们在项目列表中设计了项目状态显示功能,学生只要进入项目列表界面,就能清晰地看到所做练习的完成情况,如图 2-15:

跨文化与翻译-翻译实训1.docx(xiaoniu)　　　　　　20220223　未提交　进度 27%

图 2-15　项目状态显示

从图中可以看出,该项目尚未提交,完成度只有 27%,也就是有 73% 的句子未译。项目状态显示功能对于翻译教学中的过程监控和管理非常重要,师生可以实时了解项目进展及完成情况。

5.在线检索评注系统

平台开发了功能强大的在线检索评注系统(见图 2-16),支持两个关键词组合检索,以及排除词检索。可勾选检索结果,填写反馈评注,点击保存后系统自动将反馈评注发送到被评注学生的项目列表中。

图 2-16　在线检索评注系统

2.4.4 其他功能

1.便捷实用的项目管理菜单

可通过"发布""查看""删除""审校""下载"等功能进行相应操作(见图 2-17)。项目管理者通过发布功能可将翻译项目分发给选中的译者或学生。该项目通常用于项目管理者发布项目,或是教师布置练习。点击"查看"则可查看项目原文、译文、评注及 PE 标记。此外,还可通过"审校"功能将项目发给其他译员审校。由于操作极其简便,这些功能大大减少了学习成本,提升了平台的应用效率。

图 2-17　项目管理菜单

2.实践展示功能

平台开发了实践展示功能,学生可观摩欣赏同学的译文。(见图 2-18)在传统教学模式下,学生只能接触到教师的译文或教材中的范例,而无法得知其他同学的译文水平。然而,通过平台的实践展示功能,学生可以直接参考同学们的优秀译文,了解其他同学的翻译技巧和策略。这样一来,在学习过程中,他们可以汲取更多的经验和智慧,提高自身的翻译水平。

实践展示功能还为学生提供了互动交流的机会。通过观摩同学的译文并与他们进行交流讨论,学生可以分享彼此的学习心得和翻译经验,相互学习和改进。这种互动交流的学习模式不仅可以加深学生对翻译技能的理解,还能培养学生的团队合作精神和沟通能力。

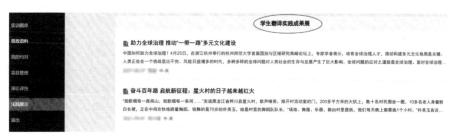

图 2-18　实践展示

2.5 在翻译教学中的应用

2.5.1 三种训练模式

1.笔译 + 平台录入 + 评注

该模式下,学生将练习手写译文,然后誊写入译后编辑教学平台,并添加评注,如图 2-19 所示。

原文	译文	评注	PE标记
到南京时,有朋友约去游逛,勾留了一日;第二日上午便须渡江到浦口,下午上车北去。	When arriving at Nanjing, I was invited by my friend to stroll and stayed for one day. The next morning I had to cross the river to Pukou and get on the train towards north in the afternoon. 翻译过程中的反思	上车在中文中是一个简略的表达,在英文中要弄清具体是何种交通工具。 研读宪益杨先生译文:A friend kept me in Nanjing for a day to see sights, and the next morning I was to cross the Yangtze to Pukou to take the afternoon train to the north. 思考汉译英如何避免"动词肿胀"。 admin	When I~~arrived~~ing at Nanjing, ~~a friend made an appointml~~ was invited by my ~~frientd~~ to ~~wander~~stroll and stayed for ~~e~~one ~~day;~~. The next morning, ~~you~~ I ha~~ve~~d to cross the river to Pukou and get on the ~~bus to the~~train towards north in the afternoon.
我们过了江,进了车站。	We crossed the river and went into station.		We crossed the river and ~~w~~entered ~~the~~ into station.

图 2-19 录入评注

学生在录入过程中,可查看平台嵌入的在线语料库及多种机译译文,并比较揣摩,对手写译文做出反思,添加评注。

2.平台笔译 + 评注

如图 2-20 所示,该模式下学生可在译文输入框进行翻译,可查看左侧 5 种机译,也可通过译文输入框下方的"机译查询"查看其他机译,下方"搜索引擎""语料库""词典""术语""百科""其他"等则提供了丰富的检索资源。学生在翻译过程中有任何疑问、心得,均可在"添加评注"框填写。

图 2-20　平台笔译＋评注

3.译后编辑＋评注

如图 2-21 所示,该模式下学生需对译文输入框的机器译文进行译后编辑。学生在译后编辑过程中有任何疑问、心得,同样可在"添加评注"框填写。

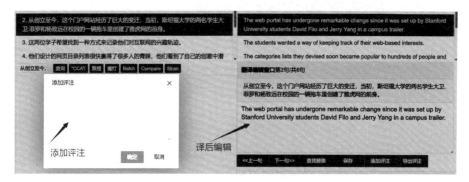

图 2-21　译后编辑＋评注

2.5.2 实时语料促学促教

CCAT 在线翻译平台支持实时生成学习者语料库。学生在提交译文后,可查看已提交的其他学生的译文以及评注(如图 2-22、图 2-23),互相借鉴,促进自主学习。

教师通过查询功能查找学生错误译文,全选后点击"添加评注",即可对选中学生的错误译文进行反馈,学生可在其翻译项目中查看教师评注。如图 2-24 所示,在查询框自动显示的原文中插入" * Wuyi Mountain",即检索出将"武夷山"翻译为"Wuyi Mountain"的错误译文(按照官方译文,应为 Mount Wuyi),教师可通过评注批量反馈。

图 2-22　查看译文

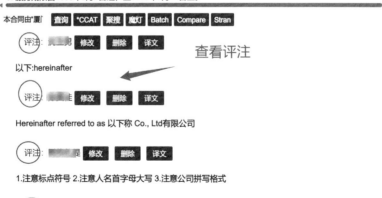

图 2-23　查看评注

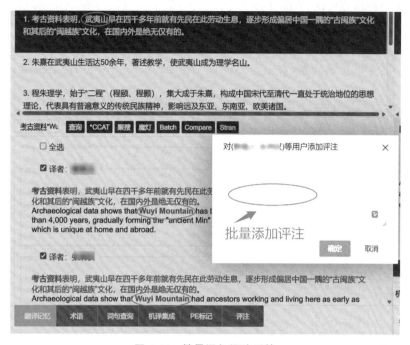

图 2-24　批量添加评注反馈

　　除批量评注外,教师可通过语料检索评注系统(见图 2-16)对学生的译文进行检索及实时评注反馈。

2.6　小结

　　CCAT 在线翻译平台的研制历经多年,共经历三个阶段。第一阶段为2009—2013 年,双语语料库融入翻译教学的微观环节(余军,王朝晖,2010)。第二阶段为 2014—2018 年。以 2014 年立项的省级教改项目"基于 Moodle 的翻译教学平台构建与应用"为依托,我们构建在线翻译教学平台,启动了在线平台的研发之路。之后,提出翻译技术应用的 CCAT 理论(王朝晖,余军,2016)。2017 年,开展基于 CCAT 的在线翻译平台研制工作,直至 2018 年人工智能翻译兴起。第三阶段为 2019—2021 年,依据 CCAT 理论及前期语料库建设和在线翻译教学平台建设经验和成果,在人工智能背景下,成功研制CCAT 在线翻译平台。

　　该平台依据 CCAT 翻译技术应用理论构建,融合第一阶段起研制的多种双语平行语料库、第二阶段研制的在线翻译教学平台、第三阶段构建的多模态双语语料库,以及 2018 年兴起的神经网络机器翻译,具备了 CCAT 界定中在线平台的全部构成要素,有助于基于 CCAT 的翻译过程的多模态研究,亦能有效促进翻译研究与教学的开展。

　　2022 年底,AIGC(AI-generated content,生成式人工智能,即生成式 AI)兴起,发展迅猛。国内具有代表性的大型语言模型相继涌现,包括文心一言、讯飞星火、通义千问、360 智脑、WPS AI 等。这些 AIGC 平台目前均处于内测或试用阶段,后续会陆续开放使用,有的会提供 API(应用程序接口)供第三方平台调用。CCAT 平台未来将接入 AIGC,在原有机器翻译的基础上加入 AIGC 的机器译文,开发基于 AIGC 的译文纠错、译文反馈、译文润饰等功能,并在此基础上进一步开展翻译过程的研究。

第 3 章　多模态双语语料库的研制

3.1　引言

本章详述了多模态双语语料库（multi-modal parallel corpus，简称 MPC）的研制过程，包括设计理念、设计原则、语料来源、建库类型、建库工具和语料标注等。此方案对其他专门用途双语语料库的构建具有参考意义。

同时，本章也讨论了术语库与记忆库的制作和转换，其涉及的技术和工具适用于任何新型专门用途双语语料库的术语库和记忆库的构建。

3.2　设计理念和原则

3.2.1　设计理念

语料库的研制通常针对特定的研究目标，这些目标决定了语料库的性质、构成、规模和后续发展等（黄立波，2013：104）。多模态双语语料库（MPC）的设计理念基于以下两个主要目标。

首先，MPC 旨在融合计算机辅助翻译（CAT）和语料库技术，以实证的方式从理论和实践两个层面深入探讨翻译过程。目前，国内关于翻译过程的研究相对较少，而将 CAT 和语料库技术应用于翻译过程研究的尝试更为罕见。因此，本研究以翻译过程为研究对象，构建双语对应语料库，以期填补这一领域的研究空白。在理论层面，本研究将探讨 CAT 和语料库技术在翻译过程研究中的应用可能性及其对翻译过程理论的启示；在实践层面，本研究将通过收集、整理和分析学习者在实际翻译过程中产生的数据，揭示其翻译过程中的问题和挑战,为翻译教学、翻译质量评估和翻译工具的开发提供有益的启示。

其次,本研究旨在通过构建多模态双语语料库,深化学习者翻译过程的研究,探索 CCAT 平台下人机协作的翻译过程,推动人工智能背景下的翻译教学改革,提升翻译人才培养质量。

MPC 的设计理念是,以应用为主导,突出兼容性,既可用于传统 CAT 工具,也可嵌入自建的 CCAT 在线翻译平台。因此,MPC 不仅包含双语对应语料库,还包括术语库和翻译记忆库;不仅包括单模态语料,还包括多模态语料。

这一新型的双语语料库,提供了与传统的双语语料库以及当代 CAT 技术的双重接口,既有利于语料库翻译学研究向应用翻译领域转向,也有助于语言服务行业人工辅助机器翻译的发展(王朝晖,余军,2016:185)。

3.2.2 设计原则

基于研究目标,MPC 的设计主要遵循以下三个原则。

首先,实施多重复合的对比模式。当前语料库翻译研究的一个显著趋势是打破传统的单语类比或单语类比加双语平行的综合模式,转向根据实际研究需求建立的多重复合对比模式,并由对比模式向过程和因果模式过渡(黄立波,王克非,2011:920)。本语料库由多个子库组成,能够实现多模态文本之间的对比;除了人工译文之间的比较,也可以进行人工译文与机器译文的比较。

其次,强调语料的多用途性。本语料库除了具有可用于检索和分析的单语及双语平行语料,还具有可以用于计算机辅助翻译软件、机器翻译的术语库和翻译记忆库。

最后,注重语料的多模态性。本语料库除了具有文本类型的语料外,还包括图片、视频等其他模态的语料。这种多模态的设计使得 MPC 能够更全面、更深入地支持翻译研究和实践。

3.3　语料界定与建库类型

3.3.1 语料界定

MPC 全部语料按其模态形式划分,包括两部分:单模态语料库,仅含文本;多模态语料库,含文本和视频。

3.3.2 建库类型

①大型通用双语语料库:包括单模态及多模态两部分,其中单模态部分约2 000 万字(词);多模态部分约 200 万字(词),含文本、视频。该通用双语语料库已嵌入 CCAT 平台,供完成翻译项目时查询之用。

②学习者双语语料库:约 120 万字(词),其中单模态部分约 80 万字(词),包含译文及屏幕录制视频的多模态部分约 20 万字(词)。全部语料来自学习者译文,以英专三年级本科生为主;练习选材多样,包括科技、财经、文化、历史、旅游等多个门类。

③参照语料库:包括参考译文语料库,约 1 万字(词),以及人工智能译文语料库,约 5 万字(词)。均为单模态的文本形式,用于与学习者译文进行比较。

④术语库及翻译记忆库:从已构建的通用双语语料库中提取的术语库,以及大约 800 万字(词)的记忆库。

3.4　建库流程

语料库的制作涉及多个环节,需要利用各种软件工具才能完成(王朝晖、余军,2016:187)。

大型通用双语语料库(单模态部分)及参考译文语料库的建库流程如下:

①搜集原文文本及其译文,包括电子文本和纸质书籍;

②电子文本进行降噪、校对,纸质书籍进行扫描识别、降噪、校对;

③原文和译文进行"句对齐";

④人工核对后入库。

在此流程中,电子文本分为可复制文字的文本和不可复制文字的扫描文本两类,其中,扫描文本需要进行光学字符识别(OCR)。整个流程涉及多个传统工具以及人工智能时代的一些新工具的应用。

大型通用双语语料库的多模态部分主要包括多模态演讲语料库。其构建流程与单模态部分有所不同,主要是通过网络获取双语字幕以及对应视频,并通过技术处理,使字幕与视频链接,再通过自建的在线多模态语料库检索平台进行检索。

　　人工智能译文语料库的构建相对简单,通过自建 CCAT 平台获取机器译文即可生成双语语料库。

　　学习者在 CCAT 在线翻译平台完成练习后,可以自动生成单模态的学习者双语语料库。如果在练习过程中进行屏幕录制,则可以将视频与译文链接,形成多模态学习者语料库,此处不予赘述。

　　以下介绍借助 CAT 软件进行的多模态语料库构建方式,该方式无需CCAT 平台,按步骤操作即可完成。

3.5　多模态学习者双语语料库的构建

　　以一次有关长春一汽的文本翻译练习为例,简要说明构建步骤。

　　1.文本预处理

　　多模态学习者语料库的构建,需要对练习文本进行预处理,步骤如下:

　　(1)将翻译练习复制到 txt 文本中,用现代汉语文本预处理软件断句并编号。如图 3-1。

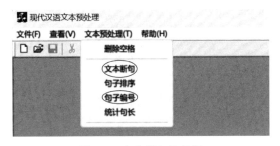

图 3-1　文本断句及编号

　　如图所示,点击文本断句,会弹出文件选择窗口;选择文件,点"打开"即可;断句后,点击句子编号,选择断句后生成的文件,点"打开"即可。

　　(2)使用 PowerGrep 软件对该文本进行处理。在软件中选择"Search and replace",在"Search"框输入"($\cdot$\d＋)(\s)"(引号内为正则表达式,不包括引号,下同),在"Replacement"框输入"＜ch\1＞",点击"Replace",即得到预处理完毕的文本。如图 3-2 所示:

　　(3)预处理后的文件命名需包括课程名称、练习序号和类别,如:汉英 2-课堂练习 2.txt。

<ch3>{00}:{00}{}{00}:{00}第六代J6重型商用车完全自主研发，具备国内领先和国际先进水平。
<ch4>{00}:{00}{}{00}:{00}今年第1000万辆汽车下线，既是辉煌时刻，又是腾飞起点，在成就面前更应保持冷静的心态，反思不足，筹划未来，这是中国汽车人的共识。

图 3-2　预处理后的文本

（4）在雪人翻译软件中新建一个中译英项目，导入练习，并保存翻译项目文件。步骤如下：运行软件，点击"文件"菜单，选择"新建—中译英项目"，在弹出的窗口点击"OK"。右键点击软件界面左边的"项目文件"，选择"导入文件"，选择预处理后的文本文件，点击"打开"。点击"文件"菜单，选择"另存为"，即可保存翻译项目文件。

2.基于 CAT 软件的翻译过程及其录制

在课堂练习环节，教师将制作好的翻译项目文件通过局域网或者因特网共享给学生。学生用雪人翻译软件打开该项目文件，在开始翻译的同时启动屏幕录制程序，将整个翻译过程录制下来。屏幕录制是制作多模态学习者双语语料库的必备环节，实现这一步的关键在于找到适用的屏幕录制软件。软件必须满足三点，一是易用，二是生成文件小，三是具备显示录制时间的录制面板。目前唯有 webex 这款免费软件符合要求。

下面简单介绍 webex 3.16 版的使用。下载安装该软件后，将 C 盘程序文件夹内的 webex 文件夹整个复制，通过局域网或者因特网将该文件夹共享给学生。学生点击文件夹内的 AtAuthor.exe 文件，即可运行录制程序。程序启动后，点击"File"，选择"Open Application"，在弹出窗口点击"Select"后自动弹出保存录制文件选项；命名文件并选择保存地址，点击"Save"后会出现录制面板，点击录制面板上的红色按钮即可开始录制。录制工作在后台进行，占用系统资源极少。学生在翻译时根据录制面板显示的时间，在每句译文的时间轴中填入翻译开始和结束的时间。由于每次练习至多 10 个句子，填入时间的操作费时至多 2 分钟，不会增加学生的负担或影响学生完成翻译。

学生完成翻译后，右键点击雪人软件左侧"项目文件"下的 txt 文件名，选择"导出双语对照文件"，按照规定的格式命名，点击"保存"。之后点击录制面板上的黑色按钮停止录制。学生将双语对照文件和录制文件通过局域网或者因特网发给教师，整个练习流程结束。

3.双语对照语料的加工

雪人翻译软件导出的双语对照文件的格式是一行原文，一行空行，一行译文，需使用正则表达式处理成检索软件支持的格式。处理步骤如下：将所有双语对照文件存入一个文件夹，用 PowerGrep 选中全部文件，进行替换操作。

选择"Search and replace",在"Search"框输入"(\r\n)(？ ＝[ˆ＜])",在"Re-placement"框输入"\t\2",点击"Replace",即得到便于检索的双语对照语料,如图 3-3 所示。

<ch5>{00}:{00}{}{00}:{00}中国已经成为汽车大国但还不是强国。　　{31}:{00}{}{32}:{00}China has become a big vehicle country but not strong.

图 3-3　加工后的双语对照语料

以上步骤,在操作熟练的情况下,可在 2 分钟内完成。与此同时,对齐文本没有任何错误,不需人工核对,较之我们前期(余军,王朝晖,2010)介绍的手工方法,极大地提高了效率。

3.6　AI 赋能:建库工具

在大型通用双语语料库的研制过程中,包括 AI 工具在内的一些建库工具起了重要作用,极大地提高了建库效率。

3.6.1 基于 AI 的文字识别工具

传统的文字识别工具 ABBYY FineReader 曾被认为是准确率最高的文字识别工具,并在语料库构建的扫描识别环节得到广泛应用(孙鸿仁,2013;王连柱,2016;秦洪武,夏云,2017;邹瑶等,2018;张政,王赟,2020;李晓倩,胡开宝,2021)。然而,对于印刷质量较差、字迹模糊的文本,ABBYY FineReader 的识别效果并不理想,需要进行大量的人工输入和校对工作(秦洪武,夏云,2017:22)。

在人工智能时代,百度、腾讯、有道等公司推出的基于 AI 的文字识别 API 接口,其准确率已经超过了 ABBYY FineReader,能够在一定程度上解决"大量的人工输入和校对工作"的问题。

尽管 ABBYY FineReader 具有强大的 PDF 文件和图片识别功能,但由于其是单机离线版,并未集成 AI 文字识别 API,因此准确率相较于使用 AI 文字识别接口的图片识别工具,如白描 OCR、天若 OCR、WPS 等,有所不及。以下是一页分辨率较低的 PDF 扫描件的识别效果比较。

从图 3-4 可以看出,该 PDF 扫描件分辨率比较低,文字较为模糊。图 3-5 为 ABBYY FineReader 的识别结果,错误较多,图中圈出的只是其中部分错误。除识别错误外,其排版也存在问题,没有保持原文的版式。这些识别错误和问题需要大量的人工校对修正。这也是语料库构建需要耗费大量人力的原因之一。

The interest of building refers to the building in the Garden. If visitors look at the building's interior, they will see that it has two stories. If visitors look at it from outside, it has only one story.

The interest of paintings refers to the colored paintings of Su style in the verandas of the Garden. And the beauty of the paintings could match that of the Long Corridor. There are more than 100 paintings on the buildings of the Garden. There are paintings of mountains and rivers as well as paintings of figures.

The interest of verandas refers to the four pavilions along the pond which have been linked up as a whole by the twisted corridor. The buildings, pavilions and verandas are linked up together by the twisted corridor. Compared with the Long Corridor, it is also very charming and interesting.

The interest of imitation refers to the Garden of Harmonious Interest is a garden within the garden of the Summer Palace. It was built in a very unique style as it imitated the Jichang Private Garden. In addition to being magnificent and dignified, it is very

山，南为绿水，细雨霏霏之时，游走于长廊之间该多么惬意呀。

长廊以排云殿为中心。向东、西延伸，东起邀月门，西止石丈亭。当人们走进长廊东端的邀月门就进入了一个一眼看不到尽头的走廊。有的地段直得像一条线，有时又曲折回转，宛如画境。从东往西，其间点缀着留佳、寄澜、秋水、滑逼四个亭子，象征春、夏、秋、冬四季。长廊的东西两部，各有一座临水敞轩，它们是对鸥舫和鱼藻轩。长廊的地基和廊身随万寿山南麓的地势高低起伏，四座八角亭是高低和变向的连接点。由于处理巧妙，利用左右的借景而转移了人们的视线。所以游长廊时并不感觉到地势不平、走向曲折。长廊不愧是我国古典园林建筑中的艺术杰作。

[在石舫]现在大家看到的这个大船就是石舫，公元 1755 年建，船体全部用大理石制作，通长 36 米。乾隆对建造这座石舫是有用意的。他引用唐朝魏征告诫唐太宗"水能载舟，亦能覆舟"的典故，勉励自己励精图治，同时也象征他的统治像石舫一样坚固，任凭风吹浪打，而无覆舟之虞。但是清王朝的腐朽统治不可能与这石舫共存。这也是北洋水师作战失利后留下的唯一一条"船"，一条不动的船。

图 3-4 低分辨率 PDF 扫描件样例

Tlu* inlerest of building refers to the building in the Garden. If visitors look at the building's interior, they will see that it has Iwo stories. If visitors look al it from outside , il has only one story.

The interest of paintings refers to the colored paintings of Su style in the verandas of the Garden. And the beauty of the paintings could malch that of the Ix ng Corridor. There are more than 100 paintings on the buildings of the Garden. There are paintings of mountains and rivers as well as paintings of figures.

The inleresl of verandas refers lo I he four pavilions along the pond which have been linked up as a whole by the wisled corridor. The buildings, pavilions and verandas arc linked up together by the twisted corridor. Compared with the ^ng Corridor, il is also very charming and interesting.

The interest of imitation refera lo the Garden of Flamionious hiterrst is a ganlen within the garden of I he Summer Palace. It was built in a very unique style as it imitated Ji *hang Private Garden. In addition lo being magnificent and dignified, it is very peaceful and elegant.

有时又曲折回转，宛如画境从东 往西。其间点缀着留佳、寄澜、秋水、滑逼四个亭子，象征春、夏、秋、冬四季。长廊的东西两部，各有一座临水敞轩，它们是对鹏舫和鱼藻轩。长廊的地基和廊身随万寿山南舱的地势高低起伏，四座八角亭是高低和变向的连接点由于处理巧妙，利用左右的借景而转移了人们的视线，所以游长廊时并不感觉到地势不平、走向曲折，长廊不愧是我国古典园林建筑中的艺术杰作

[在石舫]现在大家看到的这个大船就是石舫，公元 1755 年建，船体全部用大理石制作，通长 36 米乾隆对建造这座石舫是有用意的他引用唐朝拽征告诫唐太宗"水能载舟，亦能覆舟"的典故，勉励自己励精图治同时也象征他的统治像石舫一样坚固，任凭风吹浪打。而无■舟之虞。但是清王朝的腐朽统治不可能与这石舫共存这也是北洋水师作战失利后留下的唯一一条"船"，一条不动的船。

石舫原有中式舱楼，1860 年被烧毁后，又于光绪卜九年（公元 1893 年）改建成洋式舱楼，并在船体两侧加上两个机轮取"河清海晏"之意。名清晏舫 1903 年，慈禧又加盖了一层洋式层楼（木质结构），窗上嵌着五色琉璃，上下楼各有大镜干一块，可以反射湖里的波

图 3-5 ABBYY FineReader 识别效果

图 3-6 为 WPS 的识别结果，识别效果极佳，不仅保持了原文版式，而且基本没有识别错误。

The interest of building refers to the building in the Garden. If visitors look at the building's interior, they will see that it has two stories, If visitors look at it from outside,it has only one story.

The interest of paintings refers to the colored paintings of Su style in the verandas of the Garden. And the beauty of the paintings could match that of the Long Corridor. There are more than 100 paintings on the buildings of the Garden. There are paintings of mountains and rivers as well as paintings of figures.

The interest of verandas refers to the four pavilions along the pond which have been linked up as a whole by the twisted corridor. The buildings, pavilions and verandas are linked up together by the twisted corridor. Compared with the Long Corridor, it is also very charming and interesting.

The interest of imitation refers to the Garden of Harmonious Interest is a garden within the garden of the Summer Palace. It was built in a very unique style as it imitated the Jichang Private Garden. In addition to being magnificent and dignified, it is very

山，南为绿水，细雨霏霏之时，游走于长廊之间该多么惬意呀。

长廊以排云殿为中心。向东、西延伸，东起邀月门，西止石丈亭。当人们走进长廊东端的邀月门就进入了一个一眼看不到尽头的走廊。有的地段直得像一条线，有时又曲折回转，宛如画境。从东往西，其间点缀着留佳、寄澜、秋水、滑迤四个亭子，象征春、夏、秋、冬四季。长廊的东西两部，各有一座临水敞轩，它们是对鸥舫和鱼藻轩。长廊的地基和廊身随万寿山南麓的地势高低起伏，四座八角亭是高低和变向的连接点。由于处理巧妙，利用左右的借景而转移了人们的视线。所以游长廊时并不感觉到地势不平、走向曲折。长廊不愧是我国古典园林建筑中的艺术杰作。

[在石舫]现在大家看到的这个大船就是石舫，公元1755年建，船体全部用大理石制作，通长36米。乾隆对建造这座石舫是有用意的。他引用唐朝魏征告诫唐太宗"水能载舟，亦能覆舟"的典故，勉励自己励精图治，同时也象征他的统治像石舫一样坚固，任凭风吹浪打，而无覆舟之虞。但是清王朝的腐朽统治不可能与这石舫共存。这也是北洋水师作战失利后留下的唯一一条"船"，一条不动的船。

图 3-6　WPS 识别效果示例

以上识别中，ABBYY FineReader 的版本为 15，WPS 的版本为 12.1，不同版本可能识别效果会略有差异。

WPS 文字识别的操作步骤简述如下：

在 WPS 中打开 PDF 文件，点击左上方的 PDF 转换下拉菜单，选择"转为Word"（见图 3-7），之后逐步操作即可。

图 3-7　WPS 文字识别步骤 1：菜单选择

注意 WPS 还有一个提取文字的功能(见图 3-8),该功能无法保持原文版式,不建议用。

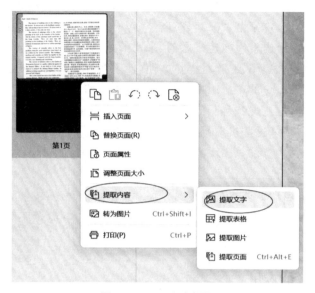

图 3-8　WPS 文字提取

3.6.2 基于 AI 的语料对齐工具

语料对齐是双语平行语料库建设的重要环节。对于百万甚至千万词级的较大规模双语语料库的构建而言,自动对齐工具至为关键。建立双语/多语对应语料库的一个目的是存储和提取语言间对译信息,从大量的对译文本中手动搜寻所有的相关句子翻译不太现实,因此,需要程序软件来自动对齐局部对译单位(王克非,2004:22-23)。最常见的对齐是在句子层次进行的,但也有对单词、多词表达(multiword expression)对齐的研究(王克非,2004:23)。常用的句对齐工具包括 WinAlign(黄立波,2013;邹瑶等,2018)、ABBYY Aligner(王连柱,2016;邹瑶等,2018;韩红梅,2019;蔡辉,2019)、雪人 CAT、Tmxmall Aligner(分在线版和离线版)、Transmate(蔡辉,2019)等。

如果常用工具不能满足需求,便需要自行开发双语对齐工具。例如,胡开宝团队自行开发了多语种平行对齐软件 SISU Aligner 1.0.0,辅以人工调整,在段对齐的基础上实现汉外多个语言对的句级对齐,并能够导出 txt 或 xml

格式(李晓倩,胡开宝,2021:85)。国家社科基金重大项目"大规模英汉平行语料库的建立与加工"课题组设计并开发了英汉双语文本自动句级对齐模块(Chinese English Text Aligner,简称 CETA),其自动对齐准确率很高,达到95%以上(梁茂成,许家金,2012:42)。

大型通用双语语料库在建设之初,采用的是 ABBYY Aligner 进行自动对齐。该工具对齐准确率较高,且操作方便,便于对齐后的人工调整。后改为使用 Tmxmall Aligner 的单机版进行对齐。该工具的独特之处在于支持接入百度翻译、腾讯翻译君、搜狗翻译、有道翻译、小牛翻译、新译等基于 AI 的神经网络机器,用户输入这些机器翻译的密钥后,便可启用机器翻译辅助对齐。相较我们曾评测并推荐的 ABBYY Aligner 和雪人软件(王朝晖,余军,2016),其准确率有一定提升。

WPS 文字识别工具和对齐工具 Tmxmall Aligner 都具有 AI 属性,性能和效率超出了传统工具。在 AI 技术迅猛发展的今天,语料库建设工具需要我们去充分挖掘利用。

3.6.3 Python 的应用

近年来,计算机技术在翻译研究和教学中的应用已成为热门话题。在众多编程语言中,Python 因其简洁、易读和丰富的库而越来越受欢迎,成为翻译研究领域的重要工具。其应用主要包括以下几个方面:

1.语料库处理

Python 具有强大的文本处理能力,可以方便地处理大量的文本数据。Python 可用于处理和分析翻译研究和教学中的平行语料库,例如,可用于对齐、清洗和预处理平行语料库,从而提高翻译质量和效率。

此外,通过使用 Python 的自然语言处理库,如 NLTK(Natural Language Toolkit,自然语言处理工具包)和 spaCy,研究者能够对语料数据进行词汇分析、词性标注、句法分析等操作,进而挖掘文本中有价值的信息。

2.翻译质量评估

翻译质量评估是翻译研究的重要组成部分。Python 可以通过 BLEU、TER 和 METEOR 等模块对译文进行质量评估。此外,Python 还可以与其他统计分析工具(如 R 语言)结合,对翻译质量评估数据进行深入分析。

3.数据可视化和分析

Python 提供了丰富的数据分析和可视化工具,如 Pandas、Matplotlib 和 Seaborn。这些工具可以帮助翻译研究人员对翻译数据进行深入分析,促进翻译教学中的有效讨论和反思。

Python 在翻译研究中的广泛应用表明,计算机技术和人工智能对于翻译领域的发展具有重要意义。Python 作为一种强大的编程语言,为翻译研究提供了便利的工具和资源,有助于提高翻译质量、拓宽研究视野。

虽然 Python 在翻译研究中的应用广泛且潜力巨大,但国内翻译界运用 Python 的情况尚不多见,仅有数位学者出版著作(雷蕾,2020;陆晓蕾,倪斌,2021;管新潮,2021;管新潮,陆晓蕾,2022),介绍其应用。

我们在多模态语料库的构建过程中,也编写了一些 Python 代码,用于语料收集、清洗、转换等流程的操作。例如,通过 OCR 识别获取的文本,往往带有多余空格;如果仅是中文文本,处理方法较为简单,直接替换删除空格即可,但如果是中英文混杂的文本,则较为麻烦。Python 代码则可轻易解决这一问题,代码如下:

```python
import os
import re


# 获取当前目录中的所有 txt 文件
files=[f for f in os.listdir()if f.endswith('.txt')]
# 遍历文件列表
for file in files:
    # 读取文件内容
    with open(file, 'r', encoding= 'utf-8')as f:
        content= f.read()
    # 删除英文单词之间的多余空格
    content= re.sub(r'\s+ ', '', content)
    # 删除中文字符之间的空格
    content= re.sub(r'([\u4e00-\u9fa5])\s+ |(\s+ [\u4e00-\u9fa5])', r'\1\2', content)
    # 将内容写回文件
    with open(file, 'w', encoding= 'utf-8')as f:
        f.write(content)
print("Alltxt files in the current directory have been processed.")
```

书末附录分享了 10 余种我们用于语料处理的 Python 代码,供参考。

关于这些代码,简要说明如下:

(1)有关 Python 的安装,请参照前述学者著作。

(2)除处理 office 文档的代码外,大部分代码处理的都是 txt 文件;txt 编码一般默认为 UTF-8 格式。

(3)Python 功能强大,主要得益于它拥有大量的标准库和第三方库。运行代码前,请先查看 import 行的代码,了解其所需库的情况(有时 import 后的名称可能不是需安装的库名称,可搜索了解);之后按 Win+R 键,然后输入 cmd,在弹出界面中输入"pip install 库名称"即可进行相关库的安装。

对于一般翻译研究人员和译者来说,学习 Python 编程可能会有一定的难度和挑战。这主要是因为编程需要一定的逻辑思维和数学基础,而且需要花费较多的时间和精力来学习。但 2022 年 11 月以来,以 ChatGPT 为代表的基于 Transformer 的大型语言模型的横空出世,将极大降低 Python 的学习和使用门槛。换言之,大型语言模型将极大降低语料库的构建与应用门槛。

3.6.4 AIGC 的应用

AIGC(AI-generated content)是通过人工智能技术自动生成内容的生成方式(翟尤等,2023:2),简称生成式 AI。AIGC 基于深度学习的大型语言模型,使用大量的语言数据进行训练,并能够生成高质量的自然语言文本。这些模型通常使用神经网络来学习文本数据中的语法、语义和上下文信息,并将这些信息编码成向量表示。在生成文本时,它们可以根据所输入文本的上下文信息,自动预测下一个最可能出现的单词或短语,从而生成连贯、流畅的文本。随着深度学习技术的飞速发展,大型语言模型在自然语言处理(NLP)领域取得了显著的进展。这些模型能够理解和生成自然语言文本,为各种 NLP 任务提供强大的支持。

基于大型语言模型,已经出现了各种 AIGC 应用,包括 ChatGPT、Claude、Bard,以及国内的文心一言、星火认知大模型、通义千问、360 智脑等,其中以 ChatGPT 4 的性能最强。

以 ChatGPT 为代表的 AIGC 横空出世后,其强大的语言能力,包括翻译和写作能力,对于外语教学构成了巨大挑战,同时也带来了机遇,在外语学界引起了热烈讨论。胡壮麟(2023)通过与 ChatGPT 对话的方式。探讨了其在外语教学中的应用,结论是 ChatGPT 可以对外语教学发挥作用,但作为人工智能模型,ChatGPT 仍需要与人类外语教师合作。张震宇、洪化清(2023)从赋能、问题与策略三个方面,讨论了 ChatGPT 支持的外语教学。秦颖(2023)以 ChatGPT 为例,探讨了人机共生场景下的外语教学方法。冯志伟、张灯柯(2023)描述了 GPT 的发展历程,分析了生成式预训练模型的特点,说明了GPT 给外语教学和语言服务行业带来的机遇和挑战。胡加圣、戚亚娟(2023)探讨了 ChatGPT 对中国外语教育政策带来的挑战和冲击。

以上讨论集中在 ChatGPT 与外语教学的宏观领域。在翻译领域,耿芳、胡健(2023)基于翻译实例文本,从错误修正、句法结构、篇章连贯及语域调整等角度分析了 ChatGPT 在英汉与汉英翻译任务中的译后编辑表现,发现人工智能辅助译后编译可提供汉译英语言对中译文校对、润色、评估、反馈及建议,同时可从译文批改等方面协助翻译教学。在语料库领域,则国内尚未见AIGC 的相关探讨。实际上,对于语料库的构建而言,AIGC 可以完成几乎全部流程的操作,从而将语料库的构建门槛降至最低。AIGC 必将带来语料库翻译学研究领域的革命。

以下简要介绍 AIGC 在语料库构建方面的一些具体应用。

3.6.4.1 机器翻译

AIGC 可以提供从一种语言到另一种语言的机器翻译,从而生成双语平行语料。我们认为,此类语料极具研究价值。AIGC 生成的机器译文与人工译文的比较研究,将成为人工智能时代翻译研究的热点之一。

以 360 智脑为例,输入相关 prompt(提示词),即可让其输出多种机器翻译,如图 3-9 所示。

将以下句子译为5种风格的英文: 北山愚公者,年且九十,面山而居。惩山北之塞, 出入之迂也,聚室而谋曰: "吾与汝毕力平险,指通豫南, 达于汉阴,可乎?"杂然相许。其妻献疑曰: "以君之力, 曾不能损魁父之丘, 如太形、王屋何?且焉置土石?"

1. Formal English Style: A man named the North Mountain Ignominious is nearly ninety years old and lives facing the mountain. He is frustrated by the blockage in the north and the roundabout route of access. So he gathered his family and discussed, "Should we strive to level the obstacles and connect the east with the west via the south, reaching Hanzhong? Will you all agree?" Everyone nodded in agreement. His wi

图 3-9　360 智脑生成的机器译文示例

我们要求 360 智脑"将以下句子译为 5 种风格的英文",这句话就是一个prompt。与神经网络机器翻译不同的是,AIGC 可以根据提示词生成译文,而且可以反复生成,每次生成的译文都不相同。

以下是 360 智脑按提示词生成的 5 种译文：

Formal English Style: A man named the North Mountain Ignominious is nearly ninety years old and lives facing the mountain. He is frustrated by the blockage in the north and the roundabout route of access. So he gathered his family and discussed, "Should we strive to level the obstacles and connect the east with the west via the south, reaching Hanzhong? Will you all agree?" Everyone nodded in agreement. His wife then offered her doubts, saying, "With your strength, can't you even damage a hill like that of Mount Chives or Mount Tai? And where will you store the earth and stones?"

Colloquial English Style: Old Man of the North Mountain is almost ninety and lives facing the mountains. He hates being blocked in the north and having to take a roundabout route for access. So he gathered his family and said, "Let us try our best to flatten the obstacles and connect the east with the west via the south, reaching Hanzhong. Will everyone agree?" Everyone agreed. His wife then asked him, "With your strength, why can't you just destroy a hill like Mount Chives or Mount Tai? And where will you put the dirt and stones?"

Animated English Style: The North Mountain Ignominious is nearly ninety and lives facing the mountain. He hates being blocked in the north and having to take a roundabout route for access. So he gathered his family and said, "We must flatten the obstacles and connect the east with the west via the south, reaching Hanzhong! Will everyone join me?" Everyone cheered in agreement. His wife then suggested, "With your incredible strength, couldn't you just destroy a hill like Mount Chives or Mount Tai? And where will you put the dirt and stones?"

Serious English Style: There is an elderly man living in the North Mountain who has been blocked in the north due to the obstacles blocking access. He decided to gather his family and discuss how they could flatten the obstacles and connect the east with the west via the south, reaching Hanzhong. They all agreed on this plan. His wife then expressed her doubt, asking if they could manage to damage a hill like Mount Chives or Mount Tai. She also wondered where they would store the earth and stones.

Casual English Style: Old Man of the North Mountain is almost ninety and lives facing the mountains. He hates being blocked in the north and having to take a roundabout route for access. So he gathered his family and said, "Let's try flattening the obstacles and connect the east with the west via the south, reaching Hanzhong. Will everyone come with me?" Everyone cheered in agreement. His wife then asked, "With your incredible strength, can't you just destroy a hill like Mount Chives or Mount Tai? And where will you put the dirt and stones?"

以上译文虽然存在少量错误,但基本可读,质量较之神经网络机器翻译有所提升。

以下是 DeepL、有道、讯飞等三种神经网络机器翻译译文。由于对原文理解存在问题,三种译文意思不通之处较多。

DeepL 译文:

The North Mountain Yugong, who was ninety years old, lived in the mountains. When he was punished for the blockage in the north of the mountain, he gathered in his room and said, "I will work with you to level the danger, and point to the south of Yu and reach Hanyin, can we?" He agreed to do so. His wife offered doubt: "with the power of the gentleman, had not been able to damage the mound of Kui father, such as too shape, Wang House what? And how to place the earth and stones?"

有道译文:

The foolish man of the North Mountain, aged ninety, lived on the mountain. Punish the north of the mountain plug, access to the imanyuan, gather room and seek to say: "I and you Bi flat risk, refers to the south of Henan, up to Hanyin, can it?" All kinds of things. His wife questioned and said, "With the strength of the king, he could not damage the hill of the Kui father, such as Tai Shape, Wang Wu? And what about earth and stone?"

讯飞译文:

The Foolish Old Man of Beishan, who was ninety years old, lived facing the mountain. To punish the fortress to the north of the mountain, and to go in and out of it, he gathered in his room and plotted, saying, "I will work with you to level the danger, and I will lead you to the south of Henan, and I will reach Hanyin. Is that all right?". His wife was suspicious, saying, "With the strength of the ruler, I have not been able to damage the hill of Kui's father, such as Taixing and Wangwu."? And how to place earth and stone?

除了对原文的理解能力更强以外,对于神经网络机器翻译存在的一些典型问题,AIGC 可以在一定程度上通过提示词解决。以汉译英中常见的重复问题为例,神经网络机器翻译不懂得避免重复,使用机器翻译的用户对此是无法事先干预的,只能通过译后编辑。

示例:

原文:这个人喜欢阿谀奉承,溜须拍马。

机器译文:

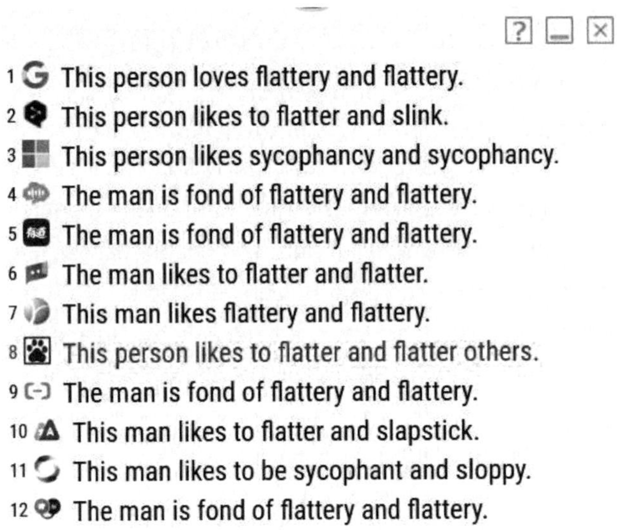

1 G This person loves flattery and flattery.
2 ● This person likes to flatter and slink.
3 ■ This person likes sycophancy and sycophancy.
4 ● The man is fond of flattery and flattery.
5 ● The man is fond of flattery and flattery.
6 ● The man likes to flatter and flatter.
7 ● This man likes flattery and flattery.
8 ● This person likes to flatter and flatter others.
9 (-) The man is fond of flattery and flattery.
10 ▲ This man likes to flatter and slapstick.
11 ● This man likes to be sycophant and sloppy.
12 ● The man is fond of flattery and flattery.

图 3-10　神经网络机器翻译的重复问题示例

如图 3-10 所示,12 种神经网络机器翻译大多都用了重复的词翻译"阿谀奉承,溜须拍马",以至出现"flattery and flattery""flatter and flatter"之类的怪异译文。

AIGC 译文:

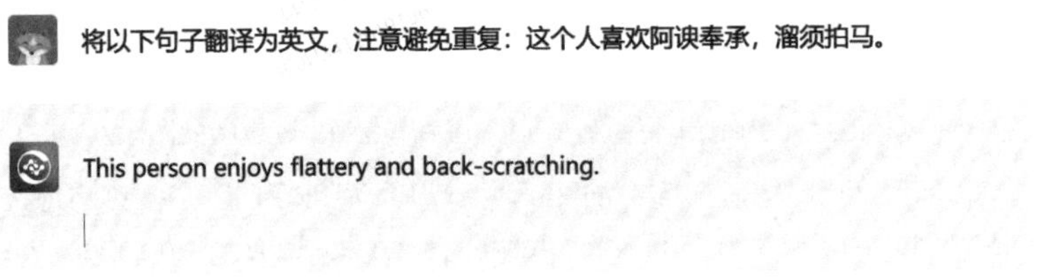

将以下句子翻译为英文, 注意避免重复: 这个人喜欢阿谀奉承, 溜须拍马。

This person enjoys flattery and back-scratching.

图 3-11　360 智脑译文

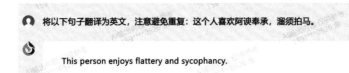

图 3-12　讯飞星火译文

360 智脑和讯飞星火都按照提示词在译文中避免了重复用词,没有出现
"flattery and flattery""flatter and flatter"之类的译文。

鉴于以上分析,我们所建参照语料库中的人工智能译文部分,将逐步用
AIGC 生成的译文替代。

3.6.4.2 语料处理

AIGC 可以对原始文本进行清洗,以及标准化和格式化处理,例如去除特
殊字符、纠正拼写错误等。

以中英文混合文本的多余空格为例,用普通的删除空格方式处理会将英
文词语之间应保留的空格删除。这是一个较难处理的问题。但对于 AIGC 而
言,这个问题颇为简单,如图 3-13 所示。

图 3-13　360 智脑删除中英文混合文本中的多余空格示例

AIGC 具有较强的理解力。以图 3-13 为例,输入的指令中,"多语"为打
字错误,应为"多余",但 360 智脑仍然理解并完成了指令。

3.6.4.3 双语对齐

下面以人机对话的形式呈现 AIGC 的双语对齐功能,Q 表示用户的提问,
A 表示 AIGC 的回答。此处所用 AIGC 为 ChatGPT。

Q：请你扮演语料库构建专家，首先你要了解双语句子对齐的要求，请你学习了解以下对齐要求：句对齐原则

句对齐依据最小句对原则，即不可割裂一个句子进行对齐。句子的标记一般为句号、问号、感叹号、省略号等，分号和冒号不视为句子标记。可出现：

1.一句对一句，如：

I am a student. 我是学生。

2.一句对多句，如：

I am here，and he is here too. 我在这。他也在这。

不能对齐为：

I am here，我在这。

and he is here too. 他也在这。

3.多句对一句，如：

I am here. He is here. 我在这，他也在这。

4.多句对多句，如：

I am here. He is here，but she is not here. 我在这，他也在这。但她不在这。

以上我给你的对齐原则，你理解了吗？

A：是的，我已经理解了您给出的句子对齐原则。简单总结如下：

1.一句对一句：源语和目标语中的一句话分别对应另一种语言中的一句话。

例如：I am a student. 我是学生。

2.一句对多句：源语中的一句话对应目标语中的多句话。

例如：I am here，and he is here too. 我在这。他也在这。

3.多句对一句：源语中的多句话对应目标语中的一句话。

例如：I am here. He is here. 我在这，他也在这。

4.多句对多句：源语中的多句话对应目标语中的多句话。

例如：I am here. He is here，but she is not here. 我在这，他也在这。但她不在这。

在进行双语句子对齐时，需要遵循这些原则，确保句子在结构和意义上的一致性。

Q：好的，下面请你对齐以下双语文本，请你以原文|||译文的格式输出对齐后的句子。

狂人日记

　　某君昆仲，今隐其名，皆余昔日在中学时良友；分隔多年，消息渐阙。日前偶闻其一大病；适归故乡，迂道往访，则仅晤一人，言病者其弟也。劳君远道来视，然已早愈，赴某地候补矣。因大笑，出示日记二册，谓可见当日病状，不妨献诸旧友。

A MADMAN'S DIARY

Two brothers, whose names I need not mention here, were both good friends of mine in high school; but after a separation of many years we gradually lost touch. Some time ago I happened to hear that one of them was seriously ill, and since I was going back to my old home I broke my journey to call on them. I saw only one of them, however, who told me that the invalid was his younger brother. "I appreciate your coming such a long way to see us," he said, "but he recovered some time ago and has gone elsewhere to take up an official post." Then, laughing, he produced two volumes of his brother's diary, saying that from these the nature of his past illness could be seen, and that there was no harm in showing them to an old friend.

A:狂人日记|||A MADMAN'S DIARY

　　某君昆仲，今隐其名，皆余昔日在中学时良友；分隔多年，消息渐阙。|||Two brothers, whose names I need not mention here, were both good friends of mine in high school; but after a separation of many years we gradually lost touch.

　　日前偶闻其一大病；适归故乡，迂道往访，则仅晤一人，言病者其弟也。|||Some time ago I happened to hear that one of them was seriously ill, and since I was going back to my old home I broke my journey to call on them. I saw only one of them, however, who told me that the invalid was his younger brother.

　　劳君远道来视，然已早愈，赴某地候补矣。|||"I appreciate your coming such a long way to see us," he said, "but he recovered some time ago and has gone elsewhere to take up an official post."

　　因大笑，出示日记二册，谓可见当日病状，不妨献诸旧友。|||Then, laughing, he produced two volumes of his brother's diary, saying that from these the nature of his past illness could be seen, and that there was no harm in showing them to an old friend.

以上双语语料的对齐难度极大,但 ChatGPT 的准确率为 100%;而其他对齐工具,包括 Tmxmall,则仍存在较多错误。

3.6.4.4 Python 代码撰写

AIGC 具备代码撰写功能,可通过 prompts 利用 AIGC 编写 Python、PHP、R 语言程序,实现较为复杂的文本处理及数据挖掘功能。

在语料库的构建及应用中,经常会涉及 txt 的编码问题。以下是请 Chat-GPT 撰写转换 txt 编码的 Python 代码的人机对话。

Q: 请写一段 txt 编码转换的 Python 代码,将同目录下的全部 txt 文件转换为 UTF-8 编码,跳过 UTF-8 格式的 txt 文件。

A: 这是一个基本的 Python 脚本,它将遍历当前目录下的所有 txt 文件,如果这些文件不是 UTF-8 编码,它将把这些文件转换为 UTF-8 编码。我在这里使用了 chardet 库来检测文件的原始编码,如果这个库还没有安装的话,你可以通过运行 pip install chardet 命令来安装。

请注意这个脚本可能会永久更改你的文件,所以在运行之前确定你已经对重要文件做好了备份。

```python
import os
importcodecs
importchardet
def convert_to_utf8(file_path):
    with open(file_path, 'rb')as f:
        content= f.read()
        detect_result = chardet.detect(content)
        original_encoding= detect_result['encoding']

        if original_encoding ! = 'utf-8':
            try:
                decoded_content= content.decode(original_encoding)
                with open(file_path, 'w', encoding= 'utf-8')as f:
                    f.write(decoded_content)
                    print(f'File {file_path} has been converted from
{original_encoding} toutf-8.')
            except Exception as e:
                print(f'Error encountered: {e}')
        else:
```

```
        print(f'File {file_path} is already inutf-8 format. Skipped.')
  if __name__ = = '__main__':
    current_directory= os.path.dirname(os.path.realpath(__file__))
    for root, _, files in os.walk(current_directory):
        for file in files:
            if file.endswith('.txt'):
                file_path= os.path.join(root, file)
                convert_to_utf8(file_path)
```

以上代码一次性运行成功。需要注意的是,ChatGPT 生成的代码可能不是最优的,也可能存在一些错误,有时候需要多轮调试修改,才能实现所需功能。

3.7　语料标注

Leech(1997:2)认为,对语料库进行标注可以使语料库增值(added value)。经过标注的语料库,其实用价值要大于无标注的语料库。

我们对多模态双语语料库进行了以下标注:

(1)文本头:文本头标注包括中文标题、英文标题、作者/文本来源、原文字数、译文字数等。

(2)词性标注:英文文本采用 CLAWS4 进行词性标注,中文文本的词性标注则采用基于 AI 的百度词法分析 API 完成。

(3)错误标注:抽取了部分典型汉英对应语料进行错误标注,制定错误标注规范,包括错误标注分类、标注赋码、标注流程,并实施严格的标注质量监控。

3.7.1 基于 AI 的中文词性标注工具

目前,对中文的词性标注研究已有 30 多年了,技术比较成熟,标注精度较高,如中国科学院计算技术研究所开发的汉语词法分析系统 ICTCLAS,词性标注正确率已达到了 97.16%(贺胜,2019:64)。在语料库建设中,ICTCLAS 常用于中文词性标注(如戴光荣,2013;秦洪武,夏云,2017)。但由于 ICTCLAS 是基于词典的词性标注系统,其对命名实体(named entity)的识别不如经过海量语料训练的 AI 词法分析工具,如百度词法分析,比较如下:

"厦门思明区中山路"包含 3 个命名实体。ICTCLAS 只识别出了"厦门",准确率不高(见图 3-14),而百度词法分析的准确率为 100%(见图 3-15):

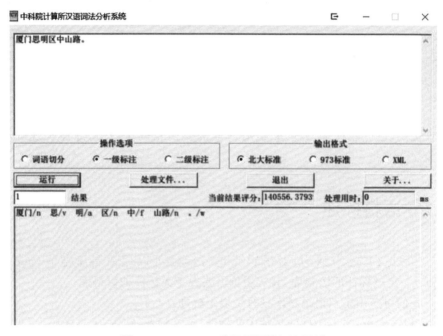

图 3-14　ICTCLAS 分词及词性标注示例

图 3-15　百度词法分析示例(网页演示版)①

---

①　https://ai.baidu.com/tech/nlp_basic/lexical

由于百度词法分析并无客户端工具,网页版也仅用于演示,至多支持 150 字,我们自制了接入百度词法分析 API 的分词工具,用于多模态双语语料库中文语料的分词及词性标注(见图 3-16):

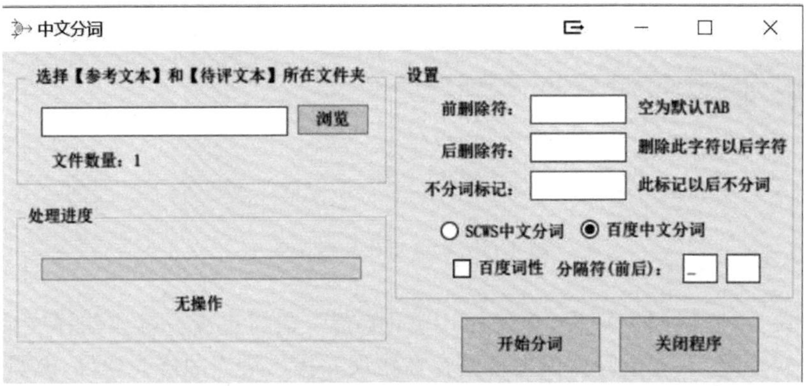

图 3-16　基于百度 AI 的自制分词及词性标注工具

3.7.2 基于 AI 的语法纠错工具

桂诗春、杨慧中(2003)在《中国学习者英语语料库》一书中把语言错误细分为 11 个类别,包括词形、动词词组、代词、形容词词组、副词、介词词组、连词、词汇、搭配和句法等错误,其中词形错误包括拼写、构词和大小写等,词汇错误包括词序、词类、替代、省略、重复、语义含糊错误;而自动批改软件 Grammarly 则把书面语篇中的错误分为 6 个大类 34 个小类,更加细致(张淑贞,2020:113)。Grammarly 是商业软件,需要按年付费才能使用。在 AI 技术应用于写作之前,我们曾使用过该工具,虽然能识别出各种错误,但误判也很多。有道推出的基于 AI 的有道写作工具,具备不逊色于 Grammarly 的纠错功能,甚至要强于以前的 Grammarly。

在学习者译文的错误标注中,我们使用了有道写作[①]这一 AI 工具,极大地提升了错误标注的效率,如图 3-17:

图 3-17 中的英文片段为随机选择的一篇学习者译文,有道写作识别出 8 个错误,并显示错误类型、简要说明及修改建议。其中第 8 个错误的说明及修

---

① 　https://write.youdao.com/#/homepage

I love natures in many aspects. I love mountains, but I love the sea even more.
Since I arrived at Xiamen. I have been in the habit of taking a walk on the seashore almost every day. When I stepped on the soft smooth sand, I felt an inexpressible comfort.
When the sea breeze rolls up snowy waves to dash against the coast, you can pick up many small and exquisite shells, and colorful small pebbles in the beautiful waves.
And those green seaweeds, which are long and smooth and glossy like women's hair, is also beautiful and lovely.
I love the sea, not only because of her beautiful color and the interesting things hiding in the bottom of the sea, but also because she has a broad-mindedness to turn dirt into clean.
I believe even a person who is fierce like a tiger or a wolf lives on the seashore for a long time, he will become as tame as a lamb.

图 3-17　有道写作纠错示例 1

改建议为"疑似词汇缺失，建议加入单词【if】"，判断正确。就该句译文而言，句式较为复杂，有道写作能发现其存在错误并提出恰当的修改建议，说明其具备较强的纠错能力。总体而言，有道写作指出的 8 个错误，全部判断正确，准确率达到了 100%。

图 3-18 为小牛机器译文，有道写作发现了一处错误——And 应为 and。与学生译文比较，小牛机器译文的语法错误少很多。就语法错误而言，目前人工智能机器译文的错误率已大幅低于学习者译文的平均错误率。

I love nature in many ways. I love mountains, but I love the sea more.
Since I came to Xiamen, I have to go for a walk on the seashore almost every day. Stepping on the soft sand has an unspeakable comfort.
When the sea breeze rolls up snow waves to attack the coast, many small and exquisite shells and colorful pebbles will be found in the beautiful waves;
And the green seaweed, which looks like hair, is beautiful and lovely.
I love the sea not only because of its beautiful colors and many interesting things hidden on the bottom of the sea, but because of its broad mind and turning filth into cleanness.
A person, even if his temper is as fierce as a tiger, I believe that if he lives on the seashore for a long time, he will become as docile as a lamb.

图 3-18　有道写作纠错示例 2

3.8　术语库制作

术语库是 CCAT 平台的一个极为重要的组成部分。在第 6 章的翻译过程研究中,我们发现术语翻译错误是比较普遍和严重的问题。制作高质量的术语库并在 CCAT 平台中应用于翻译过程,可以较好地避免术语翻译错误这一问题。

术语库的制作流程和方法见第 9 章。

3.9　翻译记忆库制作

多模态双语语料库的记忆库分为两种。一种是未经审校的生记忆库,建库过程中,起初用 ABBYY Aligner 对齐双语语料,后改为 Tmxmall Aligner,两者均可导出 tmx 文件,支持导入各种 CAT 软件,如 Trados、memoQ、Transmate 等。此类语料来源主要为时政文本、旅游文本、散文文本、应用文本等,译文质量相对较高。另一种记忆库是我们在生记忆库基础上人工审校修订的翻译记忆库。生记忆库的制作方式简要介绍如下。

3.9.1 双语对齐

启动 Tmxmall Aligner①,导入待对齐的文档(支持双语单文件或单语双文件),如图 3-19 所示。

图 3-19　Tmxmall Aligner 中导入待对齐的文件

---

① 该工具如果出现无法导入文档的问题,通过以管理员身份运行即可解决。

在对齐前,可在高级功能中设置启用机器翻译,如图 3-20。

图 3-20　设置启用机器翻译

使用机器翻译辅助对齐,可提升对齐准确率,使用前需填入机器翻译的 API 秘钥。各机器翻译引擎申请 API 的方法可在网上查询,一般均提供免费额度。选择一个已存入 API 秘钥的机器翻译,如小牛翻译,点击确定。之后点击"对齐"按钮,启动对齐,结果如图 3-21 所示。

图 3-21　对齐结果

启用机器翻译辅助对齐后的准确率极高。人工审核并纠正可能存在的对齐错误后,可导出双语对照文件。可选导出格式较全,包括 tmx、xlsx、上下对照的 docx、左右对照的 txt、上下对照的 txt(见图 3-22)。建议导出 tmx 及左右对照的 txt。

图 3-22　导出双语对照文件

3.9.2 双语文件导入

常用 CAT 软件,如 memoQ、雪人翻译软件,Transmate,均支持将 tmx 文件或 txt 文件导入翻译记忆库;Trados 则支持 tmx 文件而不支持 txt 文件。操作步骤为在 CAT 软件中建立一个空白记忆库,然后导入双语文件即可。下面以 Trados 2022 为例,简述操作过程。

(1)启动 Trados,点击左上角"文件"菜单,选择"新建""新建翻译记忆库",如图 3-23。

图 3-23　Trados 中新建翻译记忆库

（2）在弹出窗口填写翻译记忆库名称，设置源语和目标语，之后点完成即可，如图 3-24。

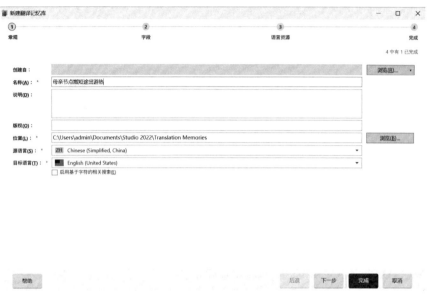

图 3-24　新建翻译记忆库设置

（3）点击该翻译记忆库，点击"导入"，在弹出窗口点击"添加文件"，将 Tmxmall Aligner 导出的 tmx 文件添加并依次点击"下一步"即可，结果如图 3-25 所示：

图 3-25　导入双语文件的翻译记忆库

3.10　语料文件转换

在术语库及翻译记忆库构建中,常用的 CAT 软件及机器翻译所支持导入的双语文件各异,如 Trados 不支持 txt 格式文件,小牛机器翻译的术语库及翻译记忆库只支持 txt 的导入。各种双语语料库检索工具支持的双语文件类型也不尽相同,如 ParaConc 和 BFSU ParaConc 只支持单语双文件,而CAT 软件一般只支持双语单文件的导入。解决以上问题,需要对语料文件进行转换;简要而言,包括以下三种类型的转换:

1.编码转换

通常而言,在语料分析或检索中出现文字乱码或不显示问题,往往是 txt编码导致,可尝试转换编码。如贾云龙检索工具[①]只支持 ANSI 编码的 txt 文件,而 Tmxmall Aligner 导出的 txt 文件为 UTF-8 编码,需转为 ANSI 编码才能使用贾云龙检索工具检索。单个 txt 文件编码的转换较为简单,用记事本打开,另存为其他编码即可,如 ANSI 另存为 UTF-8,或反之。多个 txt 文件编码的转换,可用编码转换工具批量操作,如用水淼·文件编码批量转换助手[②]。

2.文件格式转换

Trados 翻译记忆库不支持 txt 文件的导入,需转换为 tmx 格式。反之,从 ABBYY Aligner 和 LF Aligner 等对齐工具中导出的 tmx 格式文件需转换为 txt 格式,这样才可被常见双语语料检索工具检索。

如需从 tmx 格式转 txt,可用 Heartsome TMX Editor 8 转换,支持批量。启动该工具,点击 Tools 菜单,选择 Convert TMX to…,在弹出的窗口添加需转换的 tmx 文件,如图 3-26 所示:

选择 Convert to TMX…,则可将 txt、xlsx、docx 等格式文件转换为 tmx,可用于 Trados 翻译记忆库的制作。

3.对齐形式转换

有的语料检索工具,如 ParaConc 和 BFSU ParaConc,只支持单语双文件

---

① 见第 4 章介绍。

② https://www.shuimiao.net/FileCoding/

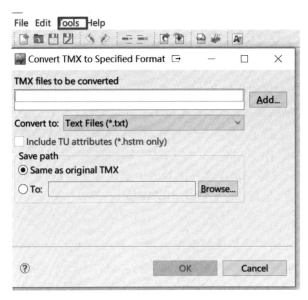

图 3-26   TMX Editor 8 中 tmx 转 txt

的检索,常见的双语单文件需转换为单语双文件,才可使用此类工具检索。

再如,Transmate 和雪人翻译软件,其翻译项目导出的双语对照文件为上下对齐形式,需转为左右对齐形式才能在贾云龙检索工具中检索,或导入其他常见 CAT 软件的翻译记忆库,等等。

对齐形式的转换可用正则表达式实现,详见下一小节。

3.11   正则表达式与对齐形式转换

正则表达式是强大的语料处理工具,相关介绍颇多,但涉及对齐形式转换的极少。此处略述对齐形式转换的正则操作,依照操作即可。

支持正则表达式的文本处理工具很多,要注意的是,不同工具的正则规则可能不同,不一定能直接套用。此处所用的正则工具为 EditPad Pro 和 PowerGrep,以下示例中的全部正则操作结果均可在这两个工具中复现。

3.11.1 原文及译文位置互换

示例:Does drag really affect a car's fuel economy more than air conditioning?
开窗的空气阻力会比开空调更耗油吗?

特征分析:原文与译文之间用 tab 间隔符区分。

正则操作:在 EditPad Pro 的 Search 栏输入(.+)(\t)(.+)[①],在 Replace 栏填入\3\2\1,点击 ,运行全部替换。

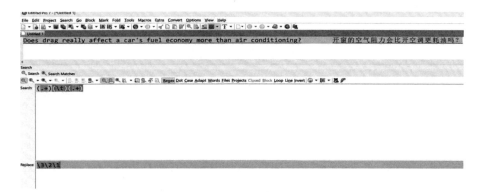

图 3-27 原文及译文位置互换的正则操作

图 3-28 原文及译文位置互换的正则操作结果

---

① 正则\t 对应 tab 间隔符。如为其他间隔符号,如|||,则对应正则为\|\|\|。

3.11.2 左右对齐双语单文件转为单语双文件

示例：

中国国产大飞机 C919 正式进入民航市场 China's C919 jetliner goes into commercial operation

5 月 28 日，国产大飞机 C919 执飞的航班由上海飞抵北京。这标志着 C919 圆满完成首个商业航班飞行，正式进入民航市场。The C919, China's self-developed large passenger aircraft, successfully completed its first commercial flight from Shanghai to Beijing on Sunday, marking its official entry into the civil aviation market.

5 月 28 日 10 时 32 分，搭载 128 名旅客的 MU9191 航班从上海虹桥国际机场起飞。The flight, operated by China Eastern Airlines, took off as MU9191 at 10:32 a.m. from Shanghai Hongqiao International Airport with 128 passengers on board.

特征分析：原文与译文用 tab 符隔开。

正则操作：在 EditPad Pro 的 Search 栏输入 (.＋)(\t)(.＋)，在 Replace 栏填入 \1，点击 ，运行全部替换，得到原文，另存为文件 A。

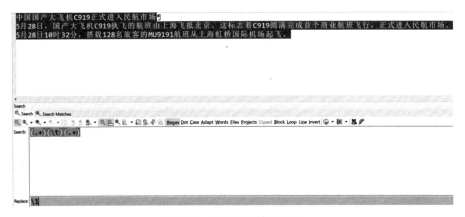

图 3-29　正则替换获取原文

撤销操作，恢复对照双语，Replace 栏正则改为 \3，点击 ，运行全部替换，得到译文，另存为文件 B。

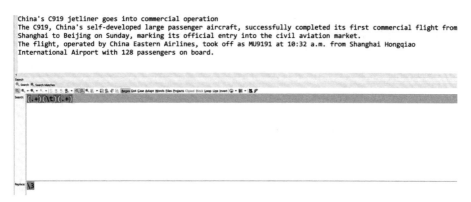

图 3-30 正则替换获取译文

建议先备份好原始文件,以免误操作导致语料丢失。

3.11.3 上下对齐双语单文件转为单语双文件

示例:

The survey was conducted on 588 top executives or decision-makers of Chinese mainland companies with an annual sales revenue of 100 million yuan to 4 billion yuan or higher.

该调查对 588 名中国大陆公司的高管或决策者进行了调查,这些公司的年销售收入在 1 亿元至 40 亿元以上。

Specifically, over 40 percent of the surveyed companies planned to expand their operations in Southeast Asia over the next three years. Singapore, Thailand and Malaysia were the top three investment destinations for Chinese companies, the survey showed.

调查显示,超过四成的受访中国企业计划未来三年向东南亚扩张,排名前三的投资目的地是新加坡、泰国和马来西亚。

特征分析:一行原文,一行译文,依次逐行排列。

正则操作:在 EditPad Pro 的 Search 栏输入(.+)(\r\n)(.+),在 Replace 栏填入\1,点击 ,运行全部替换,得到原文,另存为文件 A。撤销操作,恢复对照双语,Replace 栏正则改为\3,点击 ,运行全部替换,得到译文,另存为文件 B。

3.11.4 左右对齐转为上下对齐

Search 栏正则:(.+)(\t)(.+)

Replace 栏正则:\1\r\n\3

3.11.5 上下对齐转为左右对齐

Search 栏正则:(.+)(\r\n)(.+)

Replace 栏正则:\1\t\3

以上对齐形式转换,如涉及单个文件,使用 EditPad Pro 即可;如需批量处理多个文件,可使用 PowerGrep,选中待处理的全部文件,运行相应正则即可。

3.12　小结

近年来,国内双语语料库研究领域取得了显著的成果。但推动技术革新、提高双语语料库研制的效率,是当务之急(王朝晖,余军,2016:67)。尽管这段话是数年前所述,但在当前语料库翻译学研究和人工智能技术发展的背景下,仍然具有现实意义。

随着人工智能技术的飞速发展,各种新型工具和技术不断涌现,为双语语料库研究提供了前所未有的便利条件和广阔的发展空间。在双语语料库研究中,我们需要紧跟时代步伐,充分利用现有的先进技术和工具,实现研究的创新和突破。

在语料库工具的应用方面,我们应关注新兴技术和工具的发展趋势,挖掘其潜在价值。例如,深度学习、自然语言处理等技术的应用,可以极大地提高语料库的构建、分析和研究效率,为双语语料库研究带来新的视角和方法。此外,通过跨学科技术和工具的结合,可以实现研究创新,为双语语料库研究提供更为丰富的理论和实践资源。

总之,双语语料库研究领域的技术创新和研究方法随着人工智能技术的发展而不断演进。我们应发挥新兴技术在双语语料库研究中的应用价值,提高研究效率和推动技术革新。同时,在实践中不断创新,以在国内外学术交流中展示双语语料库研究领域的新成果,为相关领域的发展做出更大贡献。

第 4 章 多模态双语语料库的检索

4.1 引言

语料库检索工具在翻译研究和实践中具有重要价值。目前的检索工具可分为离线的单机版检索工具和在线检索平台。

1.单机版检索工具

WordSmith:广泛应用于单语检索(王立非,梁茂成,2007;毛虰,邱天河,2007;尚琼,2011),具有丰富的功能,最新版本为 8.0 版。WordSmith 4.0 版已免费提供。

AntConc:一款免费的单语和双语语料库分析工具,支持多种功能,如词频统计、关键词提取等。

LancsBox:一款强大的单语和双语语料库分析工具,提供丰富的可视化功能,便于用户分析和理解数据。

PowerConc:由许家金和贾云龙(2013)开发的一款单语检索工具,具有丰富的分析功能。

ParaConc:一款知名的双语检索工具,支持多种文件格式,便于用户快速查询双语对应关系。

2.在线检索平台

中国英汉平行语料库检索平台:由王克非(2012)开发,提供在线检索功能,方便用户查询英汉对应语料。

CQPweb:许家金、吴良平(2014)推介的在线检索平台,基于 CQP(corpus query processor)技术,支持丰富的检索和分析功能。

CCAT 在线检索平台:我们自建的在线检索平台,语料丰富,功能较多,可提供便捷的检索服务。

CCAT 在线检索评注系统:我们自建的学习者语料检索平台,支持多种检索模式,可勾选检索结果予以评注反馈。

以上检索工具和平台为翻译教学研究与实践提供了强大的支持。随着技术的发展,未来将有更多功能丰富、易用性强的语料库检索工具和平台出现,进一步推动翻译领域的发展。

王朝晖、余军(2016)在《基于 CAT 及语料库技术的电子商务翻译研究》一书中对语料库检索工具做了较为详尽的介绍,如 WordSmith、PowerGrep。本章主要介绍多模态双语语料库中单模态语料的检索,所用工具为贾云龙编制的单机版检索工具(以下简称贾云龙工具)、BFSU ParaConc 和自建 CCAT 在线检索平台;以及多模态语料的检索,所用工具为自建的多模态语料库在线检索平台以及 ELAN(EUDICO Linguistic Annotator,EUDICO 语言标注工具)。

4.2　单模态语料的检索

4.2.1 贾云龙工具

贾云龙开发的检索工具具有实用性和易用性,特别是对于双语对应语料库的检索。以下是对该工具的简要介绍。

(1)无需安装:作为一款绿色软件,该检索工具无需安装,用户只需解压缩后即可使用。

(2)数据存储:将待检索的 txt 文本文件存放在软件目录内的 data 文件夹,方便快捷。

(3)运行与检索:运行"检索.exe"文件,输入检索关键词后,工具会对 data 文件夹内的全部 txt 文件进行检索。

(4)检索方式:采用逐行检索,包含检索关键词的文本行会被提取出来,显示在检索结果中。

(5)显示结果:检索结果以网页形式呈现,方便用户查看和分析。

(6)语言支持:支持中英文单语及双语检索,满足不同用户的需求。

通过该工具,用户可以快速地找到包含关键词的文本行,从而提高翻译过程中的工作效率。尽管功能较为简单,但对于大多数用户来说,这款工具已经足够满足日常检索需求。

No	Text	Line	File
1	相传，唐贞观年间 (627-650)，名僧寒山和拾得两人由天台山来此住持，改名为 寒山寺 。 Legend has it that during the Zhenguan Years of the Tang Dynasty (627-650), two famous monks named Han Shan (meaning Cold Mountain) and Shi De came to the temple to serve as abbots. They renamed the temple Han Shan Temple, meaning Cold Mountain Temple.	1	汉英2-课堂练习11.txt
2	相传，唐贞观年间 (627-650)，名僧寒山和拾得两人由天台山来此住持，改名为 寒山寺 。 According to legend, Tang Zhenguan years (627-650) , the famous monk Han Shan and Shide two people from Mount Tiantai to this Abbot, renamed "Hanshan Temple."	2	汉英2-课堂练习11.txt
3	相传，唐贞观年间 (627-650)，名僧寒山和拾得两人由天台山来此住持，改名为 寒山寺 。 It is said that in the Tang Dynasty(618-907)two famous monks from Tiantai Mountain in today's Zhejiang Province were given charge of the temple and the name was then changed to Hanshan Temple.	3	汉英2-课堂练习11.txt
4	相传，唐贞观年间 (627-650)，名僧寒山和拾得两人由天台山来此住持，改名为 寒山寺 。 According to legend, during the Reign of Emperor Zhenguan of tang Dynasty (627-650), two famous monks, Han Shan and Shi De, came to this temple from Tiantai Mountain and changed its name to "Hanshan Temple".	4	汉英2-课堂练习11.txt
5	相传，唐贞观年间 (627-650)，名僧寒山和拾得两人由天台山来此住持，改名为 寒山寺 。 Tradition has it that two famous monks named Han Shan and Shi De, came here from Tiantai Mountain during the reign of Zhenguan of the Tang Dynasty (627-650), so they changed its names to "Hanshan Temple".	5	汉英2-课堂练习11.txt
6	相传，唐贞观年间 (627-650)，名僧寒山和拾得两人由天台山来此住持，改名为 寒山寺 。 According to legend, during the Zhenguan period of Tang Dynasty (627-650), two famous monks, Hanshan and Shide, came to the abbot from Tiantai Mountain and changed the temple's names to "Hanshan Temple".	6	汉英2-课堂练习11.txt
7	相传，唐贞观年间 (627-650)，名僧寒山和拾得两人由天台山来此住持，改名为 寒山寺 。 According to legend, during the Reign of Emperor Zhenguan of Tang Dynasty (627-650), two famous monks, Han Shan and Shi De, came to this temple from Tiantai Mountain and changed its name to "Hanshan Temple".	7	汉英2-课堂练习11.txt
8	相传，唐贞观年间 (627-650)，名僧寒山和拾得两人由天台山来此住持，改名为 寒山寺 。 It is said that in the Tang Dynasty , two famous monks Hanshan and Shide from Tiantai mountain were given charge of the temple and the name was then charged to HanshanSi.	8	汉英2-课堂练习11.txt

图 4-1　贾云龙工具双语检索

No	Text	Line	File
1	Legend has it that during the Zhenguan Years of the Tang Dynasty (627-650), two famous monks named Han Shan (meaning Cold Mountain) and Shi De came to the temple to serve as abbots. They renamed the temple Han Shan Temple, meaning Cold Mountain Temple.	1	汉英2-课堂练习11.EN.txt
2	According to legend, Tang Zhenguan years (627-650) , the famous monk Han Shan and Shide two people from Mount Tiantai to this Abbot, renamed "Hanshan Temple".	2	汉英2-课堂练习11.EN.txt
3	It is said that in the Tang Dynasty(618-907)two famous monks from Tiantai Mountain in today's Zhejiang Province were given charge of the temple and the name was then changed to Hanshan Temple.	3	汉英2-课堂练习11.EN.txt
4	According to legend, during the Reign of Emperor Zhenguan of tang Dynasty (627-650), two famous monks, Han Shan and Shi De, came to this temple from Tiantai Mountain and changed its name to "Hanshan Temple".	4	汉英2-课堂练习11.EN.txt
5	Tradition has it that two famous monks named Han Shan and Shi De, came here from Tiantai Mountain during the reign of Zhenguan of the Tang Dynasty (627-650), so they changed its names to "Hanshan Temple".	5	汉英2-课堂练习11.EN.txt
6	According to legend, during the Zhenguan period of Tang Dynasty (627-650), two famous monks, Hanshan and Shide, came to the abbot from Tiantai Mountain and changed the temple's names to "Hanshan Temple".	6	汉英2-课堂练习11.EN.txt
7	According to legend, during the Reign of Emperor Zhenguan of Tang Dynasty (627-650), two famous monks, Han Shan and Shi De, came to this temple from Tiantai Mountain and changed its name to "Hanshan Temple".	7	汉英2-课堂练习11.EN.txt
8	It is said that in the Tang Dynasty , two famous monks Hanshan and Shide from Tiantai mountain were given charge of the temple and the name was then charged to HanshanSi. I	8	汉英2-课堂练习11.EN.txt
9	It is said that during the reign of Emperor Tai Zong (627-650) of the Tang Dynasty, a famous monk Han Shan and Shide(monk) found came to this abbot from Tiantai Mountain and was renamed as "Hanshan Temple".	10	汉英2-课堂练习11.EN.txt
10	According to legend, during the Reign of Emperor Zhenguan of Tang Dynasty (627-650), two famous monks, Han Shan and Shi De, came to this temple from Tiantai Mountain and changed its name to "Hanshan Temple".	11	汉英2-课堂练习11.EN.txt

图 4-2　贾云龙工具单语检索

贾云龙工具支持对 data 文件夹内所有文件同时检索并呈现结果，此外，还支持正则检索，可以用于实验译文的初步质量评估。例如，我们用"寒山寺"作为关键词，检索汉英 2-课堂练习 11 双语语料，得到检索结果 55 条，如图 4-3：

49	相传，唐贞观年间 (627-650)，名僧寒山和拾得两人由天台山来此住持，改名为 寒山寺 。 According to legend, during the Tang Dynasty (627-650), two famous monks, Han Shan and Shi De, came from Tiantai Mountain to live here and changed the name to "Hanshan Temple."	49	汉英2-课堂练习11.txt
50	相传，唐贞观年间 (627-650)，名僧寒山和拾得两人由天台山来此住持，改名为 寒山寺 。 During the reign of Emperor Tai Zong (627-649) of the Tang Dynasty, the faous monk Hanshan and Shide came here from Mount Tiantai and changed the name into "Hanshan Temple".	50	汉英2-课堂练习11.txt
51	相传，唐贞观年间 (627-650)，名僧寒山和拾得两人由天台山来此住持，改名为 寒山寺 。 According to legend, during the Zhenguan Period of Tang Dynasty(627-650), Two famous monks, Hanshan and Shide,came to the abbot from Tiantai Mountain and changed their name to "Hanshan Temple".	51	汉英2-课堂练习11.txt
52	相传，唐贞观年间 (627-650)，名僧寒山和拾得两人由天台山来此住持，改名为 寒山寺 。 According to legend, during the The reign of Taizong in Tang Dynasty (627-650), two respectful monk named Hanshan and Shide from Tiantai Mountain became the Head Monk of this temple and renamed the temple as "Hanshan Temple".	52	汉英2-课堂练习11.txt
53	相传，唐贞观年间 (627-650)，名僧寒山和拾得两人由天台山来此住持，改名为 寒山寺 。 According to legend, during the Zhenguan Period(627-650) of the Tang Dynasty, two famous monks, Hanshan and Shide, came here from Tiantai Mountain to be the head monk and renamed it "Hanshan Temple".	53	汉英2-课堂练习11.txt
54	相传，唐贞观年间 (627-650)，名僧寒山和拾得两人由天台山来此住持，改名为 寒山寺 。 It was said that two famous monks Han, Shan and Shi De, came here from Tiantai Mountain to abbot and renamed it as Hanshan Temple during the year of 627-650, the Zhenguan period of the Tang Dynasty.	54	汉英2-课堂练习11.txt
55	相传，唐贞观年间 (627-650)，名僧寒山和拾得两人由天台山来此住持，改名为 寒山寺 。 It said that in the Tang Dynasty (618-907) two famous monks from Tiantai Mountain were given charge of the temple and the name was then changed to Hanshan Si.	55	汉英2-课堂练习11.txt

图 4-3　贾云龙工具检索"寒山寺"

而检索"寒山寺"及 Hanshan Temple,结果仅 46 条,见图 4-4:

40	相传,唐贞观年间(627-650),名僧寒山和拾得两人由天台山来此住持,改名为 寒山寺. According to the legend, a famous monk Hanshan with Shide who came here from Tiantai Mountai became its abbot and renamed it "Hanshan Temple" during the reign of Zhenguan in Tang Dynasty(627-650).	48	汉英2-课堂练习11.txt
41	相传,唐贞观年间(627-650),名僧寒山和拾得两人由天台山来此住持,改名为 寒山寺. According to legend, during the Tang Dynasty (627-650), two famous monks, Han Shan and Shi De, came from Tiantai Mountain to live here and changed the name to "Hanshan Temple".	49	汉英2-课堂练习11.txt
42	相传,唐贞观年间(627-650),名僧寒山和拾得两人由天台山来此住持,改名为 寒山寺. During the reign of Emperor Tai Zong (627-649) of the Tang Dynasty, the faous monk Hanshan and Shide came here from Mount Tiantai and changed the name into "Hanshan Temple".	50	汉英2-课堂练习11.txt
43	相传,唐贞观年间(627-650),名僧寒山和拾得两人由天台山来此住持,改名为 寒山寺. According to legend, during the Zhenguan Period of Tang Dynasty(627-650), Two famous monks, Hanshan and Shide,came to the abbot from Tiantai Mountain and changed their name to "Hanshan Temple".	51	汉英2-课堂练习11.txt
44	相传,唐贞观年间(627-650),名僧寒山和拾得两人由天台山来此住持,改名为 寒山寺. According to legend, during the The reign of Taizong in Tang Dynasty (627-650), two respectful monk named Hanshan and Shide from Tiantai Mountain became the Head Monk of this temple and renamed the temple as "Hanshan Temple".	52	汉英2-课堂练习11.txt
45	相传,唐贞观年间(627-650),名僧寒山和拾得两人由天台山来此住持,改名为 寒山寺. According to legend, during the Zhenguan Period(627-650) of the Tang Dynasty, two famous monks, Hanshan and Shide, came from Tiantai Mountain to be the head monk and renamed it "Hanshan Temple".	53	汉英2-课堂练习11.txt
46	相传,唐贞观年间(627-650),名僧寒山和拾得两人由天台山来此住持,改名为 寒山寺. It was said that two famous monks Han, Shan and Shi De, came here from Tiantai Mountain to abbot and renamed it as Hanshan Temple during the year of 627-650, the Zhenguan period of the Tang Dynasty.	54	汉英2-课堂练习11.txt

图 4-4　"寒山寺"及 Hanshan Temple 检索结果

从图 4-4 中可以看出,"寒山寺"翻译为 Hanshan Temple 的结果为 46 条,意味着 9 条"寒山寺"未译为 Hanshan Temple。虽然可以用人工查看的方式将 55 条检索结果逐一查看,找出另外 9 条译文,但这种方法效率较低,容易出错;且如果遇到要从几百甚至几千条结果中查找的情况,人工查看的方式实不可取。BFSU ParaConc 和我们自建的在线检索平台支持排除检索的功能,可解决这一问题。

4.2.2 BFSU ParaConc

BFSU ParaConc 由许家金教授、梁茂成教授和贾云龙共同设计开发。软件支持 txt 格式的单语双文件的检索,对应的两个单语文件文件名要一致,并根据文本语言分别在文件名后加上.ZH 和.EN,放入同一个文件夹。在 BFSU ParaConc 中选择文件夹,即会列出文件夹内所有对应的文件。要注意的是,该工具只支持 ANSI 编码的 txt,如为其他编码,需在检索前将 txt 文件编码转换为 ANSI。

该工具支持排除检索。前述"寒山寺"的译名查找问题,可在该工具的搜索框输入"寒山寺",勾选工具界面的"Exclude",并在其下输入 Hanshan Temple,点击 Search。共搜索到 9 条结果,如图 4-5。

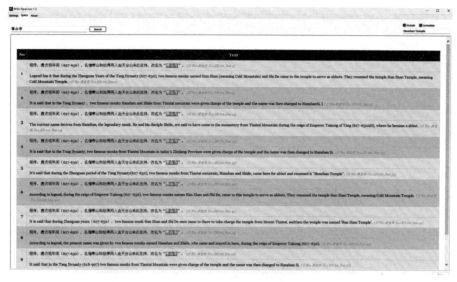

图 4-5　"寒山寺"排除检索

4.2.3 CCAT 在线检索平台

为了利用 CCAT 平台的语料库资源，我们自主开发了在线检索平台，支持单语及双语检索。平台登录界面如图 4-6。

图 4-6　CCAT 在线检索平台

该检索平台支持用户注册,即可以对外部用户开放,但目前仅在教学中面向学生开放。

该平台的语料资源包括大型通用双语语料库以及学习者语料库。已开发的功能较多,如支持两个关键词组合检索及排除检索、支持正则检索等。此外,该平台还支持一些自主学习功能。

针对前面小节中"寒山寺"的译名统计问题,可通过排除检索解决。首先在检索框输入关键词1"寒山寺",在"不含关键词 3"输入 Hanshan Temple,如图 4-7。

图 4-7   排除"Hanshan Temple"检索

点击检索,结果如图 4-8。

	CCAT在线检索平台	平台简介 使用说明

在"汉英2-课堂练习11"中共找到9项相关结果!

编号	内容	参考/出处
1 <ce000001>	相传,唐贞观年间(627-650),名僧寒山和拾得两人由天台山来此住持,改名为"寒山寺"。 Legend has it that during the Zhenguan Years of the Tang Dynasty (627-650), two famous monks named Han Shan (meaning Cold Mountain) and Shi De came to the temple to serve as abbots. They renamed the temple Han Shan Temple, meaning Cold Mountain Temple.	<汉英2-课堂练习11>
2 <ce000008>	相传,唐贞观年间(627-650),名僧寒山和拾得两人由天台山来此住持,改名为"寒山寺"。 It is said that in the Tang Dynasty , two famous monks Hanshan and Shide from Tiantai mountain were given charge of the temple and the name was then charged to HanshanSi.	<汉英2-课堂练习11>
3 <ce000013>	相传,唐贞观年间(627-650),名僧寒山和拾得两人由天台山来此住持,改名为"寒山寺"。 The current name derives from Hanshan, the legendary monk. He and his disciple Shide, are said to have come to the monastery from Tiantai Mountain during the reign of Emperor Taizong of Tang (627-650AD), where he became a abbot.	<汉英2-课堂练习11>
4 <ce000022>	相传,唐贞观年间(627-650),名僧寒山和拾得两人由天台山来此住持,改名为"寒山寺"。 It is said that in the Tang Dynasty, two famous monks from Tiantai Mountain in today's Zhejiang Province were given charge of the temple and the name was then changed to Hanshan Si.	<汉英2-课堂练习11>
5 <ce000032>	相传,唐贞观年间(627-650),名僧寒山和拾得两人由天台山来此住持,改名为"寒山寺"。 It's said that during the Zhenguan period of the Tang Dynasty(627-650), two famous monks from Tiantai mountain, Hanshan and Shide, came here for abbot and renamed it "Henshan Temple".	<汉英2-课堂练习11>
6 <ce000039>	相传,唐贞观年间(627-650),名僧寒山和拾得两人由天台山来此住持,改名为"寒山寺"。 According to legend, during the reign of Emperor Taizong (627-650), two famous monks names Han Shan and Shi De, came to this temple to serve as abbots. They renamed the temple Han Shan Temple, meaning Cold Mountain Temple.	<汉英2-课堂练习11>
7 <ce000040>	相传,唐贞观年间(627-650),名僧寒山和拾得两人由天台山来此住持,改名为"寒山寺"。 It is said that during Zhenguan years (627-650), two famous monk Han Shan and Shi De once came to there to take charge the temple from Mount Tiantai. andthen the temple was named 'Han Shan Temple'.	<汉英2-课堂练习11>
8 <ce000042>	相传,唐贞观年间(627-650),名僧寒山和拾得两人由天台山来此住持,改名为"寒山寺"。 According to legend, the present name was given by two famous monks named Hanshan and Shide, who came and stayed in here, during the reign of Emperor Taizong (627-650).	<汉英2-课堂练习11>
9 <ce000055>	相传,唐贞观年间(627-650),名僧寒山和拾得两人由天台山来此住持,改名为"寒山寺"。 It said that in the Tang Dynasty (618-907) two famous monks from Tiantai Mountain were given charge of the temple and the name was then changed to Hanshan Si.	<汉英2-课堂练习11>

第一页

图 4-8   检索结果

图中显示结果为 9 条,说明该检索方式成功地将"寒山寺"未译为 Hanshan Temple 的句子全部查出。

从以上检索结果可以看出,在"寒山寺"的翻译上,除译为 Hanshan Temple 这一正确表达外,还存在 Han Shan Temple ,Hanshansi ,Hanshan Si ,Henshan Temple ,Cold Mountain Temple 等不妥译文。从以上语料可以初步判断,Henshan Temple 属于笔误,很大可能是译者直接译出,未做查询;Hanshansi 这种拼写属于低级错误,应该不是查询得出,而是译者在音译方面的认知错误导致;至于其他几种译文,进一步追溯其对应的屏幕录像,则可以确切地了解到译者在翻译过程中的认知情况,如是否查询寒山寺的翻译,是否查询了但未能做出正确选择,等等。

4.2.4 CCAT 在线检索评注系统

为便于教师讲评反馈和学生小组讨论及相互评估反馈,我们基于 CCAT 在线翻译平台开发了在线检索评注系统。与 CCAT 在线检索平台不同的是,该系统只用于检索学习者语料,检索功能较前者更为丰富,且支持评注反馈功能。该系统功能一览如图 4-9 所示:

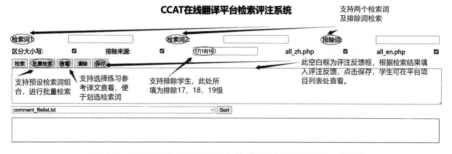

图 4-9　CCAT 在线翻译平台检索评注系统功能一览图

点击查看,出现练习译文下拉菜单,从中选择待评注的练习,则该练习的原文及参考译文会出现在阅读框内,如图 4-10 所示。

在检索词 1 框内输入"Shu King",在检索词 2 框内输入"蜀王",以查看该误译情况。

如图 4-11 所示,共检索到 11 例"蜀王"误译,此处只截取 4 例。

勾选全部误译,在评注框输入评注,点击保存,则评注会发送到被评注学生的项目列表处,如图 4-12 所示:

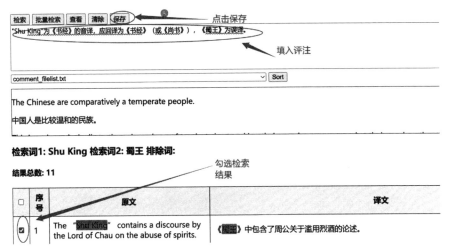

检索词1: ☐   检索词2: ☐   排除词: ☐

区分大小写: ☑   排除来源: ☑   17|18|19   all_zh.php ☑   all_en.php ☑

检索 | 批量检索 | 查看 | 清除 | 保存

comment_filelist.txt ▾ | Sort

The "Shu King" contains a discourse by the Lord of Chau on the abuse of spirits. ◀── 原文

《书经》有一篇周公谴责饮酒的训话。 ◀── 参考译文

His speech to his brother Fung, B.C. 1120, is the oldest temperance address on record, even earlier than the words of Solomon in the Proverbs.

图 4-10   练习参考译文查看

检索词1: Shu King 检索词2: 蜀王 排除词:

结果总数: 11

☑	序号	原文	译文	译者
☐	1	The "Shu King" contains a discourse by the Lord of Chau on the abuse of spirits.	《蜀王》中包含了周公关于滥用烈酒的论述。	
☐	2	The "Shu King" contains a discourse by the Lord of Chau on the abuse of spirits.	《蜀王》中包含了周公关于滥用神灵的话语。	
☐	3	The "Shu King" contains a discourse by the Lord of Chau on the abuse of spirits.	《蜀王》中有一篇周公关于虚灵的论述。	
☐	4	The "Shu King" contains a discourse by the Lord of Chau on the abuse of spirits.	《蜀王》中有一段关于周王爷滥用酒精的论述。	

图 4-11   检索误译

检索 | 批量检索 | 查看 | 清除 | (保存) ◀────── 点击保存

"Shu King"为《书经》的意译，应回译为《书经》(或《尚书》)，《蜀王》为误译。 ──▶ 填入评注

comment_filelist.txt ▾ | Sort

The Chinese are comparatively a temperate people.

中国人是比较温和的民族。

检索词1: Shu King 检索词2: 蜀王 排除词:

勾选检索结果

结果总数: 11

☐	序号	原文	译文
☑	1	The "Shu King" contains a discourse by the Lord of Chau on the abuse of spirits.	《蜀王》中包含了周公关于滥用烈酒的论述。

图 4-12   批量评注

也可排除"蜀王"误译,查看其他译文,起到展示正确译文的作用,如图 4-13:

检索词1: Shu King 检索词2:排除词: 蜀王　　　→ 排除"蜀王"

结果总数: 53

☑	序号	原文	译文	译者
☐	1	The "Shu King" contains a discourse by the Lord of Chau on the abuse of spirits.	《书经》有一篇周公谴责饮酒的训话。	admin2
☐	2	The "Shu King" contains a discourse by the Lord of Chau on the abuse of spirits.	《书经》有一篇周公谴责饮酒的训话。	阳朝杰文豪
☐	3	The "Shu King" contains a discourse by the Lord of Chau on the abuse of spirits.	《书经》有一篇周公谴责饮酒的训话。	duduw
☐	4	The "Shu King" contains a discourse by the Lord of Chau on the abuse of spirits.	《尚书》中便有周公谴责烈酒的对话。	刘永丹
☐	5	The "Shu King" contains a discourse by the Lord of Chau on the abuse of spirits.	《书经》中有一篇周公关于滥用神灵的论述。	伊一轮

图 4-13　排除词检索

还可以指定学生进行检索,可用于专门讲评某位学生译文的场合,如图 4-14。

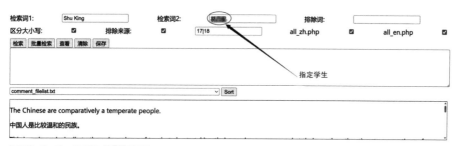

检索词1: Shu King 检索词2: 某同学 排除词:

结果总数: 1

☑	序号	原文	译文	译者
☐	1	The "Shu King" contains a discourse by the Lord of Chau on the abuse of spirits.	《尚书》中有一篇周公关于酗酒的论述。	某同学

图 4-14　指定检索示例 1

如果只输入学生姓名,不输入其他检索词,则可以检索该生的全部练习译文,可全面考察该生的翻译情况,如图 4-15。

通过语料库检索,可以发现翻译过程中比较细微的问题。例如,一次练习中,出现了"西安"一词,部分同学误译为"Xian"。在教师通过检索,统计误译数量,并予以讲评之后,多数学生印象深刻,在之后的一次包含"西安"一词的

图 4-15　指定检索示例 2

练习中,纠正了该误译。但也有学生没有切实掌握,又犯了同一错误,如图 4-16所示。

图 4-16　指定检索示例 3

图 4-16 中检索词 1 为学生姓名,检索词 2 为误译"Xian"。通过这种检索方式,可以查询学生的系统性错误,从而了解其翻译过程中的认知情况。

4.3 多模态语料的检索

4.3.1 自建在线多模态检索平台

目前多模态双语语料库在线检索的平台并不常见,网上虽然有一些多模态数据集,但都需要下载后在本地进行检索和处理。

为便于开展翻译过程的多模态研究,我们自主设计和架设了多模态双语语料库的在线检索平台。该平台基于 PHP,可在线检索双语语料,并在线播放检索结果对应的视频片段,如图 4-17。

图 4-17 在线多模态检索示例

如图所示,我们检索了"寒山寺",结果总数为 355 条。点击检索结果右侧的播放,即可定位并播放对应的视频,如图 4-18、图 4-19。

观看视频,即可了解译者的翻译过程及其后的认知机制。该译者首先利用 CCAT 平台提供的机器译文,划选并复制"寒山寺"的机译"Hanshan Temple",然后通过搜索引擎进行查询验证。这说明该译者具备较强的术语翻译意识以及查证意识。

相较于单机版检索工具,在线语料库检索平台具有一些显著优势:

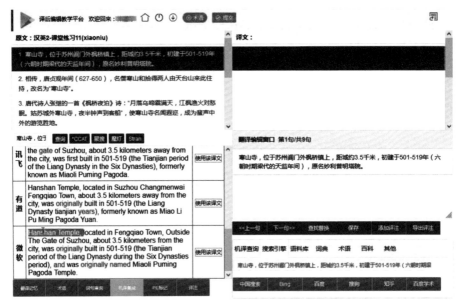

图 4-18　检索结果对应的视频片段 1

图 4-19　检索结果对应的视频片段 2

（1）可访问性：在线检索平台可以通过任何具有网络连接的设备（如台式机、笔记本电脑、平板电脑和智能手机）进行访问。这使得用户能够在任何时间、任何地点轻松获取和查询语料库资源，而无需安装特定软件。

（2）实时更新：在线平台可以实时更新数据，确保用户始终访问到最新的信息。对于动态变化的语料库，这是一个很大的优势，因为用户无需手动下载和更新数据。

（3）跨平台兼容性：在线检索平台通常可以在各种操作系统和浏览器上运行，无需考虑兼容性问题。而单机版检索工具可能需要针对不同操作系统进行优化和维护。

（4）集中式管理：在线平台将数据和检索工具集中存储在服务器上，便于统一管理和维护。这降低了数据冗余和版本不一致的风险，同时简化了系统的维护工作。

（5）多用户支持：在线检索平台可以同时支持多个用户访问和查询语料库。这使得团队成员可以轻松共享数据和资源，提高协作效率。而单机版工具通常仅支持单个用户使用，难以实现资源共享。

（6）降低硬件需求：在线平台将数据存储和计算任务托管在服务器上，这意味着用户设备的硬件需求降低。对于处理大型语料库的情况，这可以显著减轻用户设备的负担。

（7）定制化和扩展性：在线检索平台通常可以根据用户需求进行定制和扩展。例如，可以通过添加新的检索功能、分析工具或可视化组件来改进平台。而单机版工具的定制和扩展性可能受限于软件的设计和架构。

虽然在线语料库检索平台具有诸多优势，但也存在一些潜在的缺点，如对网络连接的依赖、数据安全等。因此，在选择合适的检索工具时，需要权衡这些因素以满足特定的需求和场景。

4.3.2 ELAN 检索

ELAN(EUDICO Linguistic Annotator EUDICO 语言标注工具)是一款用于创建、编辑和可视化复杂多层结构的多模态语言资源的注释及检索工具。ELAN 的主要目标是为语言学家和其他研究人员提供一种灵活的平台，以支持多媒体数据（如音频、视频和文本）的同步注释。

语料库语言学发展的一个趋势是创建多模态语料库，即语料库与音频和视频相链接，甚至是同步共现的资源库（何安平，2010:243）。ELAN 是用于多模态语料库构建、分析以及检索的重要工具,国内也已开展一些相关应用和研究,包括多模态话语分析(张立新,2012;蓝洁,2020;吴静静,2020;张雪,2022)、多模态语料库的构建(李斌,高广安,2012;刘剑,胡开宝,2015;刘剑,2019;吴蕊珠等,2019;蔡莹,2022),以及多模态互动机制研究(管乐,2021)。

我们所构建的多模态语料库也支持 ELAN 检索,主要步骤如下:

(1)下载并安装 ELAN。访问 ELAN 官方网站(https://archive.mpi.nl/tla/elan),下载适用于所用操作系统的 ELAN 版本,并按照安装说明进行安装。

(2)打开 ELAN。启动 ELAN 后,将看到一个空白的工作区。

(3)加载视频。转到菜单栏中的"文件">"新建",选择要分析的视频文件。视频将显示在左侧的媒体播放器窗口中。

(4)加载字幕。转到菜单栏中的"文件">"导入">"字幕",选择字幕文件(srt 格式),之后会在右侧窗口的"字幕"处显示字幕。

(5)进行检索。在"搜索"菜单下,点击"查找(及替换)",再点击搜索对话框"搜索"菜单下的"搜索",即可显示字幕。通过点击字幕的开始和结束时间来导航到视频中的特定部分。

4.4 小结

双语对应语料库检索工具在翻译过程中发挥着重要作用。简单易用的检索工具能够使译者在翻译过程中更加高效地查询相关信息,提高翻译质量和效率。检索工具不一定是越复杂越好,应尽量简单易用,以满足实际需求。

同时,双语语料库的构建应考虑构建的效率和格式的兼容性。在构建过程中,研究者应关注以下几个方面。

(1)界定语料范围:在构建双语语料库时,应充分考虑目标领域和应用需求,确保所收集的语料具有代表性和实用性。

(2)保持格式兼容性:在构建双语语料库时,应尽量采用通用的文件格式,以便与各种检索工具兼容。

(3)注重数据质量:在收集和整理语料时,应确保数据的准确性、完整性和一致性,以便输出高质量的检索结果。

(4)简化构建流程:在构建双语语料库时,应尽量简化构建流程,提高构建效率。这可以通过采用 AI 工具、自编 PHP 及 Python 工具等方法实现。

通过以上几个方面的考虑,可以构建出既高效又兼容的双语语料库,为简单易用的检索工具提供强大的支持。

语料库的检索工具对于语料库语言学研究具有极其重要的作用;检索软件功能是否强大、完备,是否能够满足各种统计需要,对于语料库语言学研究的影响是非常大的(王朝晖,余军,2016:198)。目前双语语料库检索工具仍以单机版居多,但随着互联网和人工智能技术的快速发展,未来在线双语语料检索平台将成为主流趋势,具备更高的开放性、兼容性和易用性。基于 AI 的检索工具和在线平台将为翻译研究和应用带来更多便利和创新。

(1)开放性:在线双语语料检索平台可以充分利用互联网资源,实现多方共享和协作,为研究者和译者提供更广泛的数据来源和更丰富的功能。

(2)兼容性:在线平台可以更好地适应不同设备和操作系统,降低技术门槛,使更多研究者和译者能够方便地使用双语语料库检索工具。

(3)易用性:在线平台可以提供更友好的用户界面和交互体验,简化检索过程,提高用户满意度。

此外,将自然语言处理 API 嵌入在线双语语料检索平台,如情感分析(sentiment analysis)和语义分析(semantic analysis),可以进一步提升检索工具的智能化水平。AI 赋能将有助于实现以下目标:

(1)提高检索效率。通过自然语言处理技术,可以实现更精确、更高效的检索,帮助用户快速找到所需信息。

(2)深度挖掘语料库。利用 AI 技术,可以对双语语料库进行深度挖掘,发现潜在的规律和特点,为翻译研究提供更多启示。

第 5 章 翻译过程中的思辨能力

5.1 引言

翻译过程是一个复杂的认知活动过程,涉及译者对源语文本的理解、分析、评估和目标语文本的生成等多个环节,需要运用多种认知能力,如语言能力、文化能力、思辨能力、技术能力、选择能力等。其中,思辨能力作为一种重要的认知能力,对翻译过程具有重要影响。

近年来,英语专业学生"思辨缺席"现象已引起外语教学界的普遍关注,培养学生的思辨能力已成为业界共识。为培养学生的思辨能力,教材的编写应向思辨倾斜,编排相应的学习内容和练习;同时教师应营造思辨性的互动课堂氛围,开展"思辨依托内容式"翻译教学,运用研究性教学,给学生提供自主学习的教学资源及指导(黄玉霞,2017:51)。

思辨能力是译者能力的核心要素,而以知识传授和技能训练为中心的传统翻译教学模式致使学生思辨能力缺失(李家坤等,2018:51)。翻译教学应放在培养批判性思维能力上(李长栓,2017:32),通过运用错误分析模式、案例教学模式、数据驱动模式等不同的教学方法和手段来有效促进大学生批判性思维的养成和提高(余国良,2010:101);在翻译教学中,始终遵循质疑反思原则、逻辑介入原则、对话合作原则与启迪创新原则(欧阳利锋,2009:50);通过分析翻译课中的学生反思日志,探索翻译教学中学生思辨能力的培养(张苇,2014:127)。

针对译者思辨能力缺失的问题,李家坤等(2017:105)构建了翻译思辨认知机制模型,并以此模型为理论框架,对译员进行了翻译思辨能力培训实验研究,有效提高了译员的翻译思辨能力。杨艳霞、王湘玲(2020:65)从译者主体思维模式、翻译课程体系、学习模式和评价体系 4 个维度,提出泛在学习时代下译者思辨能力的培养路径。

本章以思辨能力为切入点,旨在考察翻译过程中学习者的思辨能力及其对翻译质量的影响。

5.2　思辨能力在翻译认知过程中的应用

思辨能力是指分析、评估和解决问题过程中运用批判性思维的能力,包括观察能力、分析能力和创新能力等。在翻译过程中,思辨能力主要应用在以下几个方面。

5.2.1 原文文本的理解与分析

在翻译过程中,译者需要运用思辨能力对源语文本进行深入的理解和分析。这包括对文本的主题、结构、语言特点和文化内涵等方面的全面把握,以及对文本中的隐含信息、歧义现象和文化差异等问题的识别和处理。译者需要运用观察能力捕捉文本的细节信息,运用分析能力揭示文本的内在逻辑。

1.运用观察能力捕捉原文细节信息

观察能力是指译者在阅读源语文本时,关注文本中细节信息的能力。这包括对文本中的词汇、语法、修辞等方面的关注,以及对文本中的情感、态度、意图等方面的关注。通过运用观察能力,译者可以更好地理解原文文本的表层信息和深层信息,从而产出更准确的译文。

【例 1】 Our national faith has been not in propositions but in processes.

该句英文使用了头韵(alliteration)和对照(antithesis)的修辞,言简意赅,对比鲜明。译者如果缺乏观察能力,就可能会忽略这两种修辞,如图 5-1 所示的机器译文。

学生的译文与机译大同小异,大多没有意识到修辞的翻译问题。但如果换一种形式,让学生去判断该句中的修辞,则学生判断不出头韵的并不多。这一案例说明,在翻译过程中,很多学习者经常是无意识地直译,忽略了观察原文这一步。这值得引起我们的反思,在翻译教学中应注重培养和提升学生的观察能力,而案例教学就是一种较为有效的方式。在和学生讨论后,我们将该句的译文确定为"国人深信,空谈误国,实干兴邦",取得了较好的修辞效果,给学生留下了深刻印象,有助于加强其翻译过程中的观察意识。

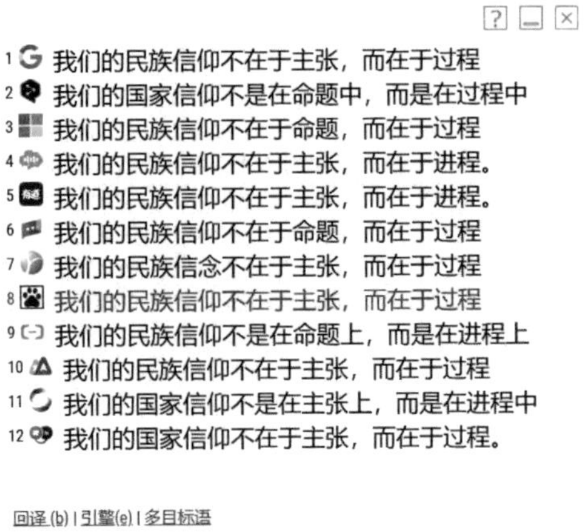

図 5-1　机译示例

2.运用分析能力揭示文本内在逻辑

分析能力是指译者在阅读源语文本时,对文本中的内在逻辑进行揭示和把握的能力。这包括对文本的结构、主题和论点等方面的分析,以及对文本中的逻辑关系和语义关系等方面的分析。通过运用分析能力,译者可以更好地理解源语文本的整体框架和内在联系,从而为翻译提供更有力的支持。

【例 2】The lighting was heavy on shadows, with frequent flashes.

例 2 摘自一篇有关全球化的文章,背景是作者在一个剧场观看莎剧《麦克白》表演,这是其描述表演的一句话。该句的翻译,需要译者具备一定的分析能力,通过逻辑思辨,发现并解决问题。我们让 30 名学生将该句英文译为中文,其中有 24 名学生将"shadows"译为"阴影""影子""暗影"等表达,只有 6 名将其译为"幽灵""鬼影"等表达。其中 2 名是因为熟悉《麦克白》,知道剧情;还有 4 名是查证了"shadow",并根据上下文做出的分析选择。除学生译文外,我们从 GT4T(吉第福第翻译工具)中选了 12 种机器翻译,获取了以下 12 种机器译文,作为比较:

译文 1:灯光阴影很重,经常闪烁。（谷歌）

译文 2:灯光的影子很重,经常有闪光灯。（DeepL）

译文 3:灯光阴影很大,闪烁频繁。（微软）

译文 4:阴影上的灯光很强,经常有闪光。（讯飞）

译文 5:阴影上的灯光很强,经常有闪光。（有道）

译文 6:灯光在阴影中很重,闪光频繁。（彩云小译）

译文 7：灯光阴影很重，经常闪光。（小牛）

译文 8：灯光笼罩在阴影中，经常闪烁。（百度）

译文 9：灯光笼罩着阴影，经常闪烁。（阿里）

译文 10：光线在阴影上很重，经常闪光。（火山）

译文 11：灯光在暗处很重，经常闪烁。（SYSTRAN）

译文 12：灯光笼罩在阴影中，闪光频繁。（腾讯）

从以上机译可以看出，神经网络机器翻译目前还不具备逻辑判断能力，无法意识到如果"shadow"的意思是"影子"，那么"The lighting was heavy on shadows"是逻辑不通的。4 位学生觉得该句意思不通，故而查阅词典，发现"shadow"还有"phantom"的意思，故将其译为"幽灵""鬼影"，都是正解。该案例说明了翻译过程中分析能力和逻辑思辨的重要性，也说明人机协作的必要性，其前提是译者能在翻译过程中充分发挥思辨能力。

【例 3】It loomed and towered in his dreams before he even saw the unaxed woods where it left its crooked print, shaggy, tremendous, red-eyed, not malevolent but just big, too big for the dogs which tried to bay it, for the horses which tried to ride it down, for the men and the bullets they fired into it; too big for the very country which was its constricting scope.

例 3 出自福克纳的中篇小说《熊》，句子的"It"指小说中的老熊。"too big for the dogs which tried to bay it"中的"bay"，所有学习者都理解为"吠叫"之意，大多将该片段翻译为"对于试图向它吠叫的狗来说，它太大了"之类。部分学生可能觉得"试图"逻辑上不妥，因为吠叫是狗的本能，似乎无需"try"，因此略去"tried"不译，译为"对它吠叫"；但可惜没有进一步查证，虽然思辨能力发挥了作用，但最终没有拿出正确译文。李文俊先生是福克纳翻译专家，他将该片段译为"对于想用一通吠叫把它吓住的猎犬来说，它是太大了"，添加了"把它吓住"，以化解逻辑上的冲突。但实际上，如果查询阅典，可以发现"bay"作为动词，还有其他意思，如图 5-2。

图中圈选的解释出自《美国传统词典》，"bay"作为动词，此处是"困住"之意。巧合的是，该释义后用的例证，就是福克纳的这句话。这一案例说明，即便是富有经验的译者，在翻译过程中发现逻辑问题之后，要做的也不是通过文字变通化解逻辑矛盾，而是查证。

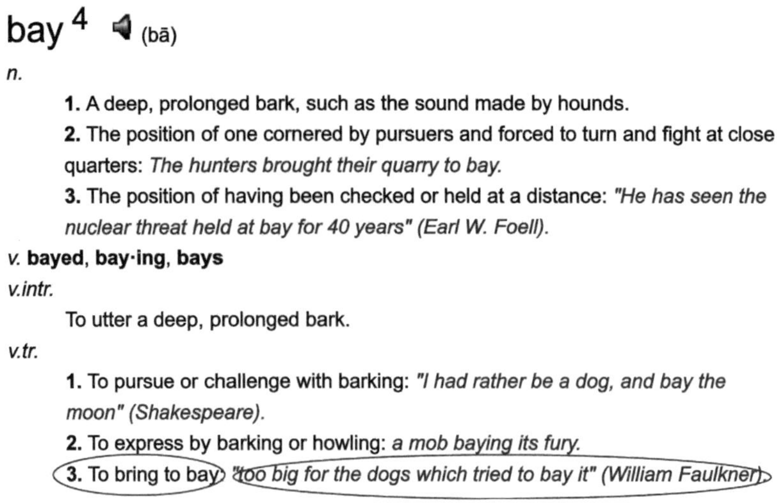

bay⁴ 🔊 (bā)

n.

1. A deep, prolonged bark, such as the sound made by hounds.
2. The position of one cornered by pursuers and forced to turn and fight at close quarters: *The hunters brought their quarry to bay.*
3. The position of having been checked or held at a distance: *"He has seen the nuclear threat held at bay for 40 years" (Earl W. Foell).*

v. **bayed, bay·ing, bays**

v.intr.

To utter a deep, prolonged bark.

v.tr.

1. To pursue or challenge with barking: *"I had rather be a dog, and bay the moon" (Shakespeare).*
2. To express by barking or howling: *a mob baying its fury.*
3. To bring to bay: *"too big for the dogs which tried to bay it" (William Faulkner).*

图 5-2　"bay"的词典释义

5.2.2 翻译问题的解决与决策

在翻译过程中,译者需要运用思辨能力解决各种翻译问题和进行翻译决策。这包括对翻译难点的识别、对翻译方案的比较和选择,以及对翻译过程中的挑战的灵活应对和策略选择。译者需要运用观察能力和分析能力发现翻译问题,运用分析能力探究问题的原因和本质,运用创新能力寻找翻译的新思路和方法,设计问题的解决方案和策略。

例如,在翻译修辞时,译者可以发挥创造性思维,解决貌似不可译的问题。以双关修辞为例,以下对话语含双关,似乎是不可译的。

【例4】——What kind of money do you like?

——Matrimony.

"Matrimony"一语双关,既可理解为一种名为"Matri"的"money",也可理解为"marriage",似乎译者只能译其一,或是用注释予以说明;但有一个译文却独辟蹊径,用增译(**黑体部分**)的方式完美地再现了该双关修辞,颇具新意,译文如下:

——你喜欢什么钱？**美元还是日元**？

——良缘。

5.3　译者思辨能力的多模态研究

本小节基于所建多模态语料库,对学习者译文、机器译文及专业译者译文进行实证研究。其中学习者语料数据包括从多模态语料库中抽取的 30 份译文、翻译过程中做的评注以及屏幕录制视频,机器译文包括微软译文、有道译文、小牛译文、百度译文和讯飞译文,专业译者译文(简称专业译文)指参考译文。

5.3.1　研究个案:原文理解

1.个案 1

原文:[杨铁心转头去看骑在马后的李氏,要瞧她在战斗之中有无受伤,突然间树丛中射出一枝冷箭,杨铁心不及闪避,这一箭直透后心。]①

李氏大惊,叫道:"叔叔,箭! 箭!"

[杨铁心心中一凉:"不料我今日死在这里! 但我死前先得把贼兵杀散,好让大嫂逃生。"]

专业译文:"Brother!" Lily Li cried.

百度译文: Li Shi was shocked and exclaimed, "Uncle, arrow! Arrow!"

讯飞译文: Li Shi is frightened greatly, cry: "Uncle, arrow! Arrows!"

小牛译文: Lee was frightened and cried, "Uncle, arrow! Arrow!"

有道译文: Li Shi was shocked and shouted,"Uncle, the arrow! Arrow!"

微软译文: Li Shi was shocked and shouted: "Uncle, arrow! Arrow!"

学习者译文 1: Li shouted out loudly, "Brother! The arrow!"②

学习者译文 2: Li was astonished and cried: "watch out for the arrows, brother! The arrows!"

学习者译文 3: Li was frightened and cried, "Uncle, arrow! Arrow!"

学习者译文 4: Li was astonished and shouted: "Brother, arrow! Arrow!"

---

①　[　]内的句子为上下文,未提供译文,后同。

②　统计分析的学习者(英语专业大三学生)译文为 30 份,限于篇幅,仅列出其中 5 份,后同。

学习者译文 5： Lee was terrified and cried: "*Uncle, arrow! There is an arrow!*"

学习者评注 1[①]：

评注: ▨▨▨ [修改] [删除] [译文]

1.《尔雅·释亲》："父之兄弟，先生为世父，后生为叔父。"又："妇谓夫之弟曰叔。"所以，已婚妇女对夫家胞弟正统的叫法应该是长辈叫"叔父"，平辈叫"叔子"。至于"叔叔"应该是在世俗变迁中渐渐以叠字表示亲昵。2.已婚妇女称呼丈夫的弟弟也叫"叔叔"，个人猜测这种平辈间得称呼是从长辈的称呼引申出来的，就是已婚女子借了自己孩子的身份来称呼丈夫的平辈，这样显得谦卑客气。由此可知，这里的"叔叔"并不是我们现在所指的叔叔。而是一种敬称。

学习者评注 2：

评注: ▨▨▨ [修改] [删除] [译文]

下文可知，叔叔，指的是小叔子

学习者评注 3：

评注: ▨▨▨ [修改] [删除] [译文]

这个叔叔不知道要怎么翻译，写个铁心。感觉不是亲叔叔。

学习者评注 4：

评注: ▨▨▨ [修改] [删除] [译文]

根据上下句的联系，若杨铁心称呼李氏为大嫂，此处李氏应称杨铁心为小叔，叔叔应译为brother-in-law

---

① 基于 CCAT 在线翻译平台，学习者可在翻译过程中实时输入评注，记录翻译过程中的思考、难点、疑点、问题、心得等。该评注功能可替代传统的有声思维法（TAPs，见 1.2 小节）。两者的差别在于有声思维法是一种人为的实验方法，受试者承担了一定的压力，有时候难免失真；而翻译过程中的评注则是有感则发，长短随意，较为真实自然。所引学习者评注均保持原样，未修改可能存在的错误。

学习者评注 5：

评注：■■文　修改　删除　译文

这里的叫是带有情绪的，因此用cry。考虑到中英文的差别，英文很少一个
单词组成句子，因此第二个箭我把它补充成了一个句子。

2.个案 2

原文：[惩山北之塞，出入之迂也，聚室而谋曰："吾与汝毕力平险，指通豫
南，达于汉阴，可乎？"]

杂然相许。

[其妻献疑曰："以君之力，曾不能损魁父之丘，如太形、王屋何？"]

专业译文：Many voices said that they agreed to the idea.

百度译文：Confused to each other.

讯飞译文：Mixed promise.

小牛译文：Miscellaneous.

有道译文：All kinds of things.

微软译文：It's mixed.

学习者译文 1：Everyone was in favor of him except his wife.

学习者译文 2：Most of them agreed the proposal.

学习者译文 3：They all agreed.

学习者译文 4：All the family members are in compatible with him.

学习者译文 5：All of them gave their support.

学习者评注 1：

评注：■■■　修改　删除　译文

结合语境，妻子并没有直接同意

学习者评注 2：

评注：■■■　修改　删除　译文

此处的意思是大家纷纷赞同。但后文妻子质疑，所以并不是所有人都同意，译为大多数人most of people
符合逻辑。

学习者评注 3:

评注:  这句话表示都赞同的意思

学习者评注 4:

评注: 这里的杂不是杂七杂八,而是指大家,所以表示众人一致赞同。

学习者评注 5:

评注: 时态应该用现在时还是过去时呢

5.3.2 分析讨论

1.个案 1

原文选自《射雕英雄传》,参考译文译者为郝玉青(Anna Holmwood)。该案例涉及原文的理解问题,"叔叔"是应该理解为一般情况下的叔叔(也就是英文的"uncle"),还是小叔子(丈夫的弟弟)? 这需要通过上下文来确定。下文杨铁心称李氏为大嫂,由此可确定此处"叔叔"为"小叔子"之意。

就以上译文来看,专业译文理解准确,机器译文全部理解错误,5 份学习者译文中 3 个理解准确,2 个理解错误。

根据学习者翻译过程中所写的评注,大体可以推断评注 2(对应译文 2,评注序号与译文对应,后同)及评注 4 的译者是联系上下文确定了小叔子这一词义,这体现出两位译者的汉语功底较为扎实,了解"叔叔"的两个词义,并且善于观察,注意到下文的"大嫂"一词,从而正确理解了原文。评注 1 的译者可能是通过查证得出对"小叔子"的理解,而其之所以查证,是因为观察到了下文的"大嫂",激发了逻辑思辨过程——"大嫂"和"叔叔"是冲突的,故而查证叔叔的含义,并通过查证理解了"小叔子"的意思。评注 5 代表了多数学习者,对上下文缺乏观察,忽略了对"叔叔"一词的理解,机械地译为"Uncle"。评注 3 的译

者注意到了上下文的矛盾之处,但并未进一步处理疑点,而是不顾前后语义冲突,译为"Uncle";可能是时间紧张,来不及查证,或也可能是没有想到此处可以通过查证解决问题。

以上基于学习者评注的分析是否属实,需要通过屏幕录制视频进行验证。我们观看了这 5 位学习者翻译过程的屏幕录制视频,发现实际情况与我们的分析大体一致。例如,评注 1 的译者是在译完"好让大嫂逃生"一句后,觉察到问题,才查证"叔叔"的含义;评注 2 和评注 4 的译者是译为"Brother"之后,直接写的评注,没有就"叔叔"进行查证;评注 5 的译者未对"大嫂"和"叔叔"予以关注,未做相关查证;评注 3 的译者虽然写了提出疑问的评注,但并未进行查证,后经询问,我们得知该译者当时未想到叔叔还可能有另一词义,故而未查证。

综合以上分析,我们将此个案所反映的思辨能力分为 4 个层次:

(1)无知无觉:缺乏对上下文的观察、判断,不能发现逻辑冲突。

(2)有觉无解:察觉到了问题,但缺乏查证能力(详见第 7 章),未能通过查证解决问题。

(3)有觉凭解:察觉到了问题,并凭借查证解决了问题。

(4)有觉直解:察觉到了问题,并凭借已有的语言文化知识储备直接解决了问题,无需查证。

2.个案 2

原文选自《愚公移山》,参考译文译者不详。文言文的汉译英一般要经过语内翻译(文言文译为白话文)及语际翻译(白话文译为英文)两个步骤,对原文的理解非常重要。原文"杂然"是"七嘴八舌"之意,"杂然相许"是"都赞同",还是"大部分都赞同"? 这要看上下文。网上的白话译文中,有将其译为"大家纷纷表示赞同"[①]的,貌似是"大家都赞同"之意,属于误译。

就以上译文而言,专业译文理解准确,机器译文全部理解错误,但这并不能说所有机器翻译都无法翻译文言文。据笔者调查,DeepL 机器翻译具有一定的文言文理解和翻译能力,将该句译为"He agreed to do so",虽然仍存在错误,但译文是可以理解的完整句子。

5 份学习者译文中 2 个理解准确,3 个理解错误。

根据学习者所做评注,可以看出评注 1 的译者通过逻辑思辨,结合语境,

---

① 　http://www.hydcd.com/guwen/gw0072.htm

正确理解了原意,是直接做出判断,没有经过查证;评注 2 的译者做了查证,查到该句是"大家纷纷赞同"的意思,但注意到下文中妻子质疑,因此最终理解为"并不是所有人都同意";评注 3 的译者是否查证,无法从其评注推断,需要查看屏幕录制视频,但该译者忽略了下文的冲突信息,缺乏思辨;评注 4 的译者与评注 3 的译者情况类似;评注 5 代表了部分学习者,缺乏对上下文的观察和思辨,忽略了"杂然相许"一句的理解,关注的是其他问题。

以上基于学习者评注的分析,存在疑问,需要通过屏幕录制视频进一步核实。我们观看了这 5 位学习者翻译过程的屏幕录制视频,发现评注 1 的译者没有查询"杂然相许"的意思,说明其对文言文的理解到位,并根据对上下文的逻辑思辨明确了该句的确切意思;评注 2 的译者做了查证,但通过对上下文的思辨对查询到的白话译文做了纠偏;评注 3 的译者没有查证,理解错误;评注 4 的译者做了查证,对该句的意思有所关注,缺乏对上下文的思辨;评注 5 的译者查证了整篇文言文的白话译文,但未关注该句的理解问题。

综合以上分析,我们将此个案所反映的思辨能力分为 4 个层次:

(1)无知无觉:缺乏对上下文的观察、判断,不能发现逻辑冲突。

(2)有查无疑:能做查证,但未察觉到问题。

(3)有查有疑:能做查证,并且通过对上下文的逻辑思辨察觉并解决了问题。

(4)有疑直解:凭借已有的语言文化知识储备及对上下文的逻辑思辨直接解决了问题,无需查证。

5.3.3 研究发现

通过查看全部 30 份译文对应的屏幕录制视频,2 个个案 4 种层次的分布如下表 5-1、表 5-2、表 5-3、表 5-4 所示:

表 5-1　个案 1 学习者的思辨能力的层次分布

层次	数量	比例
无知无觉	17	57%
有觉无解	6	20%
有觉凭解	4	13%
有觉直解	3	10%

表 5-2 个案 1 机器翻译的思辨能力的层次分布

层次	数量	比例
无知无觉	5	100%
有觉无解	0	0%
有觉凭解	0	0%
有觉直解	0	0%

表 5-3 个案 2 学习者的思辨能力的层次分布

层次	数量	比例
无知无觉	5	17%
有查无疑	7	23%
有查有疑	11	37%
有疑直解	7	23%

表 5-4 个案 2 机器翻译的思辨能力的层次分布

层次	数量	比例
无知无觉	5	100%
有查无疑	0	0%
有查有疑	0	0%
有疑直解	0	0%

综合以上统计，以下几点发现值得关注：

1.思辨能力在人机协作中具有重要作用

随着人工智能的兴起，翻译界有一种悲观观点，认为人工翻译将被机器翻译所取代。我们认为，机器翻译可能演变进化到几乎没有语法错误的程度，但至少目前仍缺乏逻辑思辨能力，在这方面只能人机协作，而其关键是译者要具有强大的思辨能力。从以上个案分析的结果来看，情况不容乐观。翻译人才培养面临着严峻挑战,需要在翻译教学中加大对学习者的思辨能力的培养力度。

2.语言文化知识的夯实极为迫切

在学习者的训练阶段,可以花费大量时间进行查证,获取某一翻译难点/疑点的解决办法,但在语言服务行业的实际操作中,译者能用于查证的时间和精力是有限的;因此需要学习者在训练阶段打下扎实的语言文化知识的基础。

3.查证能力的提升至关重要

在人工智能时代,翻译教师和学习者要清楚人与机器各自的优势。首先,在训练阶段,学习者要着力培养和提升查证能力,在查证中夯实语言文化知识,通过查证提升思辨能力,通过查证弥补机器之不足。其次,学习者要努力提高信息素养;在信息爆炸的时代,学会筛选和评估信息是提高查证能力的关键。再次,学习者还应该学会利用各种信息渠道和工具,如图书馆、网络搜索引擎、在线数据库等,来获取和检索相关信息。最后,学习者应该在学习过程中多进行实践,不断总结经验,反思自己在查证过程中的问题和不足,以促使自己不断进步。

5.4　翻译教学中思辨能力的培养

为了提高翻译质量,翻译教学应注重培养学生的思辨能力。具体措施包括:

1.强化翻译理论教学

翻译理论教学是培养学生思辨能力的基础。教师应系统地讲授翻译理论,帮助学生掌握翻译的基本原则、方法和技巧,培养学生的翻译意识和思维能力。同时,教师应鼓励学生对翻译理论进行批判性思考,培养学生的独立思考和判断能力。

2.丰富翻译实践教学

翻译实践教学是培养学生思辨能力的重要途径。教师应设计具有挑战性和针对性的翻译实践任务,确保翻译实践材料中具备充分的思辨要素,引导学生运用思辨能力解决实际翻译问题。同时,教师应关注学生的翻译过程,及时发现和纠正学生在翻译过程中缺乏思辨的问题,提升学生的思辨能力。

3.建设翻译思辨案例库

教师平时应注意收集翻译思辨案例,有条件的话,可以建设案例库,建议以师生共建的方式进行。依托翻译思辨案例,开展启发式、讨论式的案例教学,组织学生开展案例分析讨论、撰写案例分析报告。

4.加强译文修订训练

在人机协作的翻译模式下,译文修订训练非常重要;而译文修订的成败,除了取决于语言能力,更取决于思辨能力。教师通过译文修订训练,可有效提升学习者的思辨能力。

【例5】And sometimes I remembered that God was willing to spare Sodom for the sake of 10 of the righteous. Not that Keokuk was anything like wicked Sodom, or that Proust's Charlus would have been tempted to settle in Benton Harbor, Mich. I seem to have had a persistent democratic desire to find evidences of high culture in the most unlikely places.

以上原文为第 22 届韩素音国际翻译大赛(以下称"韩赛")英译汉原文第二段结尾三句。韩赛原文选材优秀,颇多需要查证思辨之处,为思辨能力的培养提供了极佳素材。在翻译教学的修订训练中,我们会鼓励学生尝试对参考译文"挑刺"。

官方参考译文及相关注解如下:有时我会想起上帝愿为十个义人而饶恕所多玛城的故事,并非基奥卡克市和邪恶的所多玛⑤有何相似之处,也并非普鲁斯特笔下的夏吕斯⑥想移居密西根州的本顿港,只不过我似乎一直有一种开明的想法,希望在最难觅高雅文化的地方找到高雅文化的证据。

⑤圣经《创世纪》第 18 章:上帝欲灭所多玛城,亚伯拉罕代为求恩,上帝允诺若城内有十名义人,便不施惩罚。

⑥夏吕斯男爵为普鲁斯特小说《追忆似水年华》中的人物,生活堕落。

我们曾多次用其进行思辨能力训练。学生先阅读译前提示,摘录如下:

> 该文句式结构并不复杂,文字也不晦涩,造成翻译障碍的主要是其中大量的文化典故和互文文本,如文中的"Sodom"和"Charlus",翻译时需要详加考证,方能明白为什么贝娄会在提到 Sodom 之后,又言及《追忆似水年华》中的 Charlus。

在修订过程中,学生一般都会推敲原文及译文,并进行相关查证。参考译文质量很高,有些学生发现不了什么问题,便会在评注中写上一些积极评价;但也有学生会对参考译文提出疑问,并下笔修改。

全体提交之后,进入讨论环节。以某届学生该次修订训练为例,有学生提出,"愿为十个义人而饶恕所多玛城"一句存在歧义,不了解《圣经》典故的读者可能会误以为上帝因为十个义人的缘故饶恕了所多玛城,但据查,所多玛城已经毁灭了。也有学生表示,看了参考译文和注解,仍不知为何作者要突然提及夏吕斯。对此,有学生提出,这几句之前,作者提到自己发现本顿港和基奥卡克市这些小地方有不少人爱好文学,因此想起难以找到十个义人的所多玛,但所多玛又是某种现象泛滥之地,可能怕招致误会,就追加一句予以澄清,而夏吕斯也属于这一情况。作者在掉书袋,参考译文及注解似乎有所欠缺,但不知怎么修改。之后,教师引导学生阅读有关"背景阐释"的技巧说明,该说明指出"背景阐释"主要有两种方式——文内阐释及文外加注。有学生建议修改注解,也有学生提出可文内阐释。讨论非常热烈,得出注解修改版和文内阐释版两种修订译文。文内阐释版译文如下:"有时我会想起所多玛城若有十个义人便可获上帝宽恕,不至毁灭的故事,并非基奥卡克市和男风泛滥的所多玛有何相似之处,也并非普鲁斯特笔下有断袖之癖的夏吕斯想移居密西根州的本顿港……",文意更为晓畅。

该类修订训练使学生思维得到启发,虽然难度极大,但有助于促进学生的独立思考和批判思维。

5.5　小结

本章以思辨能力为切入点,探讨了翻译认知过程中思辨能力的应用,并开展了译者思辨能力的多模态研究。

总体而言,学习者在翻译过程中的思辨能力运用仍有很大的提升空间。除了上述翻译教学中思辨能力的培养举措之外,还需要重视 AI 赋能。

在案例库建设的基础上,总结概括、细化翻译思辨涉及的翻译问题,以例 2"shadow"和例 3"bay"的理解和翻译为例,实际上是一个熟词偏义的问题。AIGC 是依托亿级参数训练的,是一个大型的知识库,因此可以借助 AIGC 辅助翻译,示例如下。

Q：

英文词汇往往一词多义,我想请你给出一些常见词的不常见含义,请从作为名词的 shadow 开始,比如:The light was heavy on the shadows.

A：

当作为名词时,"shadow"通常指的是物体遮挡光线所形成的暗影。然而,"shadow"还有一些不太常见的含义,以下是一些例子:

1."Shadow"作为名词,可以指代某人的隐秘伙伴或跟随者,通常用于描述特工、侦探等角色的助手或伴侣。例如:"He always works in the shadows, never revealing his true identity."(他总是在暗中工作,从不暴露真实身份。)

2."Shadow"也可以指代某人的幽灵、幻影或幽灵般的存在。例如:"She felt a shadow lurking in the corner of the room."(她感觉到一个幽灵在房间的角落潜伏。)

3."Shadow"还可以用作动词,表示跟随或监视某人的行动。例如:"He shadowed his suspect for days, gathering evidence against him."(他跟踪嫌疑人数天,收集对他不利的证据。)

需要注意的是,这些不太常见的含义在日常英语中可能不太常见,更常见的是"shadow"作为名词指代物体的暗影或作为动词表示投射阴影。

Q：

英文词汇往往一词多义,我想请你给出一些常见词的不常见含义,请从作为动词的 bay 开始,比如:The bear was too big for the dog that tried to bay it.

A：

在英语中,"bay"作为动词的常见含义是"吠叫",特别是指狗或狼的长嗥。然而,"bay"作为动词还有一些不太常见的含义,以下是一些例子:

1."Bay"作为动词,也可以表示"急切地要求"或"恳求"。例如:"The crowd was baying for justice."(人群急切地要求正义。)

2."Bay"还可以表示"围困"或"围攻"。例如:"The hunters bayed the bear in the woods."(猎人们在森林里围困了熊。)

在您给出的例句"The bear was too big for the dog that tried to bay it."

中,"bay"的含义是"围攻"或"围困",指的是狗试图围攻或围困熊,但熊的体型太大,狗无法成功。

从以上问答可以设想,在不远的将来,AIGC 的 API 得到广泛应用,将其接入在线翻译系统,在遇到熟词偏义的句子时,可一键查询 AIGC,甚至是自动弹出提示,必定能减少很多翻译错误。

要注意的是,通过以上问答中的提示词获得的答案,与直接让 AIGC 翻译的结果可能是不同的,如下所示:

Q:

译为中文:The bear was too big for the dog that tried to bay it.

A:

这只熊对于试图吠叫它的狗来说太大了。

也就是说,需要针对翻译思辨涉及的各类问题设计相应的提示词,才能让 AIGC 发挥作用。AIGC 赋能翻译思辨,大有潜力,值得深入研究和探讨。

第 6 章　翻译过程中的技术能力

6.1　引言

　　翻译作为一种跨文化的交流活动,涉及语言、文化、心理等多方面的因素,不仅需要译者具备较高的语言能力和文化素养水平,还需要掌握一定的技术能力。随着科技的飞速发展,翻译行业也在不断地发生变革。当今翻译活动的工作领域、工作内容、工作形态以及工作手段已大大超越了传统模式,皆发生了划时代的革命性变化(杨平,2012:10);译者需要不断提高自己的技术能力来适应翻译市场的需求,完成翻译任务。

　　在本章中,我们将对人工智能时代的翻译技术进行简要概述,包括语料库技术、计算机辅助翻译(CAT)技术以及机器翻译技术等领域;探讨译者所需具备的技术能力构成;通过实证案例,考察翻译过程中学习者技术能力的应用情况,并针对学习者技术能力的提升提出一些建议和方法。

6.2　人工智能时代的翻译技术概述

6.2.1 语料库技术

　　语料库技术通过对大量文本进行收集、整理、标注和分析,为翻译实践提供有力支持。自 20 世纪 90 年代以来,随着计算机技术和网络技术的飞速发展,语料库技术得到了广泛关注和应用;尤其是双语对照语料库,可以帮助译员找到相似翻译实例,从而提高翻译质量和效率。语料库技术在翻译中的作用主要体现在以下几个方面。

(1)提高翻译质量:语料库技术可以为译员提供丰富的语言资源,帮助他们找到更准确、更地道的翻译。

(2)提高翻译效率:语料库技术可以帮助译员快速定位相关信息,减少查找时间。

(3)促进翻译一致性:语料库技术可以确保译员在不同时间、不同项目中使用相同的译法,提高翻译一致性。

然而,语料库技术的应用也存在一定局限性:一方面是语料库的质量问题,语料库的质量直接影响翻译结果,而高质量的语料库建设需要投入大量人力物力;另一方面是技术门槛,语料库技术的使用需要一定的计算机技能,对于一些译员可能存在使用障碍。

6.2.2 计算机辅助翻译技术

在当今全球化进程加速的背景下,语言服务需求呈现空前增长态势,多样化和专业化趋势日益凸显;与此同时,翻译领域所面临的内容和格式也变得越来越复杂。为应对这一挑战,计算机辅助翻译(CAT)的技术应用使得原本烦琐的手工翻译过程得以逐步自动化,从而大幅提升了翻译工作的效率和质量。

得益于语言技术研发的不断创新,一系列功能强大的计算机辅助翻译工具相继涌现。这些工具包括翻译记忆工具(如 SDL Trados、memoQ 等)、术语管理工具(如 SDL MultiTerm、crossTerm、TermStar 等)以及自动质量检查工具(如 QA Distiller、ErrorSpy 等)。

如今,这些先进的 CAT 工具已经逐渐成为现代翻译工作中最为广泛应用的工具。随着这些翻译工具的广泛应用,专业翻译人员能够更加高效地处理各种类型的翻译任务,同时使翻译质量得到保障。这些工具的发展和普及不仅有助于满足日益增长的语言服务需求,而且为翻译行业的持续发展和进步提供了坚实支持。

6.2.3 机器翻译技术

随着计算机科学和人工智能领域的飞速发展,机器翻译技术逐渐成为翻译研究的焦点。自 20 世纪 50 年代起,机器翻译技术经历了基于规则、基于统计和基于神经网络的三个发展阶段。近年来,得益于深度学习技术的突破,神经机器翻译(NMT)已成为当前最先进的翻译技术,能够快速生成初步翻译结果,节省译员时间,同时提高翻译效率。

机器翻译技术与人工翻译相结合,形成了人机协作翻译模式。在此模式下,译员可以对机器翻译生成的初步结果进行修改和完善,从而提高翻译质量。此外,机器翻译技术的发展为语言服务领域提供了新的可能性,如同声传译和跨语言信息检索等,为翻译研究和实践创造了新契机。

相较于人工翻译,机器翻译在速度和大规模处理方面具有优势。机器翻译技术能够快速生成翻译结果,满足紧急翻译需求,并能处理大量文本,适用于大规模翻译项目。然而,机器翻译在质量方面仍有待提高,特别是在处理复杂、专业领域的文本时。此外,机器翻译难以处理文化差异,可能导致翻译不准确或不恰当。

随着人工智能和深度学习技术的进一步发展,机器翻译技术将不断完善,翻译质量将不断提高,人机协作的翻译模式将成为主流。

6.3　译者技术能力的构成

6.3.1　信息检索能力

信息检索能力是译者在翻译过程中查找和利用相关信息资源的关键能力,包括对信息资源的识别、评价、筛选、使用和整合等方面的知识和技能。随着互联网的普及,大量的信息资源变得触手可及,译者需要具备较强的信息素养和熟练地运用各种信息工具和渠道进行信息检索,以便在翻译过程中查找相关资料、解决翻译中遇到的问题。此外,译者还需要具备一定的信息分析和整合能力,能够根据翻译任务的要求,对检索到的信息进行有效的处理和利用。

6.3.2　计算机辅助翻译能力

计算机辅助翻译能力是指译者在翻译过程中,熟练运用计算机辅助翻译工具(如词典、术语库、翻译记忆库等)的能力,包括对这些工具的了解、操作和应用等方面的知识和技能。计算机辅助翻译工具可以帮助译者提高翻译效率、保证翻译质量,因此,译者需要熟悉各种计算机辅助翻译工具,如翻译记忆系统、术语管理系统等,并能够根据翻译任务的要求,灵活地运用这些工具进行辅助翻译。

6.3.3 术语能力

术语能力是指译者在翻译过程中对专业术语的掌握和运用能力,这包括对术语的识别、理解、翻译和使用等方面的技能。术语能力不仅体现在译者对术语的准确翻译,还包括对术语背后的概念和语境的理解。

术语能力对于翻译具有重要意义。首先,术语是专业领域知识的载体,是各个学科和行业的基础。在翻译过程中,译者需要准确地传递原文中的术语信息,以确保目标语读者能够理解原文的专业内容。其次,术语在不同语言和文化中可能存在差异,这要求译者具备跨文化沟通能力,以便在翻译过程中处理好这些差异。此外,术语在专业领域中具有规范性,译者需要遵循规范,确保翻译的一致性和准确性。

术语能力的具体体现包括以下几个方面。

1.术语识别

术语识别是指译者在阅读原文时,能够准确地识别出专业术语。这要求译者具备较高的语言敏感度和丰富的领域知识。译者需要根据语境、结构和用法等方面的信息,判断出哪些词汇属于术语,哪些属于一般词汇。

2.术语理解

术语理解是指译者能够理解术语的概念和内涵,掌握其在特定语境中的意义。这要求译者具备较强的分析和推理能力,能够通过查阅相关资料、参考典籍和专家意见等途径,获取对术语的深入理解。

3.术语翻译

术语翻译是指译者根据原文的语境和目标语的规范,选择合适的翻译策略,将术语准确地转换为目标语。这包括直译、意译、借译、创新性翻译等多种方法。在翻译过程中,译者需要综合运用语言知识、领域知识和翻译技巧,以实现对术语的恰当翻译。

4.术语工具使用能力

当代译员需具备系统化收集、描述、处理、记录、存贮、呈现与查询等术语管理的能力(冷冰冰等,2013:57),这些能力的运用,离不开术语工具。术语工具指译者能够熟练应用术语库及术语管理工具,以提高翻译效率和保证翻译质量。随着科技的发展,译者在翻译过程中可以利用各种术语工具来辅助自己的工作。这些工具包括术语数据库、术语管理软件、在线词典等。通过掌握这些工具的使用方法,译者能够更快速地查找和处理专业术语,从而提高翻译的准确性和一致性。

6.3.4 译后编辑能力

译后编辑指的是对机器翻译输出进行人工修订,以提高翻译质量,使其更符合目标语的规范和语境。

机器翻译虽然能够在短时间内处理大量文本,但其输出结果往往存在语法错误等问题。译后编辑有助于纠正这些问题,提高翻译的准确性、流畅性和可读性,减轻译者的工作量,提高翻译效率。通过对机器翻译输出进行修订,译者可以专注于解决文本中的难点和特殊问题,而不必从头开始翻译。此外,译后编辑还可以降低翻译成本,因为机器翻译的速度和规模远超过人工翻译。并且译后编辑过程中产生的修订数据可以作为训练材料,用于改进机器翻译系统。

译后编辑能力是一项综合能力,具体体现在以下几个方面。

1.语言能力

译后编辑者需要具备扎实的源语和目标语功底,能够准确理解源文,熟练掌握目标语的语法、词汇和表达习惯。

2.审校能力

译后编辑者需要具备批判性思维,能够发现并修正机器翻译输出中的错误。这包括对译文的准确性、流畅性、一致性、风格和格式进行全面审查。

3.文化适应能力

译后编辑者需要了解源语和目标语的文化背景,能够根据目标受众的需求和期望进行适当的文化调整。

4.工具能力

译后编辑者需要熟练掌握计算机辅助翻译工具和在线资源的使用方法,以便在译后编辑过程中进行有效的信息检索和处理。

6.4 译者技术能力的多模态研究

6.4.1 研究个案：术语翻译

原文：

［Chinese moralists have always inveighed against the use of spirits, and the name of I-tih, the reputed inventor of the deleterious drink, more than two thousand years before Christ, has been handed down with opprobrium, as he was himself banished by the great Yu for his discovery.］

The "Shu King" contains a discourse by the Lord of Chau on the abuse of spirits.

［His speech to his brother Fung, B.C. 1120, is the oldest temperance address on record, even earlier than the words of Solomon in the Proverbs.］

专业译文：《书经》有一篇周公谴责饮酒的训话。

百度译文：《蜀王》包含周主关于虐待神灵的论述。

讯飞译文："蜀王"包含了周公关于滥用精神的论述。

小牛译文：《蜀王》包含了周主关于虐灵的论述。

有道译文：《蜀王》中有一篇周公关于虐鬼的论述。

微软译文：《蜀王》中包含了周王关于滥用灵魂的论述。

学习者译文 1：《蜀王》中有一篇周公关于滥用酒的论述。

学习者译文 2：《尚书》中有篇目记载了周公劝诫喝酒的危害。

学习者译文 3：《书经》记载了周王关于告诫臣民不要过度饮酒的一篇演说。

学习者译文 4：《尚书》中记载着一篇周公旦禁止酗酒的文章。

学习者译文 5：《蜀王》中有一篇周公关于酗酒的论述。

学习者评注 1：

学习者评注 2:

评注: [■■■■] 修改　删除　译文

1, 专有名词书名, 人名需要考证。

学习者评注 3:

评注: [■■■■] 修改　删除　译文

1.注意 Shu King 的翻译 2.查询历史背景可知, 周王极力推行限制饮酒的措施。非纣王。

学习者评注 4:

评注: [■■■■] 修改　删除　译文

Shu King:《尚书》the Lord of Chau: 周公旦 spirits: 烈性酒

学习者评注 5:

评注: [■■■■] 修改　删除　译文

the abuse of spirits 注意 spirit 意思的选用

6.4.2 分析讨论

原文选自汉学家卫三畏所著《中国总论》,参考译文译者为陈俱。该案例集中体现了翻译过程中原文的理解与查证问题,包括"Shu King""Lord of Chau""spirits"三个点。

就以上译文来看,专业译文理解准确;机器译文"Shu King"全部理解错误,"Lord of Chau"则 3 个理解错误,"spirits"全部理解错误;5 份学习者译文中 2 份完全正确,3 份各错了 1 个点。

根据学习者翻译过程中所写的评注,大体可以推断评注 1 和 5 的译者缺乏查证意识,关注点在"spirits"词义的理解上,因此其"Shu King"误译为"蜀王"(与机器翻译的错误相同);周公译文正确(可能来自 2 个正确的机器译文);对于"spirits"的理解有其思考,并纠正了机器译文的错误。评注 2～4 的译者查证了"Shu King"和"Lord of Chau",都理解对了"Shu King"的意思;评注 3 的译者虽然做了查证,但仍将"Lord of Chau"误为周王,与另两位译者相比,体现出查证能力上的差异。

以上基于学习者评注的分析,需要通过屏幕录制视频进行验证。通过观看这 5 位学习者翻译过程的屏幕录制视频,我们发现情况与我们分析的有一致之处,也有偏差。关于前 4 位译者的判断无误,但评注 5 的译者并非没有查证;该译者在百度搜索中查证了"Shu King",但网页上出现的第一个结果是"蜀王",该译者未仔细辨别,也没有进一步查看其他结果,故未能获取正确译文。

综合以上分析,我们将此个案所反映的技术能力分为 4 个层次:

(1)无查无解:缺乏查证意识。

(2)有查无解:做了查证,但未能通过查证解决问题。

(3)查有得失:做了查证,并通过查证解决了一部分问题,但另一部分问题的查证存在失误。

(4)有查有解:做了查证,并凭借查证解决全部问题。

6.4.3 研究发现

通过查看全部 30 份译文对应的屏幕录制视频,4 种层次技术能力的分布如表 6-1 所示。

表 6-1 研究个案中学习者的技术能力的层次分布

层次	数量	比例
无查无解	6	20%
有查无解	7	23%
查有得失	8	27%
有查有解	9	30%

综合以上统计,以下几点发现值得关注:

1.搜商在人机协作中的重要作用

随着人工智能的发展,机器翻译的质量越来越高,错误越来越少,但机器翻译在术语翻译方面容易出错,准确率仍有待提高;人工译者一方面可以通过构建术语库,提升机器翻译的术语翻译准确率,一方面可以通过检索查证,纠正机器翻译的一些术语翻译错误。从以上个案分析的结果来看,学习者的搜商有待提高。就该个案而言,70％的学习者仍有提升空间,需要在翻译教学中加强搜商的培养。

2.术语库的构建亟须引起重视

术语库可以干预机器译文,提升机器翻译的准确率。例如,如果用户在小牛机器翻译的后台添加术语库,那么在机器翻译在遇到术语库中的术语时,就会采用术语库中的译文。通过构建大型的术语库,可以提升机器翻译的术语翻译质量,减少译者在翻译过程中的查询负担。

6.5　译者技术能力养成之道

6.5.1 提升搜商

译者搜商的提升对于提高翻译质量至关重要。下面从两个方面介绍如何提升译者的搜商。

6.5.1.1 掌握搜索引擎高级语法

搜索引擎是译者进行信息检索的主要工具。通过掌握高级搜索语法,译者可以更精确地定位所需信息,提高检索效率。以下为一些常用的高级搜索技巧:

1.使用引号

若使用引号将短语或句子括起来,搜索引擎将只返回包含该完整短语或句子的结果。这对于查找特定表述或引用非常有用,可以帮助译者在大量搜索结果中迅速找到所需信息。

2.使用减号

在关键词前使用减号,可以排除与特定关键词相关的搜索结果。这有助于译者在检索过程中筛选掉无关或重复的信息,提高搜索效率。

3.使用通配符

使用星号(＊)代替关键词中的部分内容,可以在搜索结果中找到多种可能的匹配。这对于查找不确定的词汇或短语非常有用,可以帮助译者找到更全面的信息。

4.使用"site:"语法

通过在关键词前加上"site:",可以将搜索结果限定于某个网站。这有助于译者在某些情况下专门检索某个网站的信息,提高搜索效率。

5.使用"filetype:"语法

通过在关键词前加上"filetype:",可以限制搜索结果为特定文件格式。这对于查找特定类型的文档(如 PDF、ppt 等)非常有用,可以帮助译者快速找到所需资料。

通过熟练掌握这些高级搜索技巧,译者可以快速、准确地找到所需信息,提高翻译效率。下表是必应和百度搜索引擎的常见搜索语法,可供参考。

表 6-2　必应、百度搜索语法

搜索引擎	语法	示例	说明
必应 (bing)	site:	site:example.com	从指定网站搜索结果
	filetype:	filetype:PDF	搜索指定文件类型的结果
	inurl:	inurl:example	搜索包含指定关键词的网页地址
	intitle:	intitle:example	搜索包含指定关键词的网页标题
	ip:	ip:192.168.1.1	搜索指定 IP 地址的网页
	" "	"search query"	搜索包含完整短语的结果
	—	example—site:example.com	从搜索结果中排除指定内容
	OR	example1 OR example2	搜索满足任一关键词的结果
百度 (Baidu)	site:	site:example.com	从指定网站搜索结果
	filetype:	filetype:PDF	搜索指定文件类型的结果
	inurl:	inurl:example	搜索包含指定关键词的网页地址
	intitle:	intitle:example	搜索包含指定关键词的网页标题
	link:	link:example.com	搜索包含指定链接的网页
	" "	"search query"	搜索包含完整短语的结果
	—	example—site:example.com	从搜索结果中排除指定内容
	OR	example1 OR example2	搜索满足任一关键词的结果

6.5.1.2 善用关键词及诱导词

1.提炼关键词

检索关键词是译者在进行信息检索时的关键。通过锻炼识别和提炼关键词的能力,译者可以更快地找到所需信息。译者需了解所翻译领域的基本术语和概念,以便在检索过程中迅速识别关键词。在阅读源文时,应注意提取与主题相关的关键信息,作为检索关键词。可尝试使用同义词或相关词汇进行检索,以便找到更广泛的信息。

2.锤炼诱导词

诱导词是指在检索过程中,能引导译者找到相关资料的词汇。通过锤炼和运用诱导词,译者可以更高效地进行信息检索。在查阅百科全书或专业词典时,注意记录与主题相关的词汇和术语,作为诱导词。在阅读相关资料时,关注作者使用的关键词和表述,以便在检索过程中运用这些诱导词。

结合所翻译领域的背景知识,译者可以尝试使用相关领域的词汇作为诱导词进行检索。通过掌握丰富的百科知识,译者可以更有针对性地选择检索关键词和诱导词,提升信息检索效率,从而提高翻译质量。

6.5.2 提升译后编辑能力

译后编辑分为两种:轻度译后编辑(light post-editing)和深度译后编辑(full post-editing)。轻度译后编辑主要着重于译文的准确性和可读性,而深度译后编辑则进一步关注译文的流畅性、一致性和文化适应性等方面。

随着机器翻译技术的不断进步,译后编辑在翻译行业中的地位越来越重要。译后编辑的作用体现在提高翻译效率、降低成本以及保持译文质量等方面。因此,对于翻译从业人员来说,提升译后编辑能力具有重要意义。为了提高学生的译后编辑能力,我们在教学中设计了一项最佳译文判断测试,并且取得了良好的效果。每次测试 10 道题目,限时 5 分钟,在基于 Moodle 的翻译平台在线完成。题目含原文及 3 个译文,要求学习者选择最佳译文。学习者需要快速阅读原文,比较译文,在 30 秒内做出判断,判断的速度及准确率取决于其掌握的术语、语言知识,对机器译文特征及错误类型的了解,对显化、隐化的认识,等等。该测试示例如下:

原文:全面依法治国是国家治理的一场深刻革命,必须坚持厉行法治,推进科学立法、严格执法、公正司法、全民守法[①]。

译文 1：Advancing law-based governance in all fields is a profound revolution in China's governance. We must promote the rule of law and work to ensure sound lawmaking, strict law enforcement, impartial administration of justice, and the observance of law by everyone.

译文 2：Ruling the country by law in an all-round way is a profound revolution in national governance. We must adhere to the rule of law, promote scientific legislation, strict law enforcement, fair justice and law-abiding by the whole people.

译文 3：Implementing the rule of law comprehensively is a profound revolution in national governance, and we must insist on strict enforcement of the law, promote scientific legislation, strict law enforcement, impartial justice, and law-abiding by all citizens.

初看三个译文差别不大，比较难以判断优劣。但经过训练的学习者可以快速判断出译文 1 为最佳译文。依据有二：一是术语翻译，"依法治国"的官方译文为"law-based governance"，明显优于累赘的"ruling the country by law"以及信息缺失的"the rule of law"；二是"国家治理"的翻译，官方译文为"China's governance"，将"国"显化为"China"，是外宣翻译中常用的处理方式，而两个机器译文不懂得显化，译为"national governance"，不妥。精通此类最佳译文判断训练之后，对于机器翻译的一些常见问题，便可洞若观火，快速命中错误并正确修改。

具体最佳译文判断测试样本见附录 1。

6.6　翻译技术融入翻译教学

为培养和提升学习者的技术能力，翻译类课程，除了包含传统的理论及技巧讲授和翻译训练之外，可以适当纳入翻译技术教学，与翻译行业需求接轨。

翻译技术是一系列技术、软件、工具、设备、语料的集合（崔启亮，2019：84），主要包括语料库、计算机辅助翻译（CAT）、本地化、机器翻译与译后编辑、翻译管理等，模块化特征明显。翻译技术融入翻译教学，会增加教学内容，需要解决技术模块的设置问题及教学课时分配问题，即选择哪些模块讲授、教

---

① 原文及译文 1 分别选自《习近平谈治国理政》第三卷中、英文版。

学课时从哪里来等。我们在翻译教学中采取精简技术模块以及视频教学的方式,较好地解决了这些问题。

6.6.1 精简模块

根据实用性、易用性、核心性、基础性这四个原则,我们在十几个翻译技术模块中去除了一些较为抽象、较为高端或实用性低的模块,并从多种翻译技术工具中选择了较为易用的几种,构成精简版的翻译技术教学模块,见表 6-3。

表 6-3　翻译技术教学模块

编号	模块	主要内容	工具	视频
1	信息搜索	关键词设定、图片搜索、学术搜索	必应、百度学术、读秀	10 分钟
2	语料库	单语检索、双语检索	AntConc、检索工具	10 分钟
3	CAT	创建项目、导出双语对照文件、术语库	雪人翻译软件	10 分钟
4	机器翻译	机器译文质量评估、译后编辑	百度、谷歌、搜狗翻译	15 分钟

以上模块的设定基于其内在关系及学生的翻译行为,将其纳入传统翻译教学,不仅不会造成教学负担,而且会对教学有较大的促进作用,原因如下:

(1)不论翻译教学中是否传授信息搜索技术及机器翻译译后编辑相关知识,学生在翻译过程中都会去使用网络搜索和机器翻译工具,这是信息技术和机器翻译发展的必然结果。将信息检索及机器翻译模块纳入翻译教学,有助于提升学生的检索能力,引导并规范学生对于机器翻译的应用。

(2)普通信息检索不能解决翻译中的细节问题,而语料库检索可以更微观地展示语言特征及提供翻译参考。

(3)CAT 可以提升翻译效率,使用 CAT 完成翻译练习,可以导出双语语料,并可用检索工具检索,提升了教学效率和讲评效果。

6.6.2 视频教学

加入技术模块后,课时会略显紧张,解决办法是利用学生课外自主学习时间,以视频教学的方式帮助学生入门。在整个课程的教学过程中,这些技术模块都会一直得到应用,学生自会逐渐掌握,乃至娴熟应用。

以 CAT 工具为例,教师只需制作十分钟左右的屏幕录制视频,便可涵盖雪人翻译工具的启动、创建项目、导出双语文件,以及筛选术语、制作术语库、导入术语库、应用术语库等操作,学生可参照视频自行演练,直到掌握操作方法。语料库和机器翻译等模块亦是如此。视频教学既节省了教师的课堂讲授时间,又促进了学生对于翻译技术的习得,实现了翻译教学中翻译技术内容的融入。

6.7　小结

翻译过程中的技术能力对于译者完成翻译任务具有重要意义。在 AIGC 时代,翻译技术将会进一步快速发展,不仅会推动翻译行业的进步,也会对翻译技术教学产生深远影响。一方面,新的翻译技术和工具的出现为翻译教学提供了更多的可能性,使得译者可以更有效地进行翻译工作,提高翻译的质量和效率;另一方面,这也对翻译教学提出了新的挑战,需要教师不断更新教学内容和方法,以适应翻译技术的发展。因此,对于翻译技术教学来说,AIGC 时代既充满机遇,也存在挑战。我们需要抓住这个机遇,积极应对挑战,以培养出能够适应新时代需求的高素质翻译人才。

第 7 章　翻译过程中的显化与隐化

7.1　引言

　　翻译作为跨文化交流的重要手段,在全球化背景下愈发显得至关重要。翻译过程中,译者需要根据源语文本和目标语读者的需求,选择适当的翻译策略。显化与隐化作为翻译过程中的两种关键策略,一直以来都是翻译研究领域的热门话题。

　　显化作为翻译研究的重要概念,早在 20 世纪 50 年代末便被学者提出。Vinay 和 Darbelnet (1958:342)将显化界定为一个把源语中所暗含的,但可以从语境或情境中推导得出的信息,在目标语中予以具体呈现的过程,但该界定未引起关注。Blum-Kulka(1986:300)提出"显化假设",认为译者对原文的解读导致译文相对原文更加冗长,主要表现为译文中衔接手段的显化程度提高。显化研究迎来了第一次飞跃。

　　在人工智能时代,显化和隐化在人机协作的翻译过程中占据重要地位,因为机器译文往往不懂得显化或隐化,需要人工译者根据情况,在必要时做出显化或隐化操作。

　　本章旨在分析这两种策略在翻译实践中的应用及其对翻译质量的影响,并考察学习者翻译过程中的显化及隐化处理情况。

7.2　显化的概念及类型

7.2.1 显化的定义

　　显化指的是在翻译过程中,译者为了使译文更易于理解,而将原文隐含的信息明确表达出来的现象。显化现象在不同程度上反映了译者对语言、文化差异的处理方式以及对译文受众需求的关注。

7.2.2 显化的类型

根据显化现象的原因和表现形式,可以将显化分为以下几种类型。

1.增译显化

增译显化指的是译者在翻译过程中,为使译文更易于理解,而在译文中增加原文未包含的信息。增译显化可分为补充性显化和阐释性显化两种。

补充性显化是指译者根据译文受众的需求和文化背景,在译文中添加有助于理解的信息。例如,译者可能会为译文受众增加一些关于事件、人物、地点等背景知识的说明。

【例 1】接着又告诉我们一个故事,说是元朝有个皇帝来游山,倦了,睡在这儿,梦见身子坐在船上,脚下翻着波浪,醒来叫人一挖脚下,果然冒出股泉水,这就是"梦赶泉"的来历。

译文:The story he then told concerned an emperor of the Yuan Dynasty (1271-1368) who fell asleep here during his trip into the hills and dreamed he was in a boat with swelling waves under his feet. When he awoke he had the ground dug up where he had stood and springs really came spurting forth. This was why the springs were called "Pursuing Dreams".

"元朝"一词,对于英语国家读者来说显然是一个文化理解的障碍点。译文增加一个括注,标明年代的起止,便于英语读者理解,否则英语国家读者仍然不清楚"元朝"是一个什么概念(魏志成,2012:104)。

阐释性显化则是译者通过增加解释性成分,使原文的意义在译文中变得更加明确。这种显化可能会涉及对原文的词汇、语法、修辞等方面的调整。

2.句法显化

句法显化是指译者在翻译过程中,对原文的句法结构进行调整,使译文符合目标语的语法规则和习惯。句法显化可以分为两种:结构显化和顺序显化。

结构显化是指译者对原文中的句子结构进行调整,使之符合目标语的语法规则。这可能涉及对原文中的名词短语、动词短语、从句等成分的重新组织。

顺序显化是指译者在翻译过程中,调整原文中成分的顺序,使之符合目标语的表达习惯。这可能包括对原文中的主语、谓语、宾语等成分的重新排列。

7.3　隐化的概念及类型

7.3.1 隐化的定义

隐化是指在翻译过程中,译者为了使译文更符合目标语的表达习惯或文化特点,将原文中明确的信息以隐含的方式表达出来的现象。与显化相反,隐化强调的是译者对原文信息的省略、精简或转换,使译文在保留原文核心意义的同时,更符合目标语和文化的特点。

7.3.2 隐化的类型

根据隐化现象的原因和表现形式,可以将隐化分为以下三种类型:

1.减译隐化

减译隐化是指译者在翻译过程中,有意或无意地省略原文中的部分信息,使译文更简洁、更符合目标语的表达习惯。减译隐化可能涉及对原文中的词汇、语法、修辞等方面的删减,但这些删减应确保不影响译文对原文核心意义的传达。

2.归纳隐化

归纳隐化是指译者在翻译过程中,将原文中的详细、具体的信息转化为更为概括、抽象的表达。归纳隐化可能涉及对原文中的实例、事例、细节等信息的概括化处理,以使译文更符合目标语的表达习惯和文化特点。

3.句法隐化

句法隐化是指译者在翻译过程中,对原文的句法结构进行调整,使译文更符合目标语的语法规则和习惯。句法隐化可能涉及对原文中的名词短语、动词短语、从句等成分的省略、转换或重新组织,以求在保留原文核心意义的同时,使译文更贴近目标语的表达特点。

7.4　显化与隐化在翻译中的应用

7.4.1 显化策略的应用

在翻译过程中,显化策略的应用主要取决于以下情况。

(1)语言习惯差异:源语和目标语在表达习惯上可能存在差异,译者需要通过显化策略使译文更符合目标语的表达习惯。

(2)文化差异:源语和目标语所代表的文化之间可能存在差异,导致某些信息在目标语环境中难以理解。译者需要通过显化策略对这些信息进行补充或解释,以便于目标语读者理解。

(3)语境信息:原文中的某些信息可能依赖于特定的语境,而在译文中这些语境信息可能无法直接呈现。此时,译者需要通过显化策略将这些隐含的语境信息显式地表达出来。

7.4.2 显化对翻译质量的影响

显化策略在翻译实践中的应用对翻译质量具有一定的影响,具体表现为:

(1)显化策略有助于理解。通过显化策略,译者可以将原文中难以理解的信息进行补充或解释,有助于目标语读者更好地理解译文。

(2)显化策略可能导致过度解释。过度使用显化策略可能导致译文过于具有解释性,使得译文失去了原文的简洁和韵味。因此,译者在使用显化策略时需要适度,以免影响翻译质量。

在翻译实践中,译者需要根据具体情况灵活运用显化策略,既要充分考虑目标语读者的需求,又要尊重原文的风格和特点,以达到翻译的最佳效果。

7.4.3 隐化策略的应用

在翻译实践中,隐化策略的应用主要取决于以下情况。

(1)冗余信息:原文中可能存在一些冗余或重复的信息,这些信息在译文中可能不必完全表达。译者可以通过隐化策略省略这些信息,使译文更为简洁。

（2）目标语习惯：目标语可能有其独特的表达习惯，某些信息在目标语境中可以隐式表达。译者可以通过隐化策略使译文更符合目标语的表达习惯。

（3）文化内在理解：目标语读者对于源语文化中的某些信息可能具有一定的了解，译者可以通过隐化策略省略这些信息，使译文更为简练。

7.4.4 隐化对翻译质量的影响

隐化策略在翻译实践中的应用对翻译质量具有一定的影响，具体表现为：

（1）隐化策略有助于增加译文的可读性。通过隐化策略，译者可以省略原文中的冗余信息或已为目标语读者所熟知的信息，使译文更为简洁，有助于增加译文的可读性。

（2）隐化策略可能导致信息丢失。过度使用隐化策略可能导致原文中的部分信息丢失，使得目标语读者难以完全理解译文的意义。因此，译者在使用隐化策略时需要谨慎，以免影响翻译质量。

在翻译实践中，译者需要根据具体情况灵活运用隐化策略，既要保持译文的简洁，又要确保译文中的重要信息得以传达，以实现翻译的最佳效果。

7.5　译者显化与隐化能力的多模态研究

7.5.1 研究个案：语境化的"显"与"隐"

1.个案1

原文：随着诺贝尔奖颁奖典礼的临近，持续2个月的"屠呦呦热"正在渐入高潮。

专业译文：

As the Nobel Prize Award Ceremony draws near, Tu Youyou's two months in the spotlight is reaching its crescendo.

百度译文：

As the Nobel Prize awarding ceremony approaches, the "Tu Youyou craze" that lasted for two months is gradually reaching its climax.

讯飞译文：

With the approaching of the Nobel Prize Award Ceremony, the "Tu Youyou *fever*" which lasted for two months is gradually reaching its climax.

小牛译文：

With the Nobel Prize awarding ceremony approaching, the "Tu Youyou *fever*", which lasted for two months, is gradually reaching a climax.

有道译文：

As the Nobel Prize Award ceremony approaches, Tu Youyou fever, which has lasted for two months, is coming to a climax.

微软译文：

With the Nobel Prize ceremony approaching, the 2-month "Tu Youyou *fever*" is gradually entering its climax.

学习者译文 1：

With the Nobel Prize awarding ceremony approaching, the discussion about Tu Youyou，which lasted for two months, is gradually reaching its crescendo.

学习者译文 2：

With the approach of the Nobel Prize awarding ceremony, the "Tu Youyou fe-ver", which lasted for two months, is gradually reaching a peak.

学习者译文 3：

As the Nobel Prize Award Ceremony draws near, Tu Youyou had been a much-talked-about name for 2 months before her popularity came to a climax.

学习者译文 4：

As the Nobel Prize ceremony approaches, a *craze* for Tu Youyou lasting for two months is gradually reaching the climax.

学习者译文 5：

With the Nobel awards ceremony approaches, the two-month bout of Tu youyou *popularity* is achieving the upsurge.

学习者评注 1：

评注：▨▨▨ 修改 删除 译文

屠呦呦热不直接翻译 要翻译出它的具体意思

学习者评注 2：

评注：▓▓▓▓　修改　删除　译文

"屠呦呦热"翻译成"Tu Youyou fever"是否可行

学习者评注 3：

评注：▓▓▓▓　修改　删除　译文

"临近"原文用的是draws near，也可以换为approaches。

学习者评注 4：

评注：▓▓▓　修改　删除　译文

…热可译为a craze for

学习者评注 5：

评注：▓▓▓　修改　删除　译文

屠呦呦热是否可以理解为受欢迎

2.个案 2[①]
原文：李氏大惊，叫道："叔叔，箭！箭！"
专业译文："Brother!"Lily Li cried.

7.5.2 分析讨论

1.个案 1

原文为第 28 届韩素音青年翻译竞赛英译汉选材，专业译文为官方提供的参考译文。原文中"屠呦呦热"，在汉语语境下，关注屠呦呦获得诺奖的读者都能理解其内涵，即获奖带来的热度，以及随之而来的争议，包括中西医之争，而

————————————

① 机器译文、学习者译文及学习者评注请参看 5.3.1 小节。

这一切都围绕着"屠呦呦",故原文作者用了一个高度概括的词"热"来形容这一现象。因此,"热"不能简单的译为"craze""fever""hot"之类词语,姑且不论这些词是否恰当,是否达意,就其词义而言,是无法概括"热"之内涵的。

从学习者的评注来看,大多关注到了"热"的英译问题,并做出了选择,有的直接译为某个与"热"有关的词,如"craze""popularity""fever";有的则选择对"热"的含义进行阐释,也就是显化,如译为"discussion""a much-talked-about name",在策略上与官方译文一致。官方译文虽然也采取了显化的策略,但手段更高明,用了"in the spotlight"这一短语,形象地传达了原文"热"的内涵,而这一显化手段是基于语境的,故称之为语境化的"显"。

2.个案 2

原文选自《射雕英雄传》,专业译文(即参考译文)译者为郝玉青(Anna Holmwood)。该案例涉及特定语境下译文的隐化问题。中英两种语言存在各种差异,包括音韵。原文的"叔叔!箭!箭!"为 4 个音节,如果如学习者的译文那样,全部译出,则都是诸如"Brother! Arrow! Arrow!"之类译文,音节较多,不符合英语语境中一个人在危急情况下的发声;换言之,箭瞬间即至,李氏只有时间喊叫一声"Brother",这么翻译既传递了惊惧之情,也给杨铁心做出了警示。

从学习者的评注来看,其译文与机器译文一样,都没有关注这一问题。而郝玉青对于该语境的理解非常到位,因此在译文中隐化了"箭!箭!",是为语境化的"隐"。

7.5.3 研究发现

通过查看全部 30 份译文对应的屏幕录制视频,两个个案学习者在"显"与"隐"方面的表现均不佳。

个案 1 中,约 30% 的学习者注意到了要阐释"热"的内涵,但结果不甚理想,选用的译文,如"discussion""a much-discussed name",都无法完全传递原文语境下"热"的内涵;约 70% 的学习者缺乏显化意识,直接选择了某个词对应"热",与原文语境下"热"的内涵相距甚远。

个案 2 中,几乎全部学习者都翻译了"箭!箭!",缺乏原文语境下对"箭!箭!"的深入分析。原因比较复杂,既是由于缺乏翻译经验,不敢略去"箭!箭!",也是由于不甚了解"隐化",不大擅长于此。只有个别学习者可能觉得译文如果过于冗长的话,不符合语境,便将译文简化为"Arrows!"。

基于以上统计与分析,我们认为,人工智能背景下,显化能力与隐化能力在翻译中极其重要,因为机器翻译的质量固然越来越高,但机器翻译的一大特点是忠实于原文,也就是机器翻译一般不会增(显化)减(隐化)原文,这在很多情况下会造成译文的意思不通透,会与"地道"有一定距离,而这正是译者可以发挥作用的地方。因此,在翻译教学中,应大力加强显化与隐化的相关训练,帮助学习者培养显化与隐化意识,并掌握显化与隐化的各种手段,如语义解释、衔接显化、语义融合等。

7.6　翻译教学中显化、隐化能力的培养

在翻译教学中,显化与隐化能力的培养主要通过两种方式。一是通过训练,帮助学习者掌握常见的显化、隐化方式。二是通过最佳译文判断测试,让学习者在人工译文和机器译文的比较鉴别中,发现显化与隐化现象;在多次循序渐进的测试之后,学习者一般都能逐渐了解和熟悉显化和隐化,具备一定的显化、隐化能力。

翻译教学中,主要围绕两类显化进行训练。一类是优化性的显化,即添加词类。不添加也不一定错,但添加之后,译文往往更具可读性,逻辑更清晰,从而起到更好的信息传递和交流效果。一类是阐释性的显化,主要是增加背景信息或必要阐释,以便于读者理解。隐化则反之,可视为一种文字上的精简,主要是为了使译文更为地道或精练而精简,以及为了避免文化冲突或误解而精简。

【例 2】[①]要强化教育引导、实践养成、制度保障,把社会主义核心价值观融入社会发展各方面,引导全体人民自觉践行。

译文 1: We should offer the people better guidance, expose them to successful practices, and provide institutional guarantees. We should see that all areas of social development are imbued with the core socialist values, and encourage the public to honor these values.

译文 2: Strengthen education guidance, practical development, and institutional guarantees, integrate socialist core values into all aspects of social development, and guide all people to consciously practice them.

---

①　本小节例证均来自《习近平谈治国理政》第 3 卷。译文 1 为官方译文。

译文 1 添加了主语"We",比译文 2 生硬的祈使句结构更顺畅地道。其他常添加的词类为表示逻辑关系的连词。

【**例 3**】中国人民相信,山再高,往上攀,总能登顶;路再长,走下去,定能到达。

译文 1: It is our firm belief that no matter how high a mountain is, if we keep climbing, we will reach the top; no matter how long a road is, if we keep walking, we will reach the destination.

译文 2: The Chinese people believe that no matter how high the mountain is, if you climb up, you can always reach the top; no matter how long the road is, if you go on, you will surely reach it.

译文 1 和译文 2 均添加连词"if",译文 1 为人工译文,译文 2 为机器译文。从这个例子可以看出,机器译文也具备一定的添加词类的显化能力。机器译文一般不具备的是阐释性的显化能力。

【**例 4**】创新从来都是九死一生,但我们必须有"亦余心之所善兮,虽九死其犹未悔"的豪情。

译文 1: In innovation the odds of failure are much higher than those of success, but we should have the determination shown by patriotic poet Qu Yuan, "For the ideal that I hold dear to my heart, I will not regret a thousand deaths to die."

译文 2: Innovation has always been a matter of life and death, but we must have the courage of "even if I have only one breath left to do what I love, I will not regret even if I die nine times".

译文 1 在引用的诗句前添加了"patriotic poet Qu Yuan",这是机器译文目前无法做到的。

【**例 5**】建设海洋强国,必须进一步关心海洋、认识海洋、经略海洋,加快海洋科技创新步伐。

译文 1: To build China into a strong maritime nation, we must take good care of, further understand, and manage the ocean, and facilitate innovation in marine science and technology.

译文 2: To build a maritime power, we must further care about the ocean, understand the ocean , develop strategies for the ocean, and accelerate the pace of marine scientific and technological innovation.

原文"海洋"出现了三次,译文 1 为了避免重复,仅出现一次"ocean",属隐化操作。机器译文(译文 2)则未隐化,出现了三次"ocean"。

最佳译文判断测试的相关阐述见 6.5.2 小节,此处不予赘述。

7.7　小结

　　显化与隐化策略在翻译过程中具有重要意义,因为它们直接影响到译文的准确性、表达效果和目标语读者的理解。显化策略可以帮助译者更明确地传达原文信息,弥合源语和目标语之间的差异;而隐化策略则有助于保持译文的简洁和流畅性,使译文更符合目标语的表达习惯。正确运用显化与隐化策略,可以使翻译更加贴近原文的意义,同时满足目标语读者的需求。

　　当前,显化与隐化策略的研究已取得了一定的成果。然而,随着全球化的发展,跨文化交流越来越频繁,对翻译质量的要求也日益提高。因此,后续研究可以从以下几个方面进行。

　　更多领域的实证研究:在不同的垂直领域开展实证研究,探讨显化与隐化策略在不同语境下的具体运用和效果。

　　翻译教学与培训:研究如何将显化与隐化策略深度融入翻译教学和培训中,以提高译者的翻译能力和水平。

　　翻译技术的发展:随着人工智能技术的迅速发展,研究如何将显化与隐化策略应用于机器翻译和翻译辅助工具中,以提高翻译质量和效率。虽然神经网络机器翻译在显化与隐化方面的表现不尽如人意,但新一代的人工智能AIGC 则不同。以例 5 为例,同一句原文,不同的提示词下效果不同。

　　对话 1:

　　Q:

　　译为英文:建设海洋强国,必须进一步关心海洋、认识海洋、经略海洋,加快海洋科技创新步伐。

　　A:

To build a strong maritime nation, we must further care for the ocean, understand the ocean, strategically manage the ocean, and accelerate the pace of marine technological innovation.

　　对话 2:

Q：

译为地道的英文，注意避免英文的重复：建设海洋强国，必须进一步关心海洋、认识海洋、经略海洋，加快海洋科技创新步伐。

A：

In order to establish a powerful maritime nation, it is essential to deepen our concern for the sea, enhance our understanding of it, strategically utilize its resources, and expedite the advancement of marine technological innovation.

对话 1 中用的是一个简单的提示词"译为英文"，AIGC 生成的译文中出现了 3 次"ocean"，没有避免重复。对话 2 增加了提示词"注意避免英文的重复"，生成的译文中只出现了 1 次"sea"；"经略海洋"译为"strategically utilize its resources"，已经不是简单的动宾结构对译，而是具有阐述性显化的翻译了。

后续研究应关注显化与隐化策略在翻译过程中的应用和发展，尤其是要探究如何让 AI 赋能，为翻译实践和翻译教学提供更多有益的实用案例。

第 8 章　翻译过程中的选择行为

8.1　引言

翻译过程是一个复杂的认知活动,涉及多个层次的语言知识和技能。在翻译过程中,译者需要根据不同的翻译任务、目标语读者和语境等因素做出一系列选择。这些选择行为对翻译质量、效果和译者的职业发展产生着重要影响。近年来,关于翻译过程中选择行为的研究逐渐成为翻译学界的关注焦点,涌现出众多有益的研究成果。

本章将对翻译过程中的选择行为进行探讨,分析选择行为的类型及影响因素,考察学习者翻译过程中的选择行为。

8.2　翻译过程中选择行为的类型

翻译过程中的选择行为可以从多个维度进行分类,如从译者的知识结构、任务特点、目标语文化等角度进行划分。

本小节主要从以下几个方面对翻译过程中的选择行为进行分析。

8.2.1 词汇选择

词汇选择是翻译过程中最基本也是最关键的选择行为之一。译者需要在源语词汇与目标语词汇之间进行选择,以实现准确、自然的表达。词汇选择涉及多种因素,如语义、语法、语用、文化等,译者需综合考虑这些因素进行选择。

以英汉翻译为例,译者在翻译英文单词"computer"时,需根据上下文和语体选择合适的汉语词汇,如"计算机""电脑"等。此外,译者还需注意词汇的多义性,如英文单词"spirits"在不同语境下可以翻译为"精神"、"酒"或"精灵"等。

8.2.2 句法选择

句法选择是翻译过程中另一个重要的选择行为。源语和目标语的语法结构往往存在差异,译者需根据源语句子的结构和意义,选择合适的目标语句法结构,以实现语义的对等和语言的通顺。

以汉英翻译为例,在主语的选择上,汉语与英语在某些情况下存在差异:汉语多用有灵主语,而英语则无灵主语用得更多,如"我没有想过他会对我撒谎"可以翻译为"It never occurred to me that he would lie to me"。译者需根据上下文和目标语读者的习惯,选择合适的句子结构。

8.2.3 修辞选择

修辞选择涉及译者在翻译过程中对比喻、拟人、排比等修辞手法的处理。不同语言和文化对修辞手法的运用和接受程度存在差异,译者需根据源语的修辞特点和目标语读者的审美习惯,选择合适的修辞手法。

以英汉翻译为例,英语中的一句谚语"The early bird catches the worm"可以直接翻译为"早起的鸟儿有虫吃",这样的翻译既保留了源语的语言形象,也符合目标语读者的审美习惯。然而,有些情况下,源语的修辞手法可能无法直接翻译,译者需采用意译、移植等手法进行处理。例如,英文中的"break a leg"在汉语中没有直接对应的成语,译者可以采用意译的方式,翻译为"祝你好运",以传达源语的含义。

8.2.4 文化选择

文化选择是指译者在翻译过程中为传达源语文本的文化信息而做出的决策。这些决策涉及源语文本中的文化特征如何在目标语中得到合适的表达。在跨文化翻译中,文化选择对于保持原文的文化内涵和使译文符合目标语文化的接受度具有重要意义。译者需根据目标语读者的文化背景、知识结构和接受能力,选择合适的翻译策略,如异化、归化、补充等。例如,将"端午节"翻译为"Dragon Boat Festival, a traditional Chinese festival celebrated on the fifth day of the fifth lunar month"，就是一种异化加阐释的翻译策略，既保留源语文化的形象，又对文化现象进行适当的解释和补充，帮助目标语读者理解。

8.2.5 策略选择

翻译策略是指译者在翻译过程中采用的一种或多种方法，以解决特定翻译问题，从而实现翻译目标。翻译策略的选择与运用直接影响翻译质量，包括译文的准确性、可读性和文化适应性等方面。

1.直译与意译

直译是指译者按照原文的字面意义和语法结构进行翻译，尽量保持源语的形式特征。直译适用于原文的表述清晰、没有难以理解的修辞手法的情况。然而，过度的直译可能导致译文忽略目标语的表达习惯，进而影响译文的可读性。

意译是指译者根据原文的意义和目标语的表达习惯进行翻译，以便更好地传达原文的意义。意译适用于原文含有难以直译的修辞手法、习语或文化特定词汇的情况。意译有助于提高译文的可读性和文化适应性，但可能导致译文与原文在形式上的差异较大。

2.增译与减译

增译是指译者在翻译过程中添加一些原文没有明确表达的信息，以便使译文更加清晰、易懂。增译适用于原文中含有较多省略或隐含的信息，以及目标语需要更明确的表达的情况。

减译是指译者在翻译过程中省略或简化一些原文中的信息，以使译文更加简洁、符合目标语的表达习惯。减译适用于原文中含有较多冗余信息，或目标语要求更简洁表达的情况。

3.归化与异化

归化是指在翻译过程中，译者将源语文本的文化元素和表达方式调整为符合目标语和目标语文化的习惯，使译文更容易为目标语文化读者接受和理解。归化有助于提高译文的可读性、通顺性和文化适应性，使译文更容易为目标文化读者接受和理解。此外，归化还有助于弥合源语文化与目标语文化之间的差异，减少文化冲突和误导。但是，过度的归化可能导致译文失去原文的文化特色和异国情调，使译文变得平庸和缺乏原创性。此外，归化还可能导致原文中的文化信息在译文中发生改变或丢失。

异化指的是在翻译过程中保留源语文本的文化特色和表达方式,使译文保持原文的异国情调,让目标语文化的读者能够体会到原文的文化背景。异化有助于保持译文的文化多样性和异国情调,使译文更具原创性和文学价值。此外,异化还有助于促进跨文化交流和理解,增强目标文化的读者对源语文化的认识和尊重。但是,过度的异化可能导致译文难以理解和被接受,降低译文的可读性和通顺性。此外,过度的异化可能导致目标语文化读者对原文的文化信息产生误解或感到困惑。

在翻译实践中,译者需要根据原文的内容、目的和目标语读者的需求,灵活运用异化策略,并在异化与归化之间寻求平衡。对于那些具有较强文化特色且需要保留异国情调的文本,译者应适当采用异化策略。而对于那些以通俗易懂为目的的文本,译者则可以更多地采用归化策略,使译文更容易为目标语文化读者接受和理解。

翻译策略选择对译者的语言能力、文化素养和翻译技巧等方面提出了较高的要求。译者需要具备扎实的源语和目标语基础,熟悉两种语言的语法规则、表达习惯和修辞手法。此外,译者还需要了解原文和译文的文化背景,能够在保留原文特点的同时,使译文符合目标语文化的要求。

8.3　影响选择行为的因素

翻译过程中的选择行为受到多种因素的影响,这些因素在不同程度上会影响翻译效果。

1.译者的语言能力

译者的源语和目标语能力是影响翻译过程中选择行为的一个关键因素。译者在翻译过程中需要对源语文本进行深入理解,并根据目标语的表达习惯进行选择。译者的语言能力越高,翻译过程中越可能做出正确的决策,从而提高翻译质量。

2.专业背景与翻译经验

译者的专业背景和翻译经验同样对翻译过程中的选择行为产生影响。具备专业背景的译者更容易理解源语文本中的专业术语和概念,从而做出更准确的翻译选择。此外,经验丰富的译者在翻译过程中更能灵活运用翻译策略,提高翻译质量。

3.文化差异

文化差异是影响翻译过程中选择行为的另一个重要因素。译者需要在翻译过程中考虑源语和目标语文化的差异,并选择合适的翻译策略来实现文化信息传递。

4.目标语读者

翻译过程中,译者需要考虑目标语读者的需求和期望。译者应根据目标语读者的文化背景、语言习惯和知识水平,选择合适的翻译策略来使译文更容易被接受和理解。例如,在翻译儿童文学作品时,译者需要使用简单明了的语言和表达方式;而在翻译专业文献时,译者则需要使用专业术语和严谨的逻辑结构。

5.翻译目的

翻译目的是影响译者翻译选择的关键因素。译者需要根据翻译任务的具体要求和目的,选择适当的翻译策略。例如,如果翻译目的是传播文化,译者可能会采用异化策略,保留原文的文化特色;而如果翻译目的是使目标语读者更容易理解,译者可能会采用归化策略,调整译文以使其适应目标语文化的习惯。

6.翻译时间和资源限制

翻译时间和资源限制也会影响译者的翻译选择。在时间紧迫的情况下,译者可能需要采取一些简化的翻译策略以提高翻译效率,如直译、意译等。而在资源充足的情况下,译者可以更加深入地研究源语和目标语文化,选择更为精细和合适的翻译策略。

影响译者翻译选择的因素有很多,译者需要在实际翻译过程中综合考虑这些因素,灵活运用各种翻译策略,以达到最佳的翻译效果。

8.4　译者选择行为的多模态研究

8.4.1 研究个案:"查"与"不查"

1.个案 1

原文: To this end, I call attention to the writings of the French philosopher

Germaine de Staël (1766-1817) because in the adaptation of her notion of progress lies possible hope for the future of the humanities and the arts.

专业译文:为此,本文呼吁关注法国哲学家斯达尔夫人(1766—1817)的著作,因为借鉴她的进步观或许可以找到人文艺术学科未来的希望。

百度译文:为此,我提请大家注意法国哲学家 *Germaine de Staël*(1766—1817)的著作,因为在对她的进步观的改编中,蕴藏着对人文和艺术未来的可能希望。

讯飞译文:为此,我提请注意法国哲学家杰曼·德·斯塔尔(Germaine de Staël,1766—1817)的著作,因为在对她的进步概念进行调整的过程中,可能存在着人文和艺术未来的希望。

小牛译文:为此,我提请注意法国哲学家杰曼·德·斯塔尔(1766—1817)的著作,因为在她对进步概念的改编中,蕴含着对人文和艺术未来的可能希望。

有道译文:为此,我提请注意法国哲学家杰曼·德 Staël(1766—1817)的著作,因为在对她的进步概念的改编中,人文和艺术的未来可能有希望。

微软译文:为此,我提请注意法国哲学家杰曼·德·斯塔尔(Germaine de Staël,1766—1817)的著作,因为在对她的进步概念的改编中,蕴藏着对人文和艺术未来的希望。

学习者译文 1:为此,我提请大家关注法国哲学家热尔梅因·德·斯塔尔(1766—1817)的著作,因为通过她对进步概念的调整,可能为人文和艺术的未来带来希望。

学习者译文 2:为此,我呼吁大家关注法国哲学家斯塔尔夫人的著作,因为她对进步概念的适应蕴含着对未来人文和艺术的希望。

学习者译文 3:为此,我想请大家去关注法国哲学家——热尔曼娜·斯塔尔(1766—1817)的著作,因为在她改良后的"进步观"里还留存着她对人文学科前途的希冀。

学习者译文 4:为此,本人呼吁各位去关注法国哲学家 *Germaine de Staël*(1766—1817)的著作,在她有关进步概念的文字中,流露出了其对人文学科未来形势所抱有的些许希望。

学习者译文 5:为此,我提请大家注意法国哲学家杰曼·德·斯泰尔(1766—1817)的著作,因为在她对进步的概念的修正中存在着对未来人文艺术可能的希望。

学习者评注 1：

评注：▨▨▨　修改　删除　译文

adaptation怎么理解和翻译？

学习者评注 2：

评注：▨▨▨　修改　删除　译文

据查，Germaine de Staël的中文译名是斯塔尔夫人。

学习者评注 3：

评注：▨▨▨　修改　删除　译文

notion of progress，进步观，比进步的概念似乎更为简练一些

学习者评注 4：

评注：▨▨▨　修改　删除　译文

人文学科，还是人文艺术？

学习者评注 5：

评注：▨▨▨　修改　删除　译文

adaptation不是改编，是修正还是改良？

2.个案 2

原文：

［随着诺贝尔奖颁奖典礼的临近,持续 2 个月的"屠呦呦热"正在渐入高潮。］

当地时间 7 日下午,屠呦呦在瑞典卡罗林斯卡学院发表题为"青蒿素——中医药给世界的一份礼物"的演讲,详细回顾了青蒿素的发现过程,并援引毛泽东的话称,中医药学"是一个伟大的宝库"。［对中医药而言,无论是自然科学"圣殿"中的这次演讲,还是即将颁发到屠呦呦手中的诺奖,自然都提供了极好的"正名"。］

专业译文：On the afternoon of December 7, Tu delivered a *speech* entitled "Artemisinin—A Gift from Traditional Chinese Medicine to the World" at the Karolinska Institute in Sweden. Quoting Mao Zedong's saying that Chinese medicine and pharmacology is "a great treasure-house", Tu walked the audience through her breakthrough discovery of the anti-malarial compound artemisinin.

百度译文：On the afternoon of the 7th local time, Tu Youyou delivered a *speech* entitled "Artemisinin—a gift of traditional Chinese medicine to the world" at the Karolinska Institute in Sweden, reviewed the discovery process of artemisinin in detail, and quoted Mao Zedong as saying that traditional Chinese medicine "is a great treasure house".

讯飞译文：On the afternoon of July 7, local time, Tu Youyou delivered a *speech* entitled "Artemisinin—a Gift of Traditional Chinese Medicine to the World" at Karolinska Institute in Sweden, reviewing in detail the discovery process of Artemisinin and quoting Mao Zedong as saying that traditional Chinese medicine "is a great treasure house".

小牛译文：On the afternoon of 7th local time, Tu Youyou delivered a *speech* entitled "Artemisinin—A Gift of Chinese Medicine to the World" in Karolinska Institute, Sweden, reviewing the discovery process of artemisinin in detail, and quoting Mao Zedong as saying that Chinese medicine is "a great treasure house".

有道译文：In a *speech* titled "Artemisinin—a Gift of traditional Chinese Medicine to the world" at Sweden's Karolinska Institute on Sunday afternoon, Tu Youyou reviewed the discovery process of artemisinin in detail and quoted Mao Zedong as saying that traditional Chinese medicine "is a great treasure house."

微软译文：On the afternoon of the 7th local time, Tu Youyou delivered a *speech* entitled "Artemisinin—A Gift of Traditional Chinese Medicine to the World" at Karolinska Institute in Sweden, reviewing the discovery process of artemisinin in detail and quoting Mao Zedong as saying that Chinese medicine "is a great treasure trove".

学习者译文 1：On the afternoon of the 7th local time，Tu Youyou gave a <u>lecture</u> under the title of "Artemisinin—a Gift of Chinese Medicine and Pharmacology to the World" at Karolinska Institute in Sweden. Tu Youyou reviewed the process of the discovery of Artemismin elaborately, quoting a saying from Mao Tse Tung that traditional Chinese medicine "is a Great Treasure House".

学习者译文 2：On the afternoon 7, Tu Youyou delivered a *speech* entitled "Artemisinin—a gift from Traditional Chinese Medicine", at the Karolinska Institutet in Sweden, the theme of which is, . The discovery process of artemisinin was reviewed in detail, citing Mao Zedong as saying, traditional Chinese medicine and pharmacy is a great treasure house.

学习者译文 3：On the afternoon of local time of the 7th, Tu Youyou gave the *speech* of Artemisinin—the gift to China from Chinese medicine, looking back at the process of discovering Artemisinin and quoting Chair Mao Zedong's saying, Chinese medicine is a great treasure.

学习者译文 4：Tu Youyou delivered a *speech* titled "Artemisinin—a gift of Traditional Chinese Medicine to the world" at the Karolinska Institute in Sweden on the afternoon of July 7 (local time). She led a detailed review of the discovery of artemisinin. She also quoted Mao Zedong as saying that "TCM is a great treasure house for the world".

学习者译文 5：On the afternoon of Decemebr 7th, Tu Youyou delivered a *speech* entitled "Artemisinin—A Gift of Chinese Medicine to the World" in Karolinska Institute, Sweden, reviewing the discovery process of artemisinin in detail, and quoting Mao Zedong as saying that Chinese medicine is "a great treasure house".

学习者评注 1：

评注：　　　修改　删除　译文

屠呦呦发表演讲。这里的演讲经查证译为"lecture"而不是"speech"。

学习者评注 2：

评注：　　　修改　删除　译文

当地时间7日下午，要查证具体的日期，查证后为2015年12月7日。注意addres和speech的使用，speech使用频率更高更正规。注意中英文语序排列，英文中的地点状语可放在后翻。

学习者评注 3：

评注：　　　修改　删除　译文

瑞典卡罗林斯卡学院 Karolinska Institute, Sweden 青蒿素artemisinin

学习者评注 4：

评注： ▇▇▇▇ 修改 删除 译文

1.涉及的专有名词要——考证, 青蒿素, 中医药, 学院等等。 2.句子中部分地方省略了部分主语和宾语, 在翻译时要注意补充。 3.要注意引用中的话标点符号的应用。

学习者评注 5：

评注： ▇▇▇▇ 修改 删除 译文

据查证可知道颁奖礼的具体时间, 应该要将时间具体化。 中医药学: traditional Chinese medicine and pharmacy "中医药, , , 。一份礼物"查证+回译, 因为屠自己用的这个标题

8.4.2 分析讨论

1.个案 1

原文为第 32 届韩素音国际翻译大赛英译汉选材,专业译文为官方提供的参考译文。本个案考察句中"Germaine de Staël"一词的翻译以及该译文背后译者所做的选择。

就以上译文来看,专业译文将"Germaine de Staël"译为斯达尔夫人,是正确的选择,因为"Germaine de Staël"在国内约定俗成的译名就是斯达尔夫人。换言之,"Germaine de Staël"的翻译,应查找其通用译名,而不是试图音译。机器译文做出的选择都是音译,由于选择错误,结果自然不可能正确。

从列出的几个学习者的评注来看,结果是令人失望的,因为这 5 位学习者在解读原文时,大多选择将注意力的重点放在"adaptation"、"notion of progress"等的理解和翻译上;并非这些点不重要,而是"Germaine de Staël"这一人名在文中出现 7 次,是必须要准确无误地译出的。5 位学习者中只有一位意识到了"Germaine de Staël"这一人名翻译的重要性,经查证将其译为斯塔尔夫人,虽然与斯达尔夫人不完全相同,但也可接受,因为这一译名也为人所知,不算误译。

2.个案 2

原文为第 28 届韩素音青年翻译竞赛英译汉选材,难度较大。专业译文为官方提供的参考译文。如同个案 1 所分析的,译者在翻译过程中,应统观全文,选择确定翻译过程中的侧重点,例如,译前利用翻译技术提取术语。此个

案也是如此,译者应有全局观,在译前做背景查询;这有助于深入理解原文,澄清疑点。

屠呦呦获奖是 2015 年的热门事件,当时中外媒体的相关报道甚多,形成了"屠呦呦现象"中的特定语境。屠呦呦在瑞典卡罗林斯卡学院发表演讲,即为该语境的重要事件之一,不乏中外媒体的相关报道。原文为屠呦呦获诺奖的新闻评论,亦属于该特定语境。在翻译该文前,如通过网络查证,则不难查到相关报道,了解相关语境的背景信息,例如:

(1)屠呦呦在瑞典发表演讲:青蒿素是中医药给世界的礼物(人民网)

(2)Youyou Tu—Nobel Lecture Discovery of Artemisinin—A Gift from Traditional Chinese Medicine to the World(www.nobelprize.org)

前文说过,译者的思辨能力中,观察能力非常重要,以上英文新闻标题中的"lecture"应不难引起译者的注意。在这种情况下,原文的"演讲"一词,其对应英文是"speech"还是"lecture",自然会激发译者的选择行为。而要在两者之间做出正确选择,查证一番即可。

"lecture"和"speech"一样,对应汉语中的"演讲",如:

He is giving a lecture on international diplomacy.[①]

【译文】:他正在做关于国际外交的演讲。

除上述证据外,屠呦呦发表诺贝尔演讲这一特定语境其实提供了完整的证据链,可以说明西方读者听众接触的有关屠呦呦的语境中,屠呦呦做的是"lecture",而非"speech",这包括现场演讲视频,以及屠呦呦本人演讲的 PPT文本,该 PPT 的标题页如图 8-1。

实际上,诺贝尔演讲的官方英文名称为"Nobel lecture",而诺贝尔颁奖晚宴致辞的官方英文名为"Nobel banquet speech",两者不宜混淆。翻译要尊重约定俗成的官方定名,如财富论坛,其英文为"Fortune Forum",就不宜译为Fortune Symposium"。

综上,此处官方译文和学习者译文的"speech"建议改为"lecture",与现场语境相符。

从 5 位学习者的评注来看,只有 1 位学习者做了查证,发现此处"演讲"应译为"lecture";其他学习者虽然都具有查证意识,但都将"演讲"直接译为"speech",并没有查证,因为对他们而言"演讲"太简单了,无需查证。官方译文亦将"演讲"误译为"speech"。原因在于,我们熟悉的是"speech",对

---

① 见陆谷孙主编《英汉大词典》第二版"lecture"词条例证。

Artemisinin– A Gift from Traditional Chinese Medicine to the World

Tu Youyou

Institute of Chinese Materia Medica, China Academy of Chinese Medical Sciences, Beijing, 100700, China

Nobel Lecture, Dec 7, 2015 Karolinska Institutet

图 8-1 屠呦呦诺贝尔演讲 ppt 英文标题页

"lecture"与"演讲"的对应关系较为陌生,因此容易先入为主,将"演讲"直接译为"speech",不会意识到还有其他译法,也自然不会进行查证,也就无从在"speech"和"lecture"之间做出选择。

这一现象引发了我们的思考,"查"与"不查",这是个问题。

8.4.3 研究发现

我们查看了 30 份学习者的屏幕录制视频,考察了个案 1 的翻译过程,得出表 8-1。

表 8-1 "Germaine de Staël"的译名统计

译文	数量	基于屏幕录制的微观分析
杰曼·德·斯戴尔	8	直接音译,未查证
斯塔尔夫人	6	有查证
杰曼·德·斯塔尔	3	据机器译文
杰曼·德·斯塔埃尔	2	直接音译,未查证

续表

译文	数量	基于屏幕录制的微观分析
热尔梅因·德·斯塔尔	1	据机器译文
热尔曼娜·德·斯塔尔	1	直接音译，未查证
杰曼·德·施塔埃尔	1	直接音译，未查证
杰曼 施太尔	1	直接音译，未查证
杰曼·德·斯特尔	1	直接音译，未查证
杰曼·德·斯泰尔	1	直接音译，未查证
杰曼·德·斯戴	1	直接音译，未查证
杰曼·斯泰尔	1	直接音译，未查证
Germaine de Staël	1	据机器译文
热尔曼娜·斯塔尔	1	直接音译，未查证
热尔梅娜·德·斯塔尔	1	直接音译，未查证

从以上表格统计来看，63.3％的学习者选择直接音译，未做查证，16.7％的学习者选择了机器译文；20％的学习者选择了查证，并选择了斯塔尔夫人这一译名。

个案 2 的统计如表 8-2 所求。

表 8-2　"演讲"的英译统计

译文	数量	基于屏幕录制的微观分析
lecture	3	有做译前背景查证，并据此选择译为"lecture"
lecture	3	未做译前背景查证，但查证了诺贝尔"演讲"的英译，并做出译为"lecture"的选择
lecture	1	未做查证，直接译为"lecture"，属于偶然
speech	5	有查证"演讲"的英译，但未查到"lecture"
speech	18	未查证"演讲"的英译

从以上表格统计来看，10％的学习者做了译前背景查证；10％的学习者未做译前背景查证，但查证了诺贝尔"演讲"的英译；16.7％的学习者有做"演讲"英译的查证，但未查到"lecture"；3.3％的学习者未查证"演讲"的英译，但译文为"lecture"，纯属偶然；60％的学习者未做有关"演讲"英译的任何查证。

综合以上统计，以下几点值得关注：

1.译者统筹全局的选择能力

个案 2 的原文为学术论文选段,篇幅相对于一般的翻译训练而言长得多,学习者缺乏充足的时间、精力和耐力进行大量查证,因此统筹全局,选择哪些词语进行查证,便至关重要。学习者首先要有术语(此处我们将"Germaine de Staël"视为术语)译名准确的责任意识,对于术语等要高度敏感,并予以重视,尤其是一个术语多次出现的情况。

2.译前背景查证的意识和习惯

学习者培养译前查证背景的意识和习惯非常重要,翻译教学中要着重培养这种习惯和能力。

3.技术能力的协调应用

多数学习者技术能力存在欠缺,尚不能允分协调运用各项技术能力。如多数学习者缺乏语篇意识和全局统筹意识,没有做好译前术语提取的准备,导致翻译过程成为完成任务式的逐句推进的翻译。

4.人机协作意识

在人工智能时代,翻译教学要充分培养学生的人机协作意识,让学生了解机器翻译的不足,将重点放在弥补机器短板方面,如术语翻译、逻辑思辨。

8.5　小结

在翻译过程中进行选择需要深入理解源语言和目标语言及其所处文化背景,是一个复杂且多样化的过程,对翻译的质量和效果具有重要的影响。

在这个过程中,译者不应是一个被动的传递者,而应是一个关键的决策者。在翻译过程中,时刻需要做出选择,以最好的方式传达原文的意义、语气和意图。这些选择的复杂性反映了语言之间固有的差异,包括语法、句法和词汇的差异,以及文化差异。译者需要具有高度的创造力和灵活性,找到创新的方式来弥合这些差距,同时保持原文的完整性。

选择的多样性反映了翻译并非一刀切的过程。不同的文本、受众和目的可能需要不同的翻译策略,这进一步强调了翻译过程中选择的重要性。

第 9 章　CCAT 平台下过程导向的比较翻译教学

9.1　引言

本章简要介绍 CCAT 平台下以翻译过程为导向的比较翻译教学。

比较翻译教学主要包括三大核心要素，一是语料库，语料库部分包括平台内嵌的大型通用语料库、多模态学习者语料库，以及网络语料。我们可在翻译过程中充分利用 CCAT 平台提供的语料库及各种搜索引擎等信息资源，进行检索查询，发现问题，解决问题，提升翻译效率和质量。二是 CAT，包括翻译记忆库、术语库、内嵌的人工智能机器翻译。我们可通过术语库提升术语翻译质量及术语译文的一致性，通过翻译记忆库避免重复翻译，通过机器译文的比较促进逻辑思辨，在翻译过程中借鉴机器译文，或是以译后编辑模式完成翻译项目，等等。三是比较法，具有两层含义。第一层含义是指翻译过程中的译文比较，包括多种机译比较，机译与参考译文比较，学习者译文与参考译文比较，学习者译文与机译比较，学习者译文相互比较等多种比较方式（见第 2 章相关小节）。译文比较可以有效提升学生翻译过程中的思辨能力、显化及隐化的应用能力以及选择行为能力。第二层含义是指比较翻译教学法，该教学法由魏志成教授（2007）首创。在人工智能时代，CCAT 平台下翻译教学各个环节的技术融入，使其得到进一步发展。

在 CCAT 平台下，语料库、CAT 与比较法三位一体，贯穿翻译过程的译前、译中、译后三个阶段，通过 AI 赋能、人机协作的方式，培养与语言服务行业接轨的翻译人才。

9.2　AI 赋能的人机协作翻译过程

9.2.1 译前阶段

9.2.1.1 术语库构建

在翻译教学中,培养学生的流程意识和规范意识非常重要。简而言之,就是翻译要严格按照一定的流程完成,不可随意略去某一流程;每个流程都要严格遵守相应的规范。认可并认真接受流程和规范训练的学生,其翻译能力和翻译质量都有明显提升。

在译前阶段,我们要求学生,翻译项目不论大小,都要制作术语库,哪怕是 300 字以内的练习。主要目的就是帮助学生了解并掌握术语库的制作,并养成翻译过程中使用术语库的习惯。

1.基于 AI 分词与 WordSmith 的中文术语提取

从原文文本中提取术语,是制作术语库的第一步。几百字的翻译练习,可能术语不多,人工阅读挑选即可,但对于较大规模的翻译项目而言,很难通过阅读从文本中提取术语。换言之,用工具提取术语是专业译者必须具备的技术能力。因此,虽然是只有几百字的练习,我们也要求学生用工具提取术语,而不是通过人工阅读挑选术语。

在 AI 技术兴起之前,传统的术语提取方法是利用 CAT 软件,如雪人翻译软件中的术语提取模块,或是通过在线版的术语提取工具,如语帆术语宝;但这两种术语提取工具主要是通过统计方式提取术语,精度不高,会提取出大量没有意义的组合搭配,需要耗费大量人力筛选术语,然而一直以来并没有更为有效的方法。

AI 技术兴起之后,百度、微软等都推出了基于文本的关键词提取 API,自然语言处理的利器 Python 也出现了很多关键词提取的方法和模块,如 RAKE、YAKE、KeyBERT 和 TextRank;但对于提取术语而言,这些关键词 API 和 Python 模块的提取效果仍不理想,提取出的词语中有很多是普通词汇,并非术语。

下面以一次翻译练习的原文文本为例,比较 CAT 软件、语帆术语宝和关键词提取 AI 的术语提取效果。

原文文本如下：

考古资料表明，武夷山早在四千多年前就有先民在此劳动生息，逐步形成偏居中国一隅的"古闽族"文化和其后的"闽越族"文化，在国内外是绝无仅有的。

朱熹在武夷山生活达 50 余年，著述教学，使武夷山成为理学名山。

程朱理学，始于"二程"（程颐、程颢），集大成于朱熹，构成中国宋代至清代一直处于统治地位的思想理论，代表具有普遍意义的传统民族精神，影响远及东亚、东南亚、欧美诸国。

孔子集前古思想之大成，开创中国文化传统之主干的儒学。

朱熹集孔子以下学术思想之大成，使程朱理学达到顶峰，为儒学注入新的生机，形成儒学思想文化的杰出代表——朱子理学，至今仍吸引着世界上几十个国家的专家、学者致力于理学思想的研究。

在中国文化史、传统思想史、教育史和礼教史上影响最大的，前推孔子、后推朱熹。

（1）雪人翻译软件提取

词频统计			✕
序号	原文		译文
1	构成中国宋代至清代一直处于统治地位的思想理论，代表具有普遍意义的传统民族精神，		
2	孔子集前古思想之大成，开创中国文化传统之主干的儒学.		
3	朱熹集孔子以下学术思想之大成，使程朱理学达到顶峰，为儒学注入		
4	达到顶峰，为儒学注入新的生机，形成儒学思想文化的杰出代表——朱子理学，至今吸引		
5	世界上几十个国家的专家、学者致力于理学思想的研究.		
6	在中国文化史、传统思想史、教育史和礼教史上影响最大的，前推孔		

序号	词语	译文	词频
11	武夷山	Wuyi Mountain	3
12	中国文化		2
13	亚、		2
14	代表	representative	2
15	史、		2
16	学思想		2
17	形成	formation	2
18	影响	influence	2
19	思想之大成，		2
20	族"文化		2
21	理学，		2
22	的"		2

清除			在线查询	热点词汇	加入词语	提取词语

图 9-1　雪人翻译软件术语提取示例

雪人翻译软件提取是基于统计的方式，因此提取效果很不理想，出现了比较多并非术语的词汇，以及"亚、"这种缺乏语义的组合。

(2)讯飞 AI 关键词提取

{ 功能体验 }

请输入一段需要分析的文本：换一个示例

考古资料表明，武夷山早在四千多年前就有先民在此劳动生息，逐步形成偏居中国一隅的"古闽族"文化和其后的"闽越族"文化，在国内外是绝无仅有的。
朱熹在武夷山生活达50余年，著述教学，使武夷山成为理学名山。

体验版最多100字

开始分析

名称	武夷山	劳动生息	名山	文化	先民	理学	著述	考古	朱熹	资料
分析结果 权重	0.625	0.597	0.577	0.576	0.575	0.572	0.571	0.562	0.560	0.556

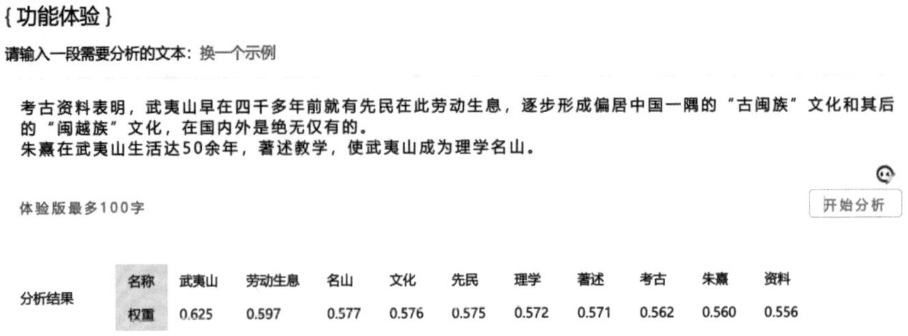

图 9-2　讯飞 AI 关键词提取

由于讯飞网页展示只支持 100 字以内的文本,故只输入了这段话的前两句。从提取情况来看,讯飞 AI 关键词提取优于雪人翻译软件的提取,但也出现了"文化""资料""劳动生息""著述"等并非术语的词汇。

(3)AI 分词＋WordSmith 提取

在以上两类工具中文术语提取效果都不理想的情况下,我们在教学中尝试将 AI 技术与传统的语料库工具结合,以求达到较好的术语提取效果。思路是用基于 AI 的百度分词先对待提取术语的文本分词,然后用 WordSmith 8.0 制作 Wordlist,制作过程中启用停用词表,排除常用词汇。

用自制的百度分词工具对文本分词,结果如下:

考古 资料 表明 ,武夷山 早 在 四千多年 前 就 有 先民 在 此 劳动 生息 ,逐步 形成 偏居 中国 一隅 的 " 古闽族 " 文化 和 其后 的 " 闽越族 " 文化 ,在 国内外 是 绝无仅有 的 。朱熹 在 武夷山 生活 达 50 余年 ,著述 教学 ,使 武夷山 成为 理学 名山 。

程朱理学 ,始于 " 二程 "（程颐 、程颢）,集大成于 朱熹 ,构成 中国 宋代 至 清代 一直 处于 统治 地位 的 思想 理论 ,代表 具有 普遍 意义 的 传统 民族 精神 ,影响 远及 东亚 、东南亚 、欧美 诸国 。

孔子 集 前古 思想 之 大成 ,开创 中国 文化 传统 之 主干 的 儒学 。

朱熹 集 孔子 以下 学术 思想 之 大成 ,使 程朱理学 达到 顶峰 ,为 儒学 注入 新 的 生机 ,形成 儒学 思想 文化 的 杰出 代表 —— 朱子 理学 ,至今 仍 吸引 着 世界 上 几十个 国家 的 专家 、学者 致力于 理学 思想 的 研究 。

在 中国 文化史 、传统 思想史 、教育史 和 礼教史 上 影响 最大 的 ,前

推 孔子 、后 推 朱熹 。

　　之后用 WordSmith 8.0 生成分词后文本的 Wordlist。这一步要注意两点，一是中文文本的 txt 编码须为 Unicode(在 Windows 11 和部分 Windows 10 系统中显示为 UTF-16)，否则 Wordlist 会出现乱码；二是要预先制作好包含中文常用字、词的停用词表。我们制作的停用词表含 45 000 多个字词。选择停用词表后，要点击 Load(加载)，显示加载的词条数量即为加载成功，如图 9-3 所示。

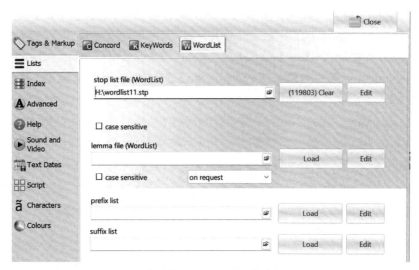

图 9-3　WordSmith 加载停用词表

提取结果如图 9-4：

N	Word	Freq.	%	Texts	%	Dispersion	Lemmas	Set
1	程朱理学	2	1.31%	1	100.00%	0.35		
2	闽越族	1	0.65%	1	100.00%	0.00		
3	程颢	1	0.65%	1	100.00%	0.00		
4	程颐	1	0.65%	1	100.00%	0.00		
5	礼教史	1	0.65%	1	100.00%	0.00		
6	朱子	1	0.65%	1	100.00%	0.00		
7	文化史	1	0.65%	1	100.00%	0.00		
8	教育史	1	0.65%	1	100.00%	0.00		
9	四千多年前	1	0.65%	1	100.00%	0.00		
10	古闽族	1	0.65%	1	100.00%	0.00		
11	前古	1	0.65%	1	100.00%	0.00		
12	二程	1	0.65%	1	100.00%	0.00		
13	#	1	0.65%	1	100.00%	0.00		

图 9-4　WordSmith 提取术语示例

WordSmith 提取出的术语未出现无意义组合,非术语词汇也相对较少,而且提取效果还可以通过增益停用词表予以不断提升。另外,以上文本较小,文本更大的话,效果更明显。

以上方法主要用于中文术语的提取。英文术语的提取可用 Trados 的 MultiTerm Extract 程序。英文术语提取的效果较好。

2.术语筛选

提取的术语需要筛选。筛选的原则主要有两点,一是关注出现频率 2 次以上的词语,二是译文必须统一的词语。如"程朱理学",出现频率达到 2 次,网上存在多种译文,如 Cheng Zhu School、Cheng-Zhu Theory、Cheng Zhu Confucianism 等等。如果不统一译文,势必造成混乱,因此要确定一个统一译名,收入术语库,以保持译文一致。

3.术语翻译

(1)多种机译比较

如上所述,筛选后的术语需要翻译。由于机器翻译术语的准确率已经较高(王朝晖,余军,2016:251),可采用机器翻译+人工修订的方式。首先用 GT4T 自动翻译筛选出的术语,然后人工审核、筛选或修改机器译文,如图 9-5:

1 Cheng Zhu Neo Confucianism
2 Ching-Chu Theory
3 Cheng Zhu Lixue
4 Cheng-Zhu Neo-Confucianism
5 Cheng-Zhu Neo-Confucianism
6 Cheng-zhu school
7 Neo-Confucianism of Cheng and Zhu
8 Cheng–Zhu school
9 Cheng Zhu Neo-Confucianism
10 Cheng Zhu Neo-Confucianism
11 Cheng Julixue
12 Cheng Zhu Neo-Confucianism

回译 (b) | 引擎(e) | 多目标语

图 9-5 "程朱理学"的多种机器译文

　　GT4T 可同时加载十几种机器翻译，用其翻译术语，可实现机器译文互补的效果，即有的机器译文错误，而有的机器译文则可能正确，译者可加以鉴别。如以上 12 个译文中，"Cheng-Zhu school"与"Cheng-Zhu Neo-Confucianism"均是正确译文。

　　如果出现机器译文均不准确的情况，则需要通过网络查询获取译文，此处不予赘述。

　　(2) AIGC 译文

　　在生成式 AI 时代，可以通过 AIGC 模型获取译文。以讯飞的星火模型为例，其提供的"程朱理学"的译文为"Cheng-Zhu Neo-Confucianism"，见图 9-6。

图 9-6　"程朱理学"的讯飞星火译文

　　值得注意的是，在输入恰当指令的情况下，AIGC 的译文往往会优于目前的各种机器翻译译文。以"瀛台会晤"为例，我们让讯飞星火模型将其翻译为英文，提示词为"将瀛台会晤翻译为英文"，结果如图 9-7：

　　⚪ 将瀛台会晤翻译为英文

　　　"瀛台会晤"的英文翻译是 "Yingtai Meeting"。

　　　○ 重新回答　　　　　　　　　　　　⯈ | 🗐 | 👍 👎

图 9-7　"瀛台会晤"的讯飞星火译文 1

　　GT4T 的机器译文如图 9-8。

　　讯飞星火译文和 GT4T 的 10 种译文缺乏背景信息，均不准确。如果我们让 GT4T 多次重译该词，结果一般是不会变的。但如果对讯飞星火模型换一种更为恰当的提示词，结果则会出乎意料，如图 9-9。

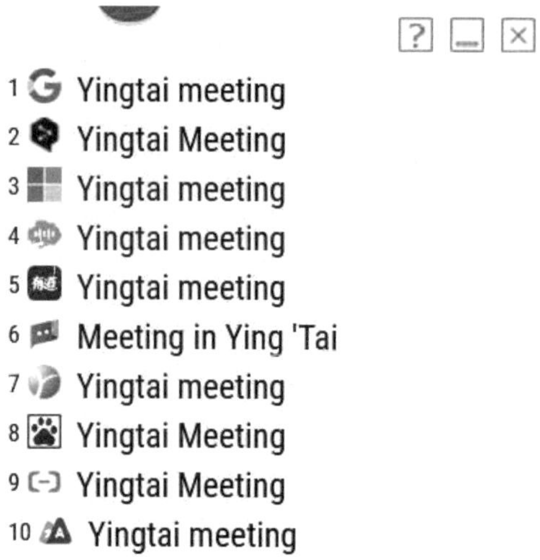

1 Yingtai meeting
2 Yingtai Meeting
3 Yingtai meeting
4 Yingtai meeting
5 Yingtai meeting
6 Meeting in Ying 'Tai
7 Yingtai meeting
8 Yingtai Meeting
9 Yingtai Meeting
10 Yingtai meeting

图 9-8　"瀛台会晤"的机器译文

瀛台会晤的官方英文名称

瀛台会晤的官方英文名称是 "Xi-Obama Meeting at Yingtai"。

重新回答

图 9-9　"瀛台会晤"的讯飞星火译文 2

该译文与官方译文一致。换言之,在翻译过程中遇到一些术语,如用恰当的指令让 AIGC 模型进行翻译,在很多情况下会比机器翻译＋人工审核＋网络查询的方式更为高效。

如何对 AIGC 模型提问,是一门技术,需要学习掌握。在翻译教学中如何科学合理地利用 AIGC,是一个全新而充满挑战的研究领域,值得关注。

需要注意的是,AIGC 生成的结果是会变化的,如果对于结果不满意,可点击"重新回答"生成新的答案。

4.术语库的制作

术语库的制作,要考虑的重要因素是兼容性。就文档格式而言,txt 是兼容性最好的。以 CAT 软件 Trados 和小牛机器翻译为例,前者支持 txt 文件转换为其术语库,后者只支持 txt。我们自建的 CCAT 平台支持的也是 txt 格式的术语库,原文和译文之间用制表符分隔即可。

在术语库制作的教学中,我们要求学生掌握三种术语库的制作方法。

一是小牛机器翻译的术语库制作。学生需自行申请免费的小牛机器翻译账号,上传 txt 格式的术语表至小牛机器翻译平台,并启用其上传的术语库。之后,不论是使用网页版的小牛机器翻译,还是 Word 插件,都会调用其自建的术语库,提升术语翻译的准确性。比较图 9-10、图 9-11:

图 9-10　"瀛台会晤"的小牛翻译(未启用术语库)

图 9-11　"瀛台会晤"的小牛翻译(启用术语库)

小牛机器翻译的术语库制作代表了机器翻译平台的术语库制作方法,其他支持术语库的机器翻译平台的术语库制作与其类似。

二是 Trados 术语库的制作。过程较为复杂,此处不予赘述。该术语库的制作代表了传统 CAT 工具这一类型,掌握了 Trados 的术语库制作方法的话,其他 CAT 工具的术语库制作一般都不成问题。

三是 CCAT 平台的术语库制作。是三种类型中最为简单的,只要上传原文和译文之间用制表符分隔的 txt 文件即可,也可以手工录入术语,如图 9-12。

从术语提取、术语翻译到术语库制作,整个流程涉及各种工具的使用、译文准确与否的判断,有助于学生掌握相关翻译技术,培养术语意识和查询意识。学生在制作术语库的过程中,思辨能力、技术能力、翻译能力可以得到提

图 9-12　CCAT 平台的术语添加功能

升,而且应用其自建的术语库,会有一种成就感,这是翻译过程中技术赋能的结果。译前阶段术语库的构建教学,值得推广。

9.2.1.2 译前编辑

译前编辑可以分为两类,一类是译者在译前对原文做一些处理,然后进行翻译,整个翻译过程属于人工翻译。例如,徐勤、吴颖(2003:80)认为,已有的翻译原则难以适用经贸外宣资料翻译,导致现实中大量存在着的、具有重要意义的经贸外宣资料翻译无章可循,通过对经贸外宣资料语篇功能和翻译事例进行分析,提出经贸外宣资料翻译应遵循"译前编辑、信息等值、译文通畅"的原则。

另一类是机器翻译的译前编辑,有关译前编辑的探讨,大多属于此类。例如,在科技文本翻译过程中,增加译前与译后编辑的互联网机器翻译完成质量优于传统人工翻译,同时也优于仅在机器翻译后进行编辑加工的翻译任务(郭高攀、王宗英,2017:76)。

译前编辑是提高机器翻译质量的重要途径之一,也是人机交互翻译的重要表现。在词级和句级层面的译前编辑方法,可以提高人机交互译前编辑模式下机译译文质量(李洋等,2021:55)。词汇的增补、删减、替代和术语提前等译前编辑方法能够提高机器英汉翻译译文质量(陈蓉等,2021:101)。汉语具有模糊特质,表现为语义外延丰富、逻辑内涵隐晦,这给机器翻译带来理解上的困难(仲文明等,2021:36);科技文本中常见的"非机器友好型"因素较多——模糊语义,包括隐喻、多义、隐性逻辑、重复结构和模糊主题词等,故在机器翻译前应考虑编辑策略。

就译前编辑而言,Trados、雪人翻译软件等传统 CAT 工具存在一个问题,即不能在翻译界面编辑原文。为避免因疏忽或误操作删改原文的情况出现,这一设定是正确且必需的,但却给译前编辑带来问题,因为译者很难预知机器翻译会出现什么结果。所谓译前编辑纯粹依赖经验,作为一个研究话题有其价值,但从翻译效率的角度而言,实际操作中有多大可行性,就另当别论了。此外,大多 CAT 工具不支持多种机器翻译同时呈现,不具备机译互补的功能。有些译前编辑,如在汉译英时政材料中添加主语"我们",在多种机器译文实时呈现的情况下,也许是不需要的,因为多种机译中,有的会在译文中添加主语 We,如图 9-13:

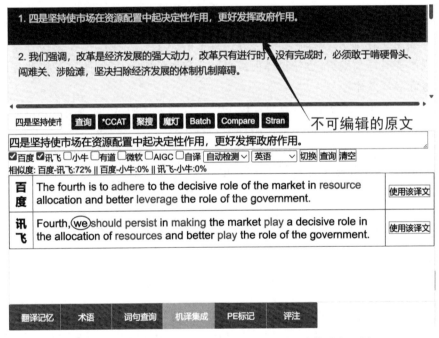

图 9-13　机器翻译自行添加主语"We"及不可编辑原文示例

如图 9-13 所示,百度译文按原句直译,未添加主语 We,而讯飞则添加了We。在这种情况下,选择讯飞译文即可,不必进行译前编辑。

针对上述问题,CCAT 平台不仅嵌入多种机器翻译引擎并实时显示多种机译,而且创新性地设计了原文实时编辑功能。这一编辑功能并非直接改动原文,而是编辑传输给机器翻译的内容。如图 9-13 所示,原文区域的原文是不可编辑的,但输送给机器翻译的原文单独显示在机器翻译界面的上方,是可以编辑的,如图 9-14:

图 9-14　译前编辑示例

如图 9-14 所示,添加"我们"之后,百度的译文也添加了"We"。这一设计实现了实时译前编辑,也使得译前编辑具有较强的可操作性,提高了机器翻译质量和翻译效率。

译前编辑主要包括增、删、改几个方面,如增加代词、连词,删除冗余,改动语序、标点,或是同义替换,语义阐释等。

我们在教学中非常重视译前编辑,会通过翻译案例传授译前编辑的各种技巧,并要求学生在翻译过程中予以实践,提升机器翻译+译后编辑的效率和质量。

9.2.2 译中阶段

9.2.2.1 术语库应用

翻译过程中,必须通过术语库确保术语翻译的准确性以及一致性,这一点至关重要。在翻译教学中,我们要求学生译前必须制作并上传术语库,养成使用术语库的习惯。

以图 9-15 的一次翻译练习为例,练习原文第一句出现了"武夷山"这一术语,其译文在网络上有多种,包括"Wuyi Mountain""Wuyi Mount""Wuyishan""Wuyishan Mountain""Mount Wuyishan",各种错误译文不胜枚举。学生在译前通过网络查询世界遗产官方网站,确定了"武夷山"的英文名称为"Mount

Wuyi"，将其加入制作的术语库并上传至 CCAT 平台。翻译时，点击原文，该术语会自动在平台界面下方的术语框中显示，只要点击"使用该术语"，术语即会自动进入译文框。

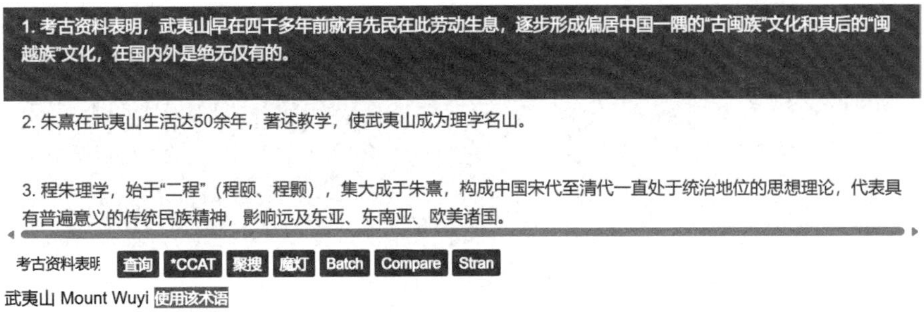

> **1. 考古资料表明，武夷山早在四千多年前就有先民在此劳动生息，逐步形成偏居中国一隅的"古闽族"文化和其后的"闽越族"文化，在国内外是绝无仅有的。**
>
> 2. 朱熹在武夷山生活达 50 余年，著述教学，使武夷山成为理学名山。
>
> 3. 程朱理学，始于"二程"（程颐、程颢），集大成于朱熹，构成中国宋代至清代一直处于统治地位的思想理论，代表具有普遍意义的传统民族精神，影响远及东亚、东南亚、欧美诸国。

考古资料表明　[查询] [*CCAT] [聚搜] [魔灯] [Batch] [Compare] [Stran]

武夷山 Mount Wuyi [使用该术语]

图 9-15　CCAT 平台的术语库应用示例

9.2.2.2 机译互补

比较翻译教学法的特色是译文比较。翻译过程中，CCAT 平台可实时提供多种机译，便于用户比较，实现机译互补。在翻译教学中，我们注重培养学生的机译查询、机译互补意识。机译互补可在一定程度上激发并增强学生的思辨意识和查询意识。以一次翻译练习为例，原文中有一句"且说贾珍方要抽身进去"，对于不熟悉《红楼梦》的译者来说，很容易将句中的"贾珍方"误读为人名，从而误译为"Jia Zhenfang"。据语料库检索，204 例学生译文中，有 42 例误译，部分误译如图 9-16：

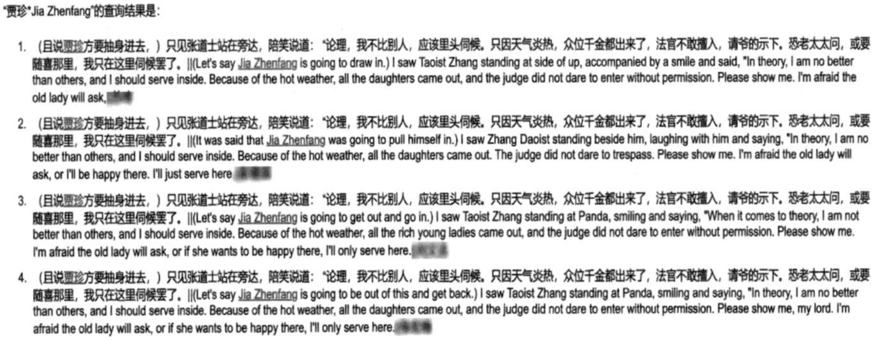

"贾珍"Jia Zhenfang"的查询结果是：

1. （且说贾珍方要抽身进去，）只见张道士站在旁边，陪笑说道："论理，我不比别人，应该里头伺候。只因天气炎热，众位千金都出来了，法官不敢撞入，请爷的示下。恐老太太问，或要随喜那里，我只在这里候罢了。||(Let's say Jia Zhenfang is going to draw in.) I saw Taoist Zhang standing at side of up, accompanied by a smile and said, "In theory, I am no better than others, and I should serve inside. Because of the hot weather, all the daughters came out, and the judge did not dare to enter without permission. Please show me. I'm afraid the old lady will ask,

2. （且说贾珍方要抽身进去，）只见张道士站在旁边，陪笑说道："论理，我不比别人，应该里头伺候。只因天气炎热，众位千金都出来了，法官不敢撞入，请爷的示下。恐老太太问，或要随喜那里，我只在这里候罢了。||(It was said that Jia Zhenfang was going to pull himself in.) I saw Zhang Daoist standing beside him, laughing with him and saying, "In theory, I am no better than others, and I should serve inside. Because of the hot weather, all the daughters came out. The judge did not dare to trespass. Please show me. I'm afraid the old lady will ask, or I'll be happy there. I'll just serve here.

3. （且说贾珍方要抽身进去，）只见张道士站在旁边，陪笑说道："论理，我不比别人，应该里头伺候。只因天气炎热，众位千金都出来了，法官不敢撞入，请爷的示下。恐老太太问，或要随喜那里，我只在这里候罢了。||(Let's say Jia Zhenfang is going to get out and go in.) I saw Taoist Zhang standing and saying, "In theory, I am no better than others, and I should serve inside. Because of the hot weather, all the rich young ladies came out, and the judge did not dare to enter without permission. Please show me. I'm afraid the old lady will ask, or if she wants to be happy there, I only serve here.

4. （且说贾珍方要抽身进去，）只见张道士站在旁边，陪笑说道："论理，我不比别人，应该里头伺候。只因天气炎热，众位千金都出来了，法官不敢撞入，请爷的示下。恐老太太问，或要随喜那里，我只在这里候罢了。||(Let's say Jia Zhenfang is going to be out of this and get back.) I saw Taoist Zhang standing at Panda, smiling and saying, "In theory, I am no better than others, and I should serve inside. Because of the hot weather, all the daughters came out, and the judge did not dare to enter without permission. Please show me, my lord. I'm afraid the old lady will ask, or if she wants to be happy there, I'll only serve here.

图 9-16　"Jia Zhenfang"误译示例

但如果学生有启用并比较多种机器翻译的习惯,就会发现有的机译为"Jia Zhenfang",有的为"Jia Zhen"(见图 9-17),从而进行思辨,进而查询,最终确定正确译文。据我们对 20 位翻译正确的学生翻译过程屏幕录像的观察统计,70%是通过比较机译并查询避免了误译。

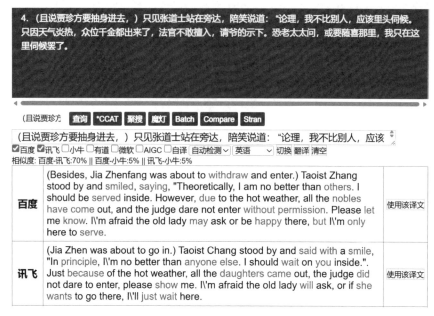

图 9-17　机译比较

9.2.2.3 语料库检索

以语料为驱动,能够提升翻译质量。CCAT 平台内嵌了大型通用语料库,并设计了便捷的查询方式。在翻译过程中,我们要求学生养成查询语料库的习惯。以图 9-18 中的"随喜"一词为例,机器译文大多错误。学生需要查询语料库进一步求证,只要鼠标划过"随喜"一词,左侧的语料库查询自动出现匹配的结果,该词的英译为"visit"。

9.2.2.4 信息检索

我们自建的通用语料库虽然规模较大,但难免会出现查询不到结果的情况。针对这一问题,我们在平台设置了便捷的网络查询入口,如图 9-19 的四张截图所示,学生可以非常便捷地查询搜索引擎、词典、百科等网络资源。

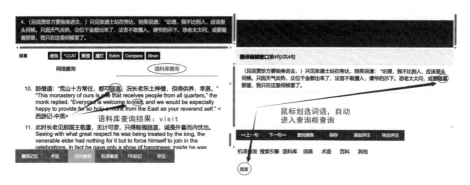

图 9-18　语料库查询示例

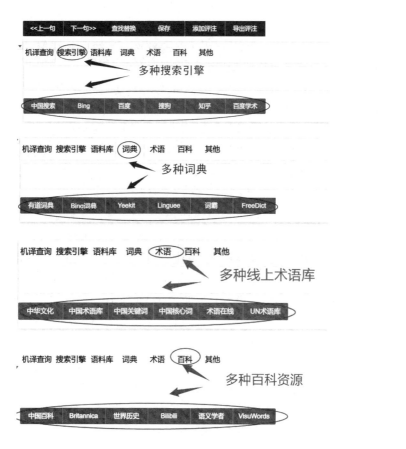

图 9-19　网络资源示例

9.2.3 译后阶段

译后阶段包括两个方面——译后编辑和译后反思,简述如下。

1.译后编辑

译后编辑指机器翻译的译后编辑。在人工智能时代,机器翻译＋译后编辑的翻译模式已经成为语言服务行业的主流翻译模式。译后编辑对于翻译教学和人才培养具有重要意义,但也带来了一些挑战。

我们在教学中给学生讲授了深度译后编辑和轻度译后编辑的区别,以及过度编辑和欠额编辑等容易出现的问题。译后编辑对于学生而言,难度较大,因为机器翻译质量越来越高,学生往往出现为译后编辑而编辑的问题,导致过度编辑甚至错误编辑,也就是出现不必要的修订甚至是错误修订;而一些隐性的问题,学生往往又难以发现,出现欠额编辑。

为提升译后编辑能力,学生需要知己知彼,了解机器翻译的常见错误类型以及存在问题,清楚自身能力,明确译后编辑的边界,并掌握译后编辑的一些技巧。经过数年的译后编辑教学实践,我们概括出最为核心的两点。

一是术语翻译。机器翻译经常出现术语翻译错误,学生通过查询大多是可以纠正的,因此,我们在教学中特别重视提升学生的查证能力,包括语料库检索和网络查询。

二是显化与隐化。以汉译英为例,经常要添加背景阐释(显化),或是略去冗余不译(隐化)。高质量的人工译文往往显化与隐化并存,而机器译文目前仍不会做出有意识的显化或隐化。在这一方面,较为有效的训练方式是进行人工译文和机器译文的比较,帮助学生鉴别人工译文和机器译文,了解翻译过程中的显化与隐化之道。经过这一训练后,学生有望通过译后编辑,进一步提升机器翻译的质量。

2.译后反思

在比较翻译教学法的比较理念下,平台提供了多种译文比较的功能。我们在教学中注重培养学生的译文比较意识,要求学生在译后进行三种比较,即自译与参考译文的比较(见图 9-20)、自译与机器译文的比较(见图 9-21),以及自译与同学译文的比较(见 9.3.2 小节)。

序号	原文	你的译文	参考译文	相似度
1	New Oxford University vice-chancellor says US 'over-reacted' to 9/11.	[1]新任牛津大学校长表示美国对9/11事件反应过度。	牛津大学新任校长称美国对9/11事件反应过度。	75.86%
2	Head & Shoulders is head and shoulders above any other.	海飞丝无人能敌。	海飞丝在同类产品中遥遥领先。	30.77%
3	An Abominable Snowman was witnessed by a naturalist last week in the Himalayas.	上周，一名自然学家目击了喜马拉雅雪人。	上周，一位博物学家在喜马拉雅山目击了雪人一样。	59.26%
4	His writings are devoured by Arabs from the casbahs of Morocco to the oil derricks of the Persian Gulf, by diplomats from Foggy Bottom to Beijing.	从摩洛哥城堡到波斯湾石油井架的阿拉伯人，从美国到中国的外交官们，都如饥似渴地拜读他的著作。	从摩洛哥城堡到波斯湾石油井架的阿拉伯人，从华盛顿到北京的外交人员，无一不拜读他的作品来满足需要。	60.42%
5	We bombed the Axis Europe.	我们轰炸了轴心国在欧洲的占领区。	我们轰炸了轴心国在欧洲的占领区。	78.95%
6	The United States has now set up a loneliness industry.	美国政府建立了一套为孤寡老人的社会服务项目。	美国现已建立起了为孤独的人服务的社会项目。	66.67%

相似度均值：61.988333333333%

图 9-20　自译与参考译文的比较

序号	原文	你的译文	机器译文	相似度
1	New Oxford University vice-chancellor says US 'over-reacted' to 9/11.	[1]新任牛津大学校长表示美国对9/11事件反应过度。	牛津大学新任校长称：美国对911事件反应过度。	82.76%
2	Head & Shoulders is head and shoulders above any other.	海飞丝无人能敌。	Head&Shouths是比其他任何东西都高的东西。	3.33%
3	An Abominable Snowman was witnessed by a naturalist last week in the Himalayas.	上周，一名自然学家目击了喜马拉雅雪人。	上周，一位博物学家在喜马拉雅山区目睹了一个可怕的雪人。	55.56%
4	His writings are devoured by Arabs from the casbahs of Morocco to the oil derricks of the Persian Gulf, by diplomats from Foggy Bottom to Beijing.	从摩洛哥城堡到波斯湾石油井架的阿拉伯人，从美国到中国的外交官们，都如饥似渴地拜读他的著作。	他的著作被阿拉伯人，从摩洛哥的城堡到波斯湾的石油井架，从华盛顿到北京的外交官所吞噬。	62.5%
5	We bombed the Axis Europe.	我们轰炸了轴心国在欧洲的占领区。	我们轰炸了轴心国欧洲。	57.89%
6	The United States has now set up a loneliness industry.	美国政府建立了一个为孤寡老人服务的社会服务项目。	美国现在建了一个孤独产业。	22.22%

相似度均值：47.376666666667%

图 9-21　自译与机器译文的比较

9.3　CCAT 平台下的比较翻译教学法

比较翻译教学法是系统地从比较翻译学的角度实施翻译教学的方法，重视语言、文化的比较，旨在通过多译本的比较，引导学生结合自己的译文参与比较评析，从而提高自主学习能力和翻译水平。魏志成教授（2007）在多年翻译教学实践中归纳出比较翻译教学在课堂教学中具体实施的"五步法"，明确了翻译课程控制过程，确立了比较翻译教学法在翻译教学法中的地位。比较翻译教学法"体现了翻译教学的一种新理念，是作者 10 多年来吸收国内外翻译教学研究新成果的结晶"（陈宏薇，2008：43），是"我国翻译教学上的一项重要突破"（杨自俭，2006：2），是国内外近年出现的 11 种优秀翻译教学法（王树槐，栗长江，2008：133）之一。

9.3.1 比较翻译教学法的五个步骤

比较翻译教学法的核心是"比较"。在比较翻译教学法的理论框架内，CCAT 完美地融入了比较翻译教学法的五个步骤之中。

1.现场翻译

比较翻译教学法的第一个步骤是现场翻译。在我们的实际教学过程中，学生在配有电脑、具备上网功能的语言实验室，使用 CCAT 翻译平台进行现场翻译，并利用屏幕录制工具录制翻译过程。现场翻译需要运用多种翻译技术能力，包括信息检索、术语库制作、语料库检索等。

2.小组讨论

比较翻译教学法的第二个步骤是小组讨论、相互评阅译文。各小组通过 CCAT 平台的检索评注系统查看指定的另一小组练习译文，结合参考译文以及其他学生的练习译文，对比讨论，从中学习并发现问题。然后在组长的组织下对所评阅的译文予以反馈（见图 9-22），被评学生可自行查看。教师查看各小组对所评译文的反馈，概括典型案例，对该次练习予以总体反馈评价。教师

图 9-22　CCAT 在线翻译平台检索评注示例

评价与小组评价自动合为一个网页文件,全部学生都可在其平台界面查看。在这一环节,学生先进行反馈评注,再阅读教师的总体反馈评价,对学生来说又是一次极好的学习机会。

3.演示报告

比较翻译教学法的第三个步骤是演示报告。每次练习均安排 2～3 组同学上台做演示报告,每组时间 5～8 分钟。演示完毕,全体同学通过基于 Moodle(余军,2017)的在线教学平台对同学演示进行评分,然后教师点评。

4.译文修改

比较翻译教学法的第四个步骤是译文修改。学生将初稿译文与参考译文及其他同学译文对比,并根据同学及教师的反馈评价,对译文进行修改,形成定稿,提交至 CCAT 平台。

5.教师点评

比较翻译教学法的第五步是教师点评。在没有 CCAT 平台(尤其是多模态语料库)之前,教师的点评往往凭经验出发,不一定能切中要害;即便是教师经过细心批改学生作业总结出存在的问题,也很难将全部原始语料整理在课件上给学生一一展示令其信服。而利用 CCAT 平台,这一切问题则迎刃而解。教师可在课堂上当场检索,借助现场语料的演示点评,不但针对性强,而且直观,令学生印象深刻,从而加深学生对错误的认识,促进他们对技巧的掌握。CCAT 的运用使教师的点评更有针对性,有利于教师对教学过程的控制。

在以上各个步骤中,学生都与 CCAT 平台和语料库密切接触,真正融入其中。

9.3.2 以"比较"为导向、语料库驱动(corpus-driven)下的自主学习

比较翻译教学法的五个教学步骤中,第一、第二和第四步骤这三个环节与语料库密切结合,充分体现了以学生为主体、发挥学生主动性的教学理念,使学生在完成翻译练习、语料自动入库的过程中充满成就感,从而也对语料库在其翻译学习中的应用产生浓厚的兴趣,积极主动地将语料库的检索对比技术运用于比较翻译学习的各个过程。

以上五个教学步骤主要有以下几个作用:

1.检索比较多种译文，自主学习不同译法

以课堂练习"背影"为例，教师为该文提供了张培基译本和杨宪益译本两种参考译文。在进行比较翻译教学法的第二步骤，即小组讨论、相互评阅译文时，学生检索参考译文和全部同学的译文，进行对比分析，普遍反映收获很大。例如，原文中有一句"这时我看见他的背影，我的泪很快地流下来了"。某小组发现该句中"看见他的背影"这一表达看似简单，其实暗藏翻译陷阱。该小组检索"背影"，共检索到 30 种译文。其中，杨宪益的译文是"at the sight of his burly back"，该组学生从中学到了将汉语的动词结构转换为英语的介词结构这一翻译技巧。同时也发现了下面所述的同学译文亮点和存在的问题。

2.发现同学译文亮点，相互学习树立信心

在上述"看见他的背影"的 30 个译文中，杨宪益译文为"at the sight of his burly back"。该小组检索"at the sight of"，结果显示有 3 位同学的译文为"at the sight of his back"，1 位的译文为"at the sight of my father's back"，与杨译类似。该组将这 4 位学生的译文视为亮点，在反馈评注中予以展示，并对所评注同学的错误译文提出了修改建议。通过同学译文的亮点展示，学生在翻译训练中树立了信心，也加强了彼此之间比较译文优劣的竞争心理，大多数学生的学习积极性有所提高。

3.比较分析客观数据，提炼演示报告主题

在上述"看见他的背影"的 30 个译文中，该小组发现有 10 位同学的译法是"watched his figure view""saw the sight of his back""saw a view of his back" "seeing the view of his back""saw the sight of his back""seeing the view of his back""watching his sight of back""seeing the sight of his father's back"等，占全部译文的 33%。该组通过讨论，确定了"汉英翻译中的逻辑思辨问题——以'看见背影'的英译为例"这一话题，在演示报告中分析了上述译文中"watch""see"等动词与同义名词"sight""view"构成动宾结构时存在的逻辑冲突，提醒同学在翻译过程中要注重逻辑思辨，提升译文质量。该组的演示报告用检索软件得出的客观数据说话，针对性强，引起了多数同学的思考，取得了很好的效果。

4.培养独立思考精神，内建翻译技巧图式

比较翻译教学法注重培养学生"不唯权威，不盲从参考译文"的独立思考精神。学生们通过语料库的检索和对比分析，除了能发现同学译文的问题外，有时还能发现参考译文的问题，提出质疑。如课堂练习"背影"参考译文中，张培基将"下午上车北去"译为"taking a train for Beijing on the afternoon of the same day",与杨译"take the afternoon train to the north"相比,显得冗长,简练不足。某小组发现了张译这一问题,以"汉英翻译中名词定语的运用"为题做演示报告。该演示报告使部分同学掌握了名词定语这一技巧,并在翻译中简练原则的驱动下运用这一技巧。这在之后的一次练习中得到了验证。该练习中有一个句子,"作为报酬,和尚把一些可吃的东西放在庙门前"。在 30 位学生的译文中,有 6 位学生将"庙门"译为"temple gate",而不是常见的"the gate of the temple",还有 4 位同学直接译为"gate",说明这些学生充分发挥了其自主判断能力,能够进行翻译策略的构建。这要归功于语料库在翻译教学中的运用,为学生提供了一个具有丰富语料的自主学习平台。学生在语料库技术驱动下的多译本对比分析中,独立思考,逐步掌握了翻译技巧。其他学生则译法各异,存在种种问题,这也说明翻译能力的培养和提升需要一个长期的训练过程,学生需要在大量语料的不断刺激下通过内省式思考总结翻译中的得失、对错,逐步形成翻译过程中可自动激发的翻译技巧图式。

9.3.3 以客观数据为依据、针对性强的教学策略与教学反馈

将 CCAT 纳入比较翻译教学法的体系,使教师摆脱了凭直觉判断学生译文质量以及存在问题的弊端。通过对学生多模态语料的检索,教师可以分析了解学生薄弱环节与强项,制定针对性强的教学策略,确定教学侧重点,及时给学生反馈;还可与低年级语言课程接轨,向低年级教师反馈学生在低年级阶段语言学习中存在的问题和薄弱环节。

1.检索功能强大,教学策略灵活调整

语料检索在翻译教学中起到了至关重要的作用。教师通过对学生译文的检索,可以了解到学生所犯错误的频率高低,灵活调整教学重点和策略,例如频率高的先讲,频率低的后讲。

2.了解学生个体,发现其系统性错误

教师利用 CCAT 平台检索学生语料,可以较为便捷地了解学生译文的语言面貌,发现其系统性问题。我们在阅览几位学生某次练习初稿时,发现"the door of temple"这种错误表达,单凭该例证不能确定是与"temple"一词有关的偶然性错误,还是系统性错误,便对这几位学生的练习检索"of"一词。检索结果显示,凡是"of＋可数名词单数"结构,这几位学生在可数名词前一概不加

定冠词,可见是系统性错误。通过检索了解学生系统性错误,可以帮助学生纠正该类错误,帮助学生提高。我们在教学中特别注重通过检索发现学生的系统性错误,因为系统性错误纠正一次,学生可能以后就不会再犯此类错误。

3.错误类别、频率统计,向低年级课程反馈

CCAT 平台的检索,使得对学生译文错误的类别、频率统计成为可能,教师从而能够将相关统计信息向低年级教师任课教师反馈,引起低年级教师对高年级频发的语法错误的重视。此外,翻译课程开发的语法错误标注系统,可以而且应该向全体语言课程教师推广。如果所有教师在评阅学生作业时使用同一套错误标注系统,全体教师和学生都手持一本配有例证说明及语法项目索引的错误标注手册,不但可以提高教学效率,而且可以大大提高学生获得错误反馈的频率;学生也可以从手册中查找到错误例证和说明,不清楚之处还可以根据语法索引进一步研习。

9.4　CCAT 平台下的过程控制策略

比较翻译教学法是以学生为中心、激发学生自主学习能力的教学法。与以教师为主的传统教学方法不同,比较翻译教学法的过程控制极其重要,甚至决定该教学法的成败。在进行本章所述的五个教学步骤的过程之中,教师都要严格监控;而引入 CCAT 平台后,学生的参与度提高,过程的控制就更为重要。

1.学习小组团队协作,人员构成合理优化

比较翻译教学法重视学生的团队合作,教学过程主要以小组为单位进行。对于学生的分组,教师要加以管理和控制,小组成员的构成不可随意。在组成小组之前,教师应对所有学生进行翻译水平和语法、词汇能力的测试,挑出水平最高的学生,成为小组的核心,再将具备一定管理能力的班干部分入每个小组。最后,每个小组再安排一个计算机技术较好的学生。水平高的同学可以带动水平较差的学生,可以对小组的反馈评注和演示报告起到一定的质量监控作用;对各小组管理和质量监控方面表现出色的学生,予以表扬并加分。

2.严格管理随时监控,因势利导灵活多变

在比较翻译教学法与 CCAT 平台相结合的各个步骤中,教师除对全体学生演示说明相关技术、要求和操作程序外,还要重点培训各小组的骨干成员,

使其熟练掌握各步骤的技术、规范和要求,如演示报告格式及要求、检索评注系统的应用等。经培训的骨干成员作为小组的项目管理者,必须调动起全体组员的积极性,对反馈评注及演示报告质量把关。

比较翻译教学法的五个步骤环环相扣,学生练习的及时提交极其重要。教师在教学中利用 CCAT 平台的自动统计功能,能够了解学生的练习完成情况,包括漏译,以及未提交作业的情况(见图 9-23)。

汉英1-课堂练习7(xiaoniu)		中英	2022-10-18-8-27-01	289	0	已提交	双语	机译	生成	查看
汉英1-课堂练习6(xiaoniu)	均已提交,漏译(缺句)为0	中英	2022-10-11-9-56-21	246	0	已提交	双语	机译	生成	查看
汉英1-课堂练习5(xiaoniu)		中英	2022-10-04-8-23-32	272	0	已提交	双语	机译	生成	查看
汉英1-课堂练习4(xiaoniu)		中英	2022-09-27-9-46-20	241	0	已提交	双语	机译	生成	查看
汉英1-课堂练习3(xiaoniu)		中英	2022-09-20-10-03-39	333	0	已提交	双语	机译	生成	查看
汉英1-课堂练习2(xiaoniu)		中英	2022-09-13-19-24-39	209	0	已提交	双语	机译	生成	查看
汉英1-课堂练习1(xiaoniu)		中英	2022-09-06-10-03-55	164	0	已提交	双语	机译	生成	查看

图 9-23　学生练习提交情况统计示例

在保证练习译文的按时提交之后,比较教学法的过程控制中最重要的环节是学生的演示报告和教师点评。教师要控制学生演示报告的时间,对演示报告的内容和质量做出评价,提出修改建议;点评时既要突出学生亮点,又要指出不足之处,引导学生深入思考。例如,上文曾提到一个例子,某小组根据语料检索结果提炼出"汉英翻译中的逻辑思辨问题——以'看见背影'的英译为例"这一话题,在演示时取得了很好的效果。教师除肯定和鼓励该组的努力外,指出该组没有深入挖掘的一个问题,即为什么学生会将"看见他的背影"译为"see the view of his back"。原因是他们都查了电子词典,词典中"背影"的英文为"view of one's back"。利用这一例子,教师提醒学生在使用电子词典或者网络资源时,要注意甄别,不能盲目照搬。这种因势利导、灵活多变的点评,要求教师平时积累较为丰富的语言文化及百科知识,熟悉各种翻译理论和技巧;不然,有可能会出现演示报告现场失控的情况。

9.5　技术驱动，以赛育人

人工翻译与翻译技术的结合，凸显了当今翻译领域的一个转向——技术转向（张霄军，贺莺，2014：74）。翻译技术的发展，对翻译教学而言，既是机遇也是挑战。近年来，我们依托 CCAT 翻译平台，以翻译技术为驱动，提高教学成效，并积极参与学科竞赛，加强学生实践能力，促进人才培养。技术驱动，以赛育人，效果较为明显。

1989 年创办的韩素音国际翻译大赛（原"韩素音青年翻译奖竞赛"，2018 年更名，以下简称"韩赛"），是国内组织时间最长、规模最大、影响最广的翻译赛事，激励和培养了一批又一批有志青年投身于翻译事业，影响广泛而深远（王朝晖，余军，2019：72）。近年来，韩赛的参与度逐年提升，以 2017—2019 年为例，2017 年共收到有效参赛译文 6 000 多份，2018 年 10 551 份，2019 年 11 900 份，呈递增趋势，反映了高校对于学科竞赛的日益重视，而获奖高校中亦不乏地方本科高校。十余年来，我们积极参与韩赛，探索并实践以韩赛为引擎驱动的翻译教学，使大赛内容贯穿翻译教学。

韩赛原文选材优秀，不论是语言还是文化层面，都涉及甚广，充满亮点；且参考译文经多位专家讨论定稿，译笔精妙；竞赛总结和译文评析探幽发微，更是富于启迪（王朝晖，余军，2019：73）。以韩赛语料为训练材料，相比一般训练材料，针对性更强，涉及的翻译要点难点更为集中。翻译课程的笔译练习一部分来自韩赛原文，为 200～300 字的语篇，短小精悍，便于学生在 30～45 分钟的时段内完成。学生用 CCAT 平台完成练习，提交译文，即可成为平行语料。

教师在讲评时通过现场在线检索，结合韩赛官方参考译文及译文评析，可对学生翻译中呈现的问题进行统计。以第 31 届韩赛为例，原文中探讨人工智能时用了 instruction 一词，指人类对人工智能发出的"指令"。学生译文五花八门，检索统计如下：

表 9-1　第 31 届韩赛练习 instruction 译文统计

译文	命令	指引	指示	指导	指引	旨意	指南	引领	指令
数量	7	3	2	3	2	1	2	3	12

现场检索呈现错误，令学生印象深刻，讲评针对性强，效率极高，效果颇佳。

　　韩赛原文难度较大,且参赛者众多,竞争激烈。参赛译文必须准确达意,简洁凝练,方有可能获奖。这便要求参赛选手具备较强的译文修订能力,能够雕琢译文。

　　人工智能背景下,未来机器翻译＋译后编辑的人机互动翻译模式将逐步取代传统的人工翻译模式。为适应人机互动翻译模式,教师在教学中有意强化学生的译文修订训练,引导学生对往届参赛译文初稿进行修订,之后对照参赛译文定稿及参考译文揣摩学习,取得了较好成效,体现在学生拿出竞赛初稿后,能通过语料库的检索比较,从往届参考译文中汲取灵感,发现差距,对初稿进行恰到好处的润饰。历届参赛定稿都是几经修订,其中不乏神来之笔。

　　韩赛是对学生整体素质的检验。完成一篇高质量的译文,需要多种能力,如查证能力、逻辑分析能力、表达能力、文字润饰能力。学生在理解原文、查询背景、拿出初稿、修订完成定稿的过程中,获益颇丰,能力得到全面提升。通过参赛实战,学生既加深了对韩赛的认识,又提高了翻译能力和水平。

　　翻译技术融入翻译教学,是"技术驱动",与之并举的是"以赛育人",两者结合,效果显著。以 2020—2021 年为例,学生参加韩赛,共获得英译汉一等奖 2 项,二等奖 6 项,三等奖 2 项,优秀奖 1 项,成绩在参赛高校中位居前列。

　　我们在翻译教学中秉承"以赛促教,以赛育才"的理念,丰富教学内容,开阔学生眼界,提升教学成效,培养翻译人才(王朝晖,余军,2019:77)。围绕着韩赛展开的课堂教学及学生的自主学习,不仅提升了学生的翻译水平,也反哺教学,为翻译教学的改革与创新提供了多维度的视角。

　　教师利用语料库的检索功能,对参赛译文初稿中存在的典型错误进行分类整理,可加深对学生错误的了解。学生译文中往往存在原文理解错误、疏于背景查证、表达啰嗦冗长、辞藻缺乏等种种问题,这给教师进行有的放矢的教学提供了依据。

　　通过在教学中设置针对性的训练,以及引导学生分析比较往届参赛初稿、定稿及参考译文,可有效纠正上述问题。学生反映,译文比较凸显了自己在翻译中存在的种种问题,使自己受益匪浅。而教师也能通过学生译文的得与失,反思教学中存在的不足,并做出相应调整和革新。

　　翻译技术尤其是语料库技术的应用,对于提升学生翻译水平,提高翻译教学质量,起到了积极作用。高难度、高水平赛事的参与与模拟,凸显了问题,开阔了学生视野,也让学生与教师收获了累累硕果,有效地取到了促教和育人的作用。

9.6　小结

　　以学生为中心,充分利用 CCAT 平台的技术优势,将比较翻译教学法的"比较"特色充分发挥,是比较翻译教学法在教学改革中的一个创新。比较翻译教学法使语料库技术在微观翻译教学过程之中得到充分应用。学习者双语语料库由单模态向多模态的发展,提供了一种新的深化翻译教学与研究的手段和方法,有助于对学生翻译过程的控制、观察、描述和分析,值得更广泛深入的探讨和研究。

参考文献

Bell, R. T., & Candlin, C. Translation and Translating: Theory and Practice [M]. London: Longman, 1991.

Blum-Kulpa, S. Shifts of Cohesion and Coherence in Translation [M]//Lawrence Venuti (ed.)The Translation Studies Reader. London & New York: Routledge, 1986: 298-313.

Holmes, J. The Name and Nature of Translation Studies [M]// L.Venuti (ed.). The Translation Studies Reader. New York and London: Routledge, 1973:78-90.

Leech, G. Introducing Corpus Annotation [M]// G. Garside, G. Leech, & A. McEnery (eds.)Corpus Annotation: Linguistic Information from Computer Text Corpora. London: Longman, 1997.

Nida, E. A., & Taber, C. R. The Theory and Practice of Translation [M]. Leiden: E. J. Brill, 1969.

Tummers, J., K. Heylen, & D. Geeraerts. Usage-based Approaches in Cognitive Linguistics: A Technical State of the Art [J]. Corpus Linguistics and Linguistic Theory, 2005(02): 225-261.

Vinay, J.-P. , & Darbelnet, J. Trans and eds. Sager, J. C., & Hamel, M.-J. Comparative Stylistics of French and English: A Methodology for Translation [M]. Amsterdam/Philadelphia: John Benjamins, 1958.

Wu, Y., et al. Google's Neural Machine Translation System: Bridging the Gap Between Human and Machine Translation [J]. arXiv reprint arXiv: 1609.08144, 2016.

D. 吉尔. 笔译训练指南[M]. 北京:中国对外翻译出版公司,2008.

包凯. 谷歌翻译汉译英错误类型及纠错方法初探[J]. 中国科技翻译,2017 (04):20-23.

蔡辉. 语料对齐工具的性能比较与选择[J]. 中国翻译,2019(03):150-155.

蔡莹. 基于 ELAN 软件的多模态语料库的构建研究——以医护英语为例 [J]. 安徽电气工程职业技术学院学报,2022(01):118-122.

曹明伦. 翻译过程是一种选择的过程[J]. 中国翻译,2021(03):176-181.

陈宏薇. 编者札记[M]// 陈宏薇. 方法·技巧·批评——翻译教学与实践研究. 上海:上海外语教育出版社,2008.

陈蓉,樊飞飞,王晓. 机器翻译过程中词汇层面的译前编辑方法[J]. 西安邮电大学学报,2021(05):101-110.

崔启亮,李闻. 译后编辑错误类型研究——基于科技文本英汉机器翻译[J]. 中国科技翻译,2015(04):19-22.

崔启亮. 论机器翻译的译后编辑[J]. 中国翻译,2014(06):68-73.

崔启亮. MTI 翻译技术教学体系设计[J]. 中国翻译,2019(05):80-86.

戴光荣. 译文源语透过效应研究[M]. 上海:上海交通大学出版社,2013.

邓志辉. 认知科学视域下西方翻译过程实证研究发展述评[J]. 外国语(上海外国语大学学报),2012(04):88-94.

邓志辉. 译者选词决策过程的影响因素分析——一项认知心理学视角的翻译过程实证研究[J]. 外国语(上海外国语大学学报),2011(05):71-76.

翟尤,郭晓静,曾宣玮. AIGC 未来已来:迈向通用人工智能时代[M]. 北京:人民邮电出版社,2023.

冯佳,王克非. 探悉翻译过程的新视窗:键盘记录和眼动追踪[J]. 中国翻译,2016(01):12-18.

冯全功,李嘉伟. 新闻翻译的译后编辑模式研究[J]. 外语电化教学,2016(06):74-79.

冯志伟,张灯柯. GPT 与语言研究[J]. 外语电化教学,2023(02):3-11,105.

耿芳,胡健. 人工智能辅助译后编辑新方向——基于 ChatGPT 的翻译实例研究[J]. 中国外语,2023(03):41-47.

管新潮,陆晓蕾. 基于 Python 的语料库翻译:数据分析与理论探索[M]. 上海:上海交通大学出版,2022.

管新潮. Python 语言数据分析[M]. 上海:上海交通大学出版社,2021.

管乐. 基于 ELAN 的演讲视频多模态互动机制研究——以一则 TED 教育类演讲视频为例[J]. 北京科技大学学报(社会科学版),2021(05):499-510.

桂诗春,杨惠中. 中国学习者英语语料库[M]. 上海:上海外语教育出版社,2003.

郭高攀,廖华英. 框架语义的建构与翻译过程的概念整合——基于认知语料库"FrameNet"的翻译教学研究[J]. 上海翻译,2016(04):33-36.

郭高攀,王宗英. 机器翻译的译前与译后编辑在科技文本翻译中的探究

[J].浙江外国语学院学报,2017(03):76-83.

韩红梅.中国政治特色词的翻译:一项基于语料库的研究[J].齐齐哈尔大学学报(哲学社会科学版),2019(03):127-130.

贺胜.现代汉语深度语义标注研究[M].长春:吉林大学出版社,2019.

侯林平,郎玥,何元建.语料库辅助的翻译认知过程研究模式:特征与趋势[J].外语研究,2019(06):69-75.

胡庚申.适应与选择:翻译过程新解[J].四川外语学院学报,2008(04):90-95.

胡加圣,戚亚娟.ChatGPT时代的中国外语教育:求变与应变[J].外语电化教学,2023(01):3-6,105.

胡开宝,李晓倩.语料库翻译学与翻译认知研究:共性与融合[J].山东社会科学,2016(10):39-44.

胡开宝,李翼.机器翻译特征及其与人工翻译关系的研究[J].中国翻译,2016(05):10-14.

胡朋志.翻译能力的自然化研究:生物认知视角[M]杭州:浙江大学出版社,2016.

胡壮麟.ChatGPT谈外语教学[J].中国外语,2023(03):1,12-15.

黄立波,王克非.语料库翻译学:课题与进展[J].外语教学与研究,2011(03):911-923.

黄立波.中国现当代小说汉英平行语料库:研制与应用[J].外语教学,2013(06):104-109.

黄玉霞.翻译教学中学生思辨能力的培养[J].教育理论与实践,2017(06):51-53.

何安平.语料库的教学加工理念与应用[J]//语料库语言学与中国外语教学,现代外语,2010(04):419&426.

蓝洁.基于ELAN软件的多模态动态视频个案的话语分析[J].九江学院学报(社会科学版),2020(03):90-97.

雷蕾.基于Python的语料库数据处理[M].北京:科学出版社,2020.

冷冰冰,王华树,梁爱林.MTI术语课程构建[J].中国翻译,2013(1):55-59.

李斌,高广安.基于Elan的湖南省普通话水平测试等级标准样本库建设探索[J].语言文字应用,2012(03):126-133.

李长栓.以批判性思维贯穿翻译始终[J].上海翻译,2017(05):32-36,95.

李德超.TAPs翻译过程研究二十年:回顾与展望[J].中国翻译,2005(01):29-34.

李家坤,李琳琳,徐淑玉.行业译员培养中思辨缺乏症对策实证研究[J].外国语文,2017(04):105-114.

李家坤,李琳琳,徐淑玉.依托翻译实训的 MTI 学生思辨能力提升机制研究[J].上海翻译,2018(01):51-57.

李梅,朱锡明.英汉机译错误分类及数据统计分析[J].上海理工大学学报(社会科学版),2013(03):201-207.

李庆明,刘婷婷.译者主体性与翻译过程的伦理思考——以文学翻译为例[J].外语教学,2011(04):101-105.

李晓倩,胡开宝.《习近平谈治国理政》多语平行语料库的建设与应用[J].外语电化教学,2021(03):83-88,13.

刘晓东,李德凤.翻译认知过程加工路径:基于汉英双语平行语料库的实证研究[J].外国语(上海外国语大学学报),2022(02):102-110.

李洋,孙宁,梁玉静.基于机器翻译的人机交互译前编辑模式研究[J].语言教育,2021(02):55-62.

李翼.汉学家译者身份对翻译过程的影响——澳大利亚汉学家杜博妮的中国现当代文学翻译研究[J].中国翻译,2022(05):87-94.

梁茂成,许家金.双语语料库建设中元信息的添加和段落与句子的两级对齐[J].中国外语,2012(06):37-42,63.

刘剑,胡开宝.多模态口译语料库的建设与应用研究[J].中国外语,2015(05):77-85.

刘剑.四款可用于多模态口译语料库建设的软件功能比较研究[J].文化创新比较研究,2019(31):63-64.

刘绍龙.论双语翻译的认知心理研究——对"翻译过程模式"的反思和修正[J].中国翻译,2007(01):11-16,95.

刘艳春,胡显耀.国外翻译过程研究 30 年——翻译过程研究的理论模型回顾与展望[J].外语电化教学,2022(01):75-80,112.

刘泽权,朱利利.国内外语料库翻译认知研究对比考察——基于 Web of Science 和中国知网数据库的可视化分析[J].解放军外国语学院学报,2019(01):29-38,159.

陆晓蕾,倪斌.Python 3:语料库技术与应用[M].厦门:厦门大学出版社,2021.

卢植,孙娟.人工翻译和译后编辑中认知加工的眼动实验研究[J].外语教学与研究,2018(05):760-769,801.

马会娟. 汉译英翻译能力研究[M]. 北京:北京师范大学出版社,2013.

毛鑫,邱天河. WordSmith 在翻译批评中的应用——借助 WordSmith 工具分析《匆匆》译文的风格[J]. 科技信息(学术研究),2007(34):14-16.

聂炜,许明武. 学者译史与史家译史:译者身份对翻译过程影响举隅——以《资治通鉴》方志彤、张磊夫译本为例[J]. 西安外国语大学学报,2022(04):81-86.

欧阳利锋. 论译者的批判性思维[J]. 外语与外语教学,2009(08):50-53.

潘文国. 翻译过程研究的重要成果——序郑冰寒《英译汉过程中选择行为的实证研究》[J]. 山东外语教学,2012(02):90-92.

秦洪武,夏云. 基于历时语料的翻译与现代汉语互动研究[M]. 上海:上海交通大学出版社,2017.

秦颖. 基于神经网络的机器翻译质量评析及对翻译教学的影响[J]. 外语电化教学,2018(2):51-56.

秦颖. 人机共生场景下的外语教学方法探索——以 ChatGPT 为例[J]. 外语电化教学,2023(02):24-29,108.

尚琼. WordSmith 软件界面下的《石油勘探英语》词汇检索[J]. 江汉石油职工大学学报,2011(03):91-93.

宋志平,程力. 论翻译过程研究的心理认知视角[J]. 东北师大学报,2006(06):128-132.

宋志平. 论翻译过程中的主体性意识[J]. 东北师大学报,2000(06):84-88.

苏雯超,李德凤,曹洪文. 论口译认知负荷的眼动研究[J]. 外语学刊,2021(03):109-114.

孙鸿仁. 鲁迅小说词汇统计研究[J]. 绍兴文理学院学报(哲学社会科学),2013(06):26-30.

孙逸群. 材料类文摘机助翻译的错误剖析. 中国科技翻译,2018(03):15-18.

王克非. 双语对应语料库:研制与应用[C]. 北京:外语教学与研究出版社,2004.

谭业升. 翻译认知过程研究[M]. 北京:外语教学与研究出版社,2020.

谭业升. 认知翻译学探索:创造性翻译的认知路径与认知制约[M]. 上海:上海外语教育出版社,2012.

王恒兰,孙崇飞. 实证性翻译研究的困境与出路[J]. 外语研究,2022(06):89-95.

王怀贞. 翻译过程的认知心理描述——Bell 翻译过程的信息加工模式评介

[J]. 山东大学学报(哲学社会科学版),2008(01):70-75.

王娟. 国外翻译过程实证研究中的眼动跟踪方法述评[J]. 外语学刊,2016(04):124-129.

王均松,钱家骏,郭亚玲. 翻译过程研究中的眼动实验效度:问题与对策[J]. 外国语(上海外国语大学学报),2022(02):93-101.

王克非. 中国英汉平行语料库的设计与研制[J]. 中国外语,2012(06):23-27.

王立非,梁茂成. WordSmith 方法在外语教学研究中的应用[J]. 外语电化教学,2007(03):3-7+12.

王连柱. 汉英平行语料库的构建及其在医学文献翻译教学中的应用[J]. 中国医学教育技术,2016(05):613-618.

王树槐,栗长江. 翻译教学方法述评[J]. 外语教育,2008(00):133-138.

王天翼,王寅. 翻译隐喻观的认知分析——以"变异"和"损耗"两条支隐喻机制为例[J]. 外语研究,2018(03):82-86.

王湘玲,贾艳芳. 21 世纪国外机器翻译译后编辑实证研究[J]. 湖南大学学报(社会科学版),2018(2):82-87.

王湘玲,王立阳. 国际翻译过程研究前沿动态的可视化分析(2001—2020)[J]. 上海翻译,2022(04):17-22.

王一方,郑冰寒. 英译汉过程中译者的认知资源分配模式——基于眼动、键击和反省法的实证研究[J]. 中国外语,2020(04):87-94.

王一方. 翻译过程研究中眼动数据的收集、呈现与分析[J]. 外语研究,2017(06):76-81.

王寅. 基于认知语言学的翻译过程新观[J]. 中国翻译,2017(06):5-10,17,129.

王朝晖,余军. 基于 CAT 及语料库技术的电子商务翻译研究[M]. 厦门:厦门大学出版社,2016.

王朝晖,余军. 韩素音国际翻译大赛语料库构建及翻译教学应用[J]. 中国翻译,2019(05):72-79.

魏志成. 比较翻译教学法的过程控制[C]// 杨仁敬,吴建平. 华东外语教学论坛(第 2 辑). 上海:上海外语教育出版社,2007:345-359.

魏志成. 汉英比较翻译教程[M]. 北京:清华大学出版社,2012.

吴静静. 基于 ELAN 的多模态话语分析——以第九届"外教社杯"全国高校外语教学大赛获奖视频为例[J]. 湖北文理学院学报,2020(12):68-72.

吴蕊珠,李晗静,吕会华等. 面向 ELAN 软件的手语汉语平行语料库构建

[J].中文信息学报,2019(02):43-50.

夏锡华.翻译过程中的主体间性[J].国外理论动态,2007(05):59-62.

许多.译者身份对翻译过程的影响——以罗慕士译本中的曹操形象为例[J].外语教学,2018(06):85-89.

许家金,贾云龙.基于R-gram的语料库分析软件PowerConc的设计与开发[J].外语电化教学,2013(01):57-62.

许家金,吴良平.基于网络的第四代语料库分析工具CQPweb及应用实例[J].外语电化教学,2014(05):10-15,56.

徐勤,吴颖.经贸外宣资料的翻译探索[J].中国翻译,2003(03):80-82.

杨平.拓展翻译研究的视野与空间 推进翻译专业教育的科学发展[J].中国翻译,2012(04):9-10.

杨艳霞,王湘玲.泛在学习时代译者思辨能力培养路径研究[J].外语学刊,2020(05):65-70.

俞敬松,杨超,李静雅.基于眼动追踪的语块翻译教学研究[J].外语电化教学,2020(03):100-105,16.

郑冰寒.英译汉过程中选择行为的实证研究[M].北京:外语教学与研究出版社,2012.

杨自俭.关于翻译教学的几个问题——《汉英比较翻译教程》序言一[M]// 魏志成汉英比较翻译教程.北京:清华大学出版社,2006.

叶文兴.译者翻译过程认知路径——基于语料库方法的《红楼梦》"死亡隐喻"翻译研究[J].西安外国语大学学报,2023(01):101-105.

余国良.翻译教学中批判性思维的培养模式研究[J].外语学刊,2010(05):101-104.

余军,王朝晖.基于比较翻译教学法的教学型语料库构建与应用[J].中国翻译,2010(05):57-62.

余军.基于Moodle的翻译教学平台构建与应用[J].重庆电子工程职业学院学报,2017(04):125-127.

张爱玲,杨子靖,刘晨璇等.人工智能技术发展与专业口笔译实践耦合机制路径初探[J].外语电化教学,2018(03):88-94.

张立新.基于ELAN的多模态话语研究——以大学英语教师课堂话语为例[J].现代教育技术,2012(07):54-56.

张淑贞.学习者错误研究[M].长春:吉林大学出版社,2020.

张霄军,贺莺.翻译的技术转向——第20届世界翻译大会侧记[J].中国翻译,2014(06):74-77.

张雪.基于 ELAN 的多模态外语微课话语分析[J].黑河学院学报,2022(04):102-104.

张苇.翻译教学与思辨能力的培养——基于翻译教学中反思日志作用的思考[J].合肥学院学报(社会科学版),2014(06):127-130.

张震宇,洪化清.ChatGPT 支持的外语教学:赋能、问题与策略[J].外语界,2023(02):38-44.

张政,王赟.MTI 项目化翻译教学与翻译能力培养:理论与实践[J].外语界,2020(02):65-72.

仲文明,徐佳敏,李芸昕.机译中汉语科技文本的模糊特质与译前编辑[J].中国科技翻译,2021(04):36-39+42.

邹瑶,郑伟涛,杨梅.冬奥会冰雪项目英汉平行语料库研制与平台建设探究[J].外语电化教学,2018(05):19-22.

附录 1　最佳译文判断样题

说明:答案默认为 A,采用在线测试方式,测试时系统会随机调整选项显示顺序。该测试有助于提升学生对于译文优劣的判断能力;学生通过比较人工译文和机器译文的差异,掌握翻译技巧,提升译后编辑能力(见 6.5.2 小节)和显化、隐化的运用能力(见 7.6 小节)。

1.工商登记前置审批精简 85%,全面实施三证合一、一照一码。

> A. The number of items which require government approval for new businesses prior to registration was cut by 85%, and the system of a separate business license, organization code certificate, and taxation registration certificate was replaced by a unified business license with a unified social credit code.
>
> B. Before the registration of business, the pre-approval process has been streamlined by 85%, and the comprehensive implementation of the integration of the three certificates into one, with one license and one code.
>
> C. The pre-examination and approval of industrial and commercial registration has been streamlined by 85%, and three certificates in one, one license and one yard have been fully implemented.

2.推广上海自贸试验区经验,新设广东、天津、福建自贸试验区。

> A. Pilot free trade zones were established in Guangdong, Tianjin, and Fujian based on the model of the China (Shanghai) Pilot Free Trade Zone.
>
> B. Promote the experience of the Shanghai Free Trade Zone and establish new Free Trade Zones in Guangdong, Tianjin, and Fujian.
>
> C. We will promote the experience of the Shanghai Pilot Free Trade Zone and set up new pilot free trade zones in Guangdong, Tianjin and Fujian.

3.人民币加入国际货币基金组织特别提款权货币篮子。

A. The RMB was included in the IMF's Special Drawing Rights basket.

B. Chinese Yuan joins the International Monetary Fund's Special Drawing Rights currency basket.

C. The RMB was included in the SDR basket of the International Monetary Fund.

4.亚洲基础设施投资银行正式成立,丝路基金投入运营。

A. The Asian Infrastructure Investment Bank was officially inaugurated, and the Silk Road Fund opened for business.

B. Asian Infrastructure Investment Bank officially established, Silk Road Fund put into operation.

C. The Asian Infrastructure Investment Bank was formally established and the Silk Road Fund was put into operation.

5.签署中韩、中澳自贸协定和中国-东盟自贸区升级议定书。

A. China signed free trade agreements with the Republic of Korea and Australia, respectively, and signed the Protocol to Amend the Framework Agreement on Comprehensive Economic Cooperation between China and ASEAN.

B. Sign the China-Korea, China-Australia Free Trade Agreements and the Upgraded Protocol of China-ASEAN Free Trade Area.

C. China-ROK and China-Australia free trade agreements and a protocol to upgrade the China-ASEAN Free Trade Area were signed.

6.继续推动东、中、西、东北地区"四大板块"协调发展,重点推进"一带一路"建设、京津冀协同发展、长江经济带发展"三大战略"。

A. Work continued to promote the coordinated development of the eastern region, the central region, the western region, and the northeast; priority was placed on moving forward with the Three Initiatives—the Belt and Road Initiative, the Beijing-Tianjin-Hebei Integration Initiative, and the Yangtze Economic Belt Initiative.

B. Continue to promote the coordinated development of the four major regions of East, Central, West, and Northeast China, with a focus on advancing the "Belt and Road" initiative, the coordinated development of the Beijing-Tianjin-Hebei region, and the development of the Yangtze River Economic Belt.

C. We will continue to promote the coordinated development of the "four major plates" in the eastern, central, western and northeastern regions, focusing on the "three major strategies" of "one belt and one road" construction, the coordinated development of Beijing, Tianjin and Hebei, and the development of the Yangtze River Economic Belt.

7.城镇保障性安居工程住房基本建成 772 万套,棚户区住房改造开工 601 万套,农村危房改造 432 万户,一大批住房困难家庭圆了安居梦。

A. Over the course of the year, 7.72 million government-subsidized housing units were basically completed in urban areas, work started on the reconstruction of 6.01 million housing units in rundown urban areas, and 4.32 million dilapidated houses in rural areas were rebuilt, helping large numbers of families that are struggling with housing realize their dream of having a home to settle in.

B. 7.72 million affordable housing units in urban areas have been completed as part of the government's Urban Affordable Housing Project. Additionally, construction has commenced on 6.01 million housing units to transform shanty towns, while 4.32 million rural dilapidated houses have been renovated. These efforts have helped numerous families facing housing difficulties realize their dream of a secure and comfortable home.

C. A total of 7.72 million government-subsidized housing units have been basically completed in urban areas, 6.01 million housing units have been renovated in shanty towns, 4.32 million dilapidated houses have been renovated in rural areas, and a large number of families with housing difficulties have realized their dream of living in peace.

8.服务业成为第一大产业,工业化与信息化融合加深,农业综合生产能力明显增强。

A. Service industries have grown to be the largest economic sector, information technology has been further integrated into industrialization, and overall agricultural production capacity has notably improved.

B. The service industry has become the largest industry, the integration of industrialization and informatization has deepened, and the comprehensive production capacity of agriculture has significantly increased.

C. The service industry has become the largest industry, the integration of industrialization and informatization has deepened, and the comprehensive agricultural production capacity has increased significantly.

9.抓紧制定收入分配体制改革总体方案。努力提高居民收入在国民收入分配中的比重,提高劳动报酬在初次分配中的比重。

A. We will promptly formulate a master plan for reforming the income distribution system, strive to raise the proportion of individual income in national income, and raise the proportion of remuneration in the primary distribution.

B. Urgently formulate an overall plan for income distribution system reform. Strive to increase the proportion of residents' income in national income distribution, and increase the proportion of labor compensation in initial distribution.

C. We will promptly formulate an overall plan for the reform of the income distribution system. Efforts should be made to increase the proportion of residents' income in the distribution of national income and the proportion of labor remuneration in the primary distribution.

10.完善工资制度,建立工资正常增长机制,稳步提高最低工资标准。

A. We will improve the salary system, put in place a mechanism for regular salary increases, and steadily raise the minimum wage.

B. Improve the salary system, establish a mechanism for normal salary growth, and steadily increase the minimum wage standard.

C. We should improve the wage system, establish a normal wage growth mechanism, and steadily raise the minimum wage standard.

11.稳定出口退税政策,扩大贸易融资和信用保险,改进海关、质检、外汇等方面的监管和服务,帮助企业克服订单不足、成本升高、摩擦增多等多重困难和压力。

A. We will continue to implement the export tax rebate policy; increase trade financing and credit insurance; ensure that customs, quality inspectors, and foreign exchange authorities improve their supervision and services; and help enterprises overcome difficulties and pressures resulting from falling orders, rising costs, and increasing trade friction.

B. Stable export tax refund policy, expand trade financing and credit insurance, improve supervision and services in customs, quality inspection, foreign exchange, etc., help enterprises overcome multiple difficulties and pressures such as insufficient orders, rising costs, and increased friction.

C. We will stabilize the export tax rebate policy, expand trade financing and credit insurance, improve the supervision and services of customs, quality inspection and foreign exchange, and help enterprises overcome multiple difficulties and pressures such as insufficient orders, rising costs and increasing frictions.

12.大力发展服务贸易,承接服务外包。

A. We will work hard to promote trade in services and undertake more services outsourced by other countries.

B. Vigorously develop service trade and undertake service outsourcing.

C. We will vigorously develop trade in services and undertake service outsourcing.

13.实施新修订的外商投资产业指导目录,引导外资更多投向先进制造业、高新技术产业、节能环保产业、现代服务业和中西部地区。

A. We will implement the newly revised Proposed List of Industries for Foreign Investment, and encourage more foreign investment in advanced manufacturing, new and high technologies, energy conservation, environmental protection, new service industries, and the central and western regions.

B. Implement the newly revised Catalogue of Industries for Foreign Investment, guiding more foreign investment towards advanced manufacturing, high-tech industries, energy-saving and environmental protection industries, modern service industries, and the central and western regions.

C. We will implement the newly revised Catalogue for the Guidance of Foreign Investment Industries and guide more foreign investment in advanced manufacturing, high-tech industries, energy-saving and environmental protection industries, modern service industries and the central and western regions.

14. 创新境外经贸合作区发展模式,支持"走出去"的企业相互协同、集群发展。

A. We will explore new models for overseas economic and trade cooperation zones, and support companies making overseas investments in coordinating their growth and forming clusters.

B. Innovate the development model of overseas economic and trade cooperation zones, support the coordinated and clustered development of "going global" enterprises.

C. We should innovate the development model of overseas economic and trade cooperation zones and support the mutual coordination and cluster development of "going out" enterprises.

15. 衔接和落实好支持港澳经济社会发展的系列政策措施,大幅提升内地对港澳服务贸易开放水平,加快推进港珠澳大桥等基础设施建设和对接,深化合作,支持港澳参与国际和区域经济合作。

A. We will implement coordinated policies and measures for supporting the economic and social development of Hong Kong and Macao, open the mainland much wider to trade in services with the two regions, accelerate the construction of the Hong Kong-Zhuhai-Macao Bridge and other shared infrastructure projects, and deepen cooperation with Hong Kong and Macao to support them in participating in international and regional economic cooperation.

B. Coordinate and implement a series of policy measures to support the economic and social development of Hong Kong and Macau, significantly enhance the level of openness of the mainland to trade in services with Hong Kong and Macau, accelerate the construction and connection of infrastructure such as the Hong Kong-Zhuhai-Macao Bridge, deepen cooperation, and support the participation of Hong Kong and Macau in international and regional economic cooperation.

C. We will link up and implement a series of policies and measures to support the economic and social development of Hong Kong and Macao, substantially increase the level of opening up of trade in services between the mainland and Hong Kong and Macao, accelerate the construction and docking of infrastructure such as the Hong Kong-Zhuhai-Macao Bridge, deepen cooperation, and support Hong Kong and Macau in participating in international and regional economic cooperation.

16.我们圆满完成"十一五"规划,顺利实施"十二五"规划。

A. We successfully completed the Eleventh Five-Year Plan and got off to a good start in implementing the Twelfth Five-Year Plan.

B. We successfully completed the "Eleventh Five-Year Plan" and smoothly implemented the "Twelfth Five-Year Plan".

C. We have successfully completed the Eleventh Five-Year Plan and smoothly implemented the Twelfth Five-Year Plan.

17.我们沉着应对,及时果断调整宏观调控着力点,出台进一步扩大内需、促进经济平稳较快增长的十项措施,全面实施一揽子计划。

A. We responded to the crisis calmly, made timely and decisive adjustments to the focus of macro-control, adopted ten measures to increase domestic demand and promote steady and rapid economic growth, and implemented a comprehensive package plan.

B. We respond calmly, make timely and decisive adjustments to the focus of macro-control, introduce ten measures to further expand domestic demand and promote stable and rapid economic growth, and fully implement a package plan.

C. We responded calmly, promptly and decisively adjusted the focus of macro-control, introduced ten measures to further expand domestic demand

and promote stable and rapid economic growth，and comprehensively implemented a package plan.

18.这些举世瞩目的成就,对我们有效应对国际金融危机严重冲击发挥了至关重要的作用,为经济社会长远发展打下了坚实基础。

A. These impressive achievements played a vital role in our effective response to the severe impact of the global financial crisis，and laid a solid foundation for sustaining China's economic and social development.

B. These remarkable achievements have played a crucial role in our effective response to the severe impact of the international financial crisis，and have laid a solid foundation for the long-term development of the economy and society.

C. These remarkable achievements have played a vital role in our effective response to the severe impact of the international financial crisis and laid a solid foundation for long-term economic and social development.

19.推动科技、教育、文化事业全面发展,为国家长远发展奠定了坚实基础。

A. This gave impetus to all-around progress in science and technology，education，and culture and laid a solid foundation for ensuring China's long-term development.

B. Promote the comprehensive development of science and technology，education，and cultural undertakings，laying a solid foundation for the long-term development of the country.

C. The comprehensive development of science，technology，education and culture has laid a solid foundation for the long-term development of the country.

20.全面实现城乡九年免费义务教育,惠及 1.6 亿学生。

A. We made free nine-year compulsory education universal across the country，benefiting 160 million students.

B. Fully implement free compulsory education for nine years in both urban and rural areas，benefiting 160 million students.

C. Nine-year free compulsory education in urban and rural areas has been fully realized，benefiting 160 million students.

21.国际金融危机深层次影响持续显现,世界经济复苏充满不确定性、不稳定性。

A. The profound impact of the global financial crisis persists，and the recovery of the world economy is full of uncertainty and not yet on a stable footing.

B. The deep-seated impact of the global financial crisis continues to manifest，and the world economy's recovery is filled with uncertainty and instability.

C. The deep-seated impact of the international financial crisis continues to emerge，and the recovery of the world economy is full of uncertainty and instability.

22.实现上述目标,必须继续实施积极的财政政策和稳健的货币政策,保持政策连续性和稳定性,增强前瞻性、针对性和灵活性。

A. To reach the above targets，we must continue to implement a proactive fiscal policy and a prudent monetary policy，maintain continuity and stability of our policies，and make them more forward-looking，targeted and flexible.

B. To achieve the above goals, it is necessary to continue implementing proactive fiscal policies and prudent monetary policies，maintaining policy continuity and stability, and enhancing foresight，targeting, and flexibility.

C. To achieve the above objectives，we must continue to implement a proactive fiscal policy and a prudent monetary policy，maintain policy continuity and stability, and enhance foresight，pertinence and flexibility.

23.创新是引领发展的第一动力,必须摆在国家发展全局的核心位置,深入实施创新驱动发展战略。

A. Innovation is the primary driving force for development and must occupy a central place in China's development strategy，which is why we must implement a strategy of innovation-driven development.

B. Innovation is the first driving force for development and must be placed at the core of the national development agenda, and the innovation-driven development strategy must be implemented thoroughly.

C. Innovation is the primary driving force for development, which must be placed at the core of the overall national development situation and thoroughly implement the strategy of innovation-driven development.

24.我们要持之以恒,建设天蓝、地绿、水清的美丽中国。

A. We must work to build, through tireless efforts, a Beautiful China where the sky is blue, the land is green, and the water runs clear.

B. We must persevere and build a beautiful China with blue skies, green land, and clear water.

C. We must persevere in building a beautiful China with blue sky, green land and clear water.

25.使市场在资源配置中起决定性作用和更好发挥政府作用,加快形成引领经济发展新常态的体制机制和发展方式。

A. It should be ensured that the market plays the decisive role in resource allocation and the government better plays its role, and work should be accelerated to create the systems, mechanisms, and growth model that will guide the new normal in economic development.

B. To make the market play a decisive role in resource allocation and better exert the role of the government, accelerate the formation of a new system and development mode that leads the economic development in a new normal.

C. Make the market play a decisive role in the allocation of resources and better play the role of the government, and accelerate the formation of institutional mechanisms and development modes leading the new normal of economic development.

26.全面实行准入前国民待遇加负面清单管理制度,逐步构建高标准自由贸易区网络。

A. We should put into force across the board the management system for pre-establishment national treatment plus a negative list, and progressively build a network of high-standard free trade areas.

　　B. Fully implement the system of national treatment plus negative list for market access, and gradually build a high-standard network of free trade zones.

　　C. We will fully implement the management system of pre-establishment national treatment plus negative list, and gradually build a network of high-standard free trade zones.

27.发展如逆水行舟,不进则退。

　　A. Pursuing development is like sailing against the current: you either forge ahead or drift downstream.

　　B. Development is like rowing against the current, if you don't move forward, you will go backward.

　　C. Development is like sailing against the current, not to advance is to fall behind.

28.运用信息网络等现代技术,推动生产、管理和营销模式变革,重塑产业链、供应链、价值链,改造提升传统动能,使之焕发新的生机与活力。

　　A. We will use network-based information technology and other modern technologies to drive changes in models of production, management, and marketing, create new industry chains, supply chains, and value chains, and transform and upgrade conventional drivers, thus injecting them with new vitality.

　　B. Using modern technologies such as information networks to promote changes in production, management, and marketing models, reshaping industry chains, supply chains, and value chains, transforming and enhancing traditional driving forces, and revitalizing them with new vitality.

　　C. We should use modern technologies such as information networks to promote the transformation of production, management and marketing modes, reshape industrial chains, supply chains and value chains, transform and upgrade traditional kinetic energy, and make it glow with new vitality and vitality.

29.实现新旧动能转换,推动发展转向更多依靠人力人才资源和创新,既是一个伴随阵痛的调整过程。

> A. Obviously, replacing old drivers of growth with new ones and achieving a shift in development toward greater reliance on human resources, human capital, and innovation is a process of painful adjustment.
>
> B. Promoting the transformation of old and new driving forces and shifting development towards greater reliance on human resources, talent, and innovation is both an adjustment process accompanied by birth pains.
>
> C. It is a painful adjustment process to realize the transformation of new and old kinetic energy and promote development to rely more on human resources and innovation.

30.从国际看,世界经济深度调整、复苏乏力,国际贸易增长低迷,金融和大宗商品市场波动不定。

> A. Internationally, the global economy is experiencing profound changes and struggling to recover; growth in trade is weak; there are fluctuations in the financial and commodity markets;
>
> B. From an international perspective, the world economy is undergoing a deep adjustment and a weak recovery, international trade growth is sluggish, and the financial and commodity markets are volatile.
>
> C. Internationally, the world economy is undergoing deep adjustment and weak recovery, the growth of international trade is sluggish, and the financial and commodity markets are volatile.

31.经过多年的快速发展,我国物质基础雄厚,经济韧性强、潜力足、回旋余地大。

> A. Thanks to years of rapid development, China has laid a solid material foundation, and its economy is hugely resilient and has enormous potential and ample room for growth.
>
> B. After years of rapid development, our country has a solid material foundation, strong economic resilience, abundant potential, and ample room for maneuver.

C. After years of rapid development, China has a strong material foundation, strong economic resilience, sufficient potential and great room for manoeuvre.

32.建立规范的地方政府举债融资机制,对财政实力强、债务风险较低的,按法定程序适当增加债务限额。

A. We will establish a well-regulated mechanism for local governments to secure financing through bond issuance and make moderate upward adjustments to debt ceilings for local governments with strong financial resources and low debt risks through statutory procedures.

B. Establish a standardized local government debt financing mechanism, and for those with strong fiscal strength and low debt risks, appropriately increase the debt limit according to legal procedures.

C. Establish a standardized local government debt financing mechanism, and appropriately increase the debt limit in accordance with legal procedures for those with strong financial strength and low debt risk.

33.大力弘扬创新文化,厚植创新沃土,营造敢为人先、宽容失败的良好氛围。

A. We will foster a culture of innovation and create an enabling environment for innovation in which people venture to break new ground and failure is tolerated.

B. Vigorously promote a culture of innovation, cultivate a fertile ground for innovation, and create a good atmosphere of daring to be the first and being tolerant of failure.

C. We should vigorously promote the culture of innovation, cultivate the fertile soil for innovation, and create a good atmosphere of daring to be the first and tolerant of failure.

34.分批取消和下放了 416 项行政审批等事项,修订政府核准的投资项目目录,推动工商登记制度改革。

A. We abolished or delegated to lower-level governments 416 items previously subject to State Council review and approval in batches, revised the list of investment projects requiring government review and approval，and carried forward reform of the business registration system.

B. Delegated and cancelled 416 administrative approval matters in batches，revised the list of investment projects approved by the government，and promoted the reform of the industrial and commercial registration system.

C. 416 items of administrative examination and approval have been cancelled and released in batches，the catalogue of investment projects approved by the government has been revised，and the reform of the industrial and commercial registration system has been promoted.

35.让市场吃了"定心丸"，成为经济稳中向好的关键一招。

A. All these efforts reassured the market and played a vital role in sustaining steady economic growth.

B. Let the market eat the "reassurance pill" and become the key move for the stable and positive development of the economy.

C. Let the market eat the "reassurance pill" and become the key to economic stability.

36.要牢记责任使命,增强忧患意识,敢于担当,毫不懈怠,扎实有效解决问题,决不辜负人民的厚望。

A. We must firmly bear in mind our duties and mission, increase our sense of vigilance against potential dangers, be eager to take on challenges, work tirelessly and effectively to solve problems, and truly live up to people's expectations.

B. To remember responsibilities and missions, enhance awareness of potential risks, dare to take on responsibilities, never slack off, solidly and effectively solve problems, and never let down the high expectations of the people.

C. We should bear in mind our responsibilities and missions, enhance our sense of hardship, dare to shoulder them, never slacken our efforts, solve problems effectively and never fail to live up to the expectations of the people.

37.历史性地解决了绝对贫困问题,为全球减贫事业作出了重大贡献。

A. We have，once and for all，resolved the problem of absolute poverty in China，making significant contributions to the cause of global poverty reduction.

B. Historically solved the problem of absolute poverty and made significant contributions to global poverty reduction efforts.

C. It has historically solved the problem of absolute poverty and made great contributions to the cause of global poverty reduction.

38.人民群众获得感、幸福感、安全感更加充实、更有保障、更可持续,共同富裕取得新成效。

A. We have ensured a more complete and lasting sense of fulfillment，happiness，and security for our people，and we have made further progress in achieving common prosperity for all.

B. The people have a greater sense of gain，happiness，and security，which are more substantial，more guaranteed，and more sustainable. New achievements have been made in achieving common prosperity.

C. The sense of happiness and security of the people is more substantial，more secure and more sustainable，and new achievements have been made in common prosperity.

39.我们坚持绿水青山就是金山银山的理念。

A. We have acted on the idea that lucid waters and lush mountains are invaluable assets.

B. We adhere to the concept that "green waters and green mountains are as valuable as mountains of gold and silver."

C. We adhere to the concept that lucid waters and lush mountains are invaluable assets.

40.让金融成为一池活水,更好地浇灌小微企业、"三农"等实体经济之树。

A. We will ensure that financial services play an active role in meeting the needs of the real economy，including small and micro businesses，agriculture，rural areas，and farmers.

B. Let finance become a pool of living water, better nourishing the tree of real economy such as small and micro enterprises and agriculture.

C. Let finance become a pool of living water to better irrigate the trees of the real economy such as small and micro enterprises, agriculture, rural areas and farmers.

41.深入贯彻依法治国基本方略,把政府工作全面纳入法治轨道,用法治思维和法治方式履行职责。

A. We will fully implement the basic strategy of law-based governance, act in accordance with the law in all our government work, and be guided by law in both thinking and action in performing our duties.

B. Fully implement the basic strategy of governing the country according to law, comprehensively bring government work into the track of the rule of law, and fulfill responsibilities with legal thinking and legal methods.

C. We should thoroughly implement the basic strategy of governing the country according to law, bring the work of the government into the orbit of the rule of law in an all-round way, and perform our duties with the thinking and way of the rule of law.

42.所有公务员都要以人民利益至上,廉洁奉公,勤勉尽责,真正当好人民公仆。

A. All public servants must put people's interests first and perform their duties honestly, diligently and faithfully.

B. All civil servants must prioritize the interests of the people, be honest and upright, diligent and responsible, and truly serve as the servants of the people.

C. All civil servants should put the interests of the people first, be honest, diligent and responsible, and truly be good public servants.

43.必须增强"四个意识",坚定"四个自信",做到"两个维护",坚定斗争意志,当严峻形势和斗争任务摆在面前时,骨头要硬,敢于出击,敢战能胜。

A. We must enhance the Four Consciousnesses, reinforce the Four-sphere Confidence, and ensure the Two Upholds. Furthermore, we need to strengthen our will to confront the grim challenges that lie in front of us; we must steel ourselves, take proactive action, and dare to fight and win.

B. We must strengthen the "four consciousness", strengthen the "four self-confidence", achieve the "two safeguards" and strengthen the will to struggle. When the grim situation and the task of struggle are in front of us, we must be tough, dare to attack, dare to fight and win.

C. We must strengthen the "four consciousnesses", firm up the "four confidences", achieve the "two maintenances", strengthen our will to fight, and when faced with severe situations and struggle tasks, we must be tough, dare to attack, and be able to win.

44.领导干部要把践行"三严三实"贯穿于全部工作生活中,养成一种习惯、化为一种境界。

A. Officials must practice the Three Guidelines for Ethical Behavior and Three Basic Rules of Conduct at work, as well as in their daily life. Furthermore, they should turn the practice into a habit.

B. Leading cadres should put the practice of "Three Strictness and Three Realities" throughout their work and life, cultivate a habit and turn it into a realm.

C. Leaders and cadres should integrate the practice of "Three Stricts and Three Earnests" into all aspects of their work and life, forming a habit and reaching a state of mind.

45.依法治国首先要坚持依宪治国,依法执政首先要坚持依宪执政。

A. In pursuing law-based governance, we must first uphold Constitution-based governance; in pursuing law-based exercise of state power, we must first uphold Constitution-based exercise of state power.

B. To govern the country according to law, we must first adhere to the rule of constitution, and to govern according to law, we must first adhere to the rule of constitution.

C. "Adhering to the rule of law requires first and foremost adhering to the rule of the constitution, and governing by law requires first and foremost adhering to governing by the constitution."

46.全面依法治国是国家治理的一场深刻革命,必须坚持厉行法治,推进科学立法、严格执法、公正司法、全民守法。

A. Advancing law-based governance in all fields is a profound revolution in China's governance. We must promote the rule of law and work to ensure sound lawmaking, strict law enforcement, impartial administration of justice, and the observance of law by everyone.

B. Ruling the country by law in an all-round way is a profound revolution in national governance. We must adhere to the rule of law, promote scientific legislation, strict law enforcement, fair justice and law-abiding by the whole people.

C. Implementing the rule of law comprehensively is a profound revolution in national governance, and we must insist on strict enforcement of the law, promote scientific legislation, strict law enforcement, impartial justice, and law-abiding by all citizens.

47."四风"问题具有顽固性反复性,纠正"四风"不能止步,作风建设永远在路上。

A. The Four Malfeasances are difficult to eradicate. Therefore, we should never slacken our efforts in rectifying these problems, and there is no end to the task of improving our conduct.

B. The "Four Winds" problem is stubborn and repetitive, and the correction of the "Four Winds" can not stop, and the style construction is always on the way.

C. "The 'Four Winds' problem is persistent and recurrent; rectifying the 'Four Winds' cannot be stopped, and the improvement of work style is always ongoing."

48.要更大力度转变政府职能,深化简政放权、放管结合、优化服务改革,全面提升政府治理能力。

A. We need to make greater efforts to transform government functions, further streamline administration, and delegate powers, striking the right balance and optimizing services to improve our governance capacity in all sectors.

B. Greater efforts should be made to transform government functions, deepen the reform of simplification and decentralization, combination of decentralization and optimization of services, and comprehensively enhance the government's governance capacity.

C. "We need to make greater efforts to transform government functions, deepen reforms in streamlining administration, delegating power, improving regulation and services, and comprehensively enhance government governance capabilities."

49.同时,大家要关心国家发展全局,维护国家政治体制,积极参与国家经济、政治、文化、社会、生态文明建设,自觉维护国家安全。

A. Meanwhile, you should pay close attention to the country's overall development, safeguard the country's political system, actively engage in furthering the country's economic, political, cultural, social, and eco-environmental progress, and conscientiously safeguard national security.

B. At the same time, we should be concerned about the overall development of the country, safeguard the national political system, actively participate in the construction of national economic, political, cultural, social and ecological civilization, and consciously safeguard national security.

C. At the same time, everyone should care about the overall development of the country, safeguard the national political system, actively participate in the construction of the country's economy, politics, culture, society, and ecological civilization, and consciously maintain national security.

50.推进全球互联网治理体系变革是大势所趋、人心所向。

A. Reforming global internet governance is an irresistible and desirable trend.

B. Promoting the reform of the global Internet governance system is the trend of the times and the aspiration of the people.

C. Promoting the reform of the global Internet governance system is an irresistible trend and the will of the people.

51.要倡导环保意识、生态意识,构建全社会共同参与的环境治理体系,让生态环保思想成为社会生活中的主流文化。

A. Additionally, it is essential to raise people's awareness of environmental and ecological protection, and develop an environmental governance system in which the whole of society participates, so that the eco-environment will become a primary focus of daily life.

B. We should advocate environmental awareness and ecological awareness, build an environmental governance system with the participation of the whole society, and make the idea of ecological environmental protection the mainstream culture in social life.

C. Promote environmental protection awareness and ecological consciousness, build an environmental management system with the participation of the whole society, and make ecological and environmental protection ideas the mainstream culture in social life.

52.要高举构建人类命运共同体旗帜,推动全球治理体系朝着更加公正合理的方向发展。

A. We should continue to champion the cause of building a global community of shared future, and work for greater fairness and equity in global governance.

B. We should hold high the banner of building a community of human destiny and promote the development of the global governance system in a more just and rational direction.

C. "Uphold the banner of building a shared future for mankind, and promote the development of a more just and reasonable global governance system."

53.全球治理体系的走向,关乎各国特别是新兴市场国家和发展中国家发展空间,关乎全世界繁荣稳定。

A. Thus, the evolution of the global governance system will have a profound impact on all nations, particularly emerging markets and developing countries, and indeed on the prosperity and stability of the whole world.

B. The direction of the global governance system is related to the development space of all countries, especially emerging market countries and developing countries, and to the prosperity and stability of the world.

C. The direction of the global governance system is related to the development space of all countries, especially emerging market countries and developing countries, and is closely connected to the prosperity and stability of the world.

54.共建"一带一路"顺应了全球治理体系变革的内在要求,彰显了同舟共济、权责共担的命运共同体意识,为完善全球治理体系变革提供了新思路新方案。

A. The Belt and Road Initiative (BRI) was launched in response to the call for reforming the global governance system. The BRI promotes partnership and a community of shared future, shared rights and joint responsibilities. It offers a new approach to reform and improvement of the global governance system.

B. The joint construction of "Belt and Road" conforms to the inherent requirements of the reform of the global governance system, demonstrates the sense of a community of shared destiny, and provides new ideas and new solutions for improving the reform of the global governance system.

C. Co-building the "Belt and Road Initiative" conforms to the inherent requirements of the global governance system reform, demonstrates the sense of a community of shared future with shared responsibilities, and provides new ideas and solutions for improving the transformation of the global governance system.

55.我们要发挥负责任大国作用,支持广大发展中国家发展,积极参与全球治理体系改革和建设,共同为建设持久和平、普遍安全、共同繁荣、开放包容、清洁美丽的世界而奋斗。

A. China will continue to play its part as a major and responsible country. It will support the development of the vast number of developing countries, take an active part in reforming and developing the global governance system, and join the global endeavor to build an open, inclusive, clean and beautiful world that enjoys lasting peace, universal security, and common prosperity.

B. We should play the role of a responsible big country, support the development of developing countries, actively participate in the reform and construction of the global governance system, and work together to build a world of lasting peace, universal security, common prosperity, openness, inclusiveness, cleanliness and beauty.

C. We should play the role of a responsible major country, support the development of developing countries, actively participate in the reform and construction of the global governance system, and work together to build a world of lasting peace, universal security, common prosperity, openness, inclusiveness, cleanliness, and beauty.

56.中国支持二十国集团、亚太经合组织、上海合作组织、金砖国家等机制发挥更大作用,推动全球经济治理体系朝着更加公正合理的方向发展。

A. China supports a greater role for mechanisms such as the G20, APEC, the Shanghai Cooperation Organization, and the BRICS in building a fairer and more equitable global economic governance system.

B. China supports the G20, APEC, Shanghai Cooperation Organization, BRICS and other mechanisms to play a greater role in promoting the development of the global economic governance system in a more just and rational direction.

C. China supports the greater role of mechanisms such as the G20, Asia-Pacific Economic Cooperation, Shanghai Cooperation Organization, and BRICS countries, promoting the development of the global economic governance system in a more just and reasonable direction.

57.要持续巩固壮大主流舆论强势,加大舆论引导力度,加快建立网络综合治理体系,推进依法治网。

A. We should continue to consolidate and strengthen the preponderance of mainstream opinions, and intensify guidance on public opinion. At the same time we need to accelerate the establishment of a system for integrated internet management to promote a law-based cyberspace.

B. We should continue to consolidate and strengthen the mainstream public opinion, strengthen the guidance of public opinion, speed up the establishment of a comprehensive network governance system, and promote the rule of law.

C. Strengthen and expand the mainstream public opinion, increase the guidance of public opinion, accelerate the establishment of a comprehensive network governance system, and promote the rule of law on the internet.

58.农村现代化既包括"物"的现代化,也包括"人"的现代化,还包括乡村治理体系和治理能力的现代化。

A. Rural modernization involves both material and people, and covers the rural governance system and governing capability.

B. Rural modernization includes not only the modernization of "things" and "people", but also the modernization of rural governance system and governance capacity.

C. Rural modernization includes not only the modernization of "things," but also the modernization of "people," as well as the modernization of rural governance systems and governance capabilities.

59.我们要坚持创新驱动,打造富有活力的增长模式;坚持协同联动,打造开放共赢的合作模式;坚持公平包容,打造平衡普惠的发展模式,让世界各国人民共享经济全球化发展成果。

A. We need to pursue innovation-driven development to foster dynamic growth. We need to take a well-coordinated and interconnected approach to enhance open and win-win cooperation. We need to uphold equity and inclusiveness to promote balanced and inclusive development so that people across the world can all benefit from economic globalization.

B. We need to pursue innovation-driven and dynamic growth, pursue coordinated and interconnected development and open and win-win cooperation, and pursue equitable, inclusive, balanced and inclusive development to deliver the benefits of economic globalization to people around the world.

C. We must adhere to innovation-driven development, creating a dynamic growth model; persist in coordinated linkage, forging an open and mutually beneficial cooperation model; insist on fairness and inclusiveness, creating a balanced and universally beneficial development model, allowing people from all countries in the world to share the fruits of economic globalization.

60.新技术、新产品、新产业、新业态蓬勃发展,创新驱动力越来越大,新动能对经济的支撑作用明显增强。

A. New technologies, new products, new industries and new business models have flourished, and innovation has played a more obvious role as the major driving force of the economy.

B. With the vigorous development of new technologies, new products, new industries and new formats, the driving force of innovation is growing, and the role of new momentum in supporting the economy has been significantly enhanced.

C. New technologies, new products, new industries, and new business formats are flourishing, with increasing innovation-driven momentum, and the supporting role of new drivers in the economy is significantly enhanced.

61.要加快海洋科技创新步伐,提高海洋资源开发能力,培育壮大海洋战略性新兴产业。

A. We need to speed up innovation in marine science and technology, improve the ability to develop marine resources, and cultivate and strengthen strategic emerging industries in this sector.

B. We should accelerate the pace of marine science and technology innovation, improve the capacity of marine resources development, and foster and strengthen marine strategic emerging industries.

C. Accelerate the pace of marine technology innovation, improve the ability to develop marine resources, and cultivate and grow the strategic emerging marine industries.

62.面对世界经济复苏乏力、局部冲突和动荡频发、全球性问题加剧的外部环境,面对我国经济发展进入新常态等一系列深刻变化,我们坚持稳中求进工作总基调,迎难而上,开拓进取,取得了改革开放和社会主义现代化建设的历史性成就。

A. Outside China, we have been confronted with sluggish global economic recovery, frequent outbreaks of regional conflicts and disturbances, and intensifying global issues. At home, we have encountered profound changes as China has entered a new normal in economic development. We have upheld the underlying principle of pursuing progress while ensuring stability, risen to challenges, pioneered and pushed ahead, and made historic achievements in reform, opening up, and socialist modernization.

B. Faced with the external environment of sluggish world economic recovery, frequent local conflicts and turbulence, and intensified global issues, as well as a series of profound changes such as China's economic development entering a new normal, we adhered to the general tone of steady progress, faced difficulties, forged ahead, and made historic achievements in reform, opening up and socialist modernization.

C. Faced with the external environment of weak global economic recovery, frequent local conflicts and turbulence, and intensified global issues, as well as profound changes such as China's economic development entering a new normal, we adhere to the general principle of seeking progress while maintaining stability, rise to the challenge, forge ahead, and achieve historic achievements in reform, opening up, and socialist modernization construction.

63.要强化教育引导、实践养成、制度保障,把社会主义核心价值观融入社会发展各方面,引导全体人民自觉践行。

A. We should offer the people better guidance, expose them to successful practices, and provide institutional guarantees. We should see that all areas of social development are imbued with the core socialist values, and encourage the public to honor these values.

B. We should strengthen education guidance, practice cultivation and system guarantee, integrate socialist core values into all aspects of social development, and guide all people to consciously practice them.

C. Strengthen education guidance, practical development, and institutional guarantees, integrate socialist core values into all aspects of social development, and guide all people to consciously practice them.

64.要大力弘扬社会主义核心价值观,加强思想教育、道德教化,改进见义勇为英雄模范评选表彰工作,让全社会充满正气、正义。

A. We need to promote the core socialist values, strengthen political and moral education, improve the nomination and commendation of role models who act bravely for justice, and let integrity and justice prevail in the whole society.

B. We should vigorously promote socialist core values, strengthen ideological education and moral education, improve the selection and recognition of heroic models, and make the whole society full of righteousness and justice.

C. We must vigorously promote the core values of socialism, strengthen ideological education and moral edification, improve the selection and recognition of heroic models who perform courageous deeds, and fill the whole society with righteousness and justice.

65.社会主义核心价值观是当代中国精神的集中体现,凝结着全体人民共同的价值追求。

A. The core socialist values represent the contemporary Chinese spirit and are a crystallization of the values shared by all Chinese people.

B. Socialist core values are the concentrated embodiment of the spirit of contemporary China and condense the common value pursuit of all the people.

C. The core values of socialism are a concentrated embodiment of the contemporary Chinese spirit, condensing the common value pursuits of all people.

66.用新时代中国特色社会主义思想铸魂育人

A. Raise Students' Awareness of the Thought on Socialism with Chinese Characteristics for a New Era

B. Casting the Soul and Educating People with the Socialist Thought with Chinese Characteristics in the New Era

C. "Cultivate people's souls with the ideology of Socialism with Chinese characteristics for a new era"

67.中国特色社会主义进入新时代,我国社会主要矛盾已经转化为人民日益增长的美好生活需要和不平衡不充分的发展之间的矛盾。

A. As socialism with Chinese characteristics has entered a new era, the principal challenge facing Chinese society has evolved. What we now face is the gap between unbalanced and inadequate development and the ever-growing expectation of the people for a better life.

B. As socialism with Chinese characteristics enters a new era, the main contradictions in our society have been transformed into the contradiction between the people's growing need for a better life and the unbalanced and inadequate development.

C. "Socialism with Chinese characteristics has entered a new era, and the main contradiction in our society has now transformed into the contradiction between the people's ever-growing needs for a better life and the unbalanced and inadequate development."

68.兴文化,就是要坚持中国特色社会主义文化发展道路,推动中华优秀传统文化创造性转化、创新性发展,继承革命文化,发展社会主义先进文化,激发全民族文化创新创造活力,建设社会主义文化强国。

A. Developing Chinese culture means orienting culture towards socialism. We must promote the creative evolution and development of traditional Chinese culture, inherit our revolutionary cultural traditions, and develop an advanced socialist culture. We must inspire the cultural creativity of our whole nation, and develop a great socialist culture in China.

B. Promoting culture means adhering to the road of socialist cultural development with Chinese characteristics, promoting the creative transformation and development of excellent traditional Chinese culture, inheriting revolutionary culture, developing advanced socialist culture, stimulating the cultural innovation and creativity of the whole nation, and building a strong socialist cultural country.

C. Promoting culture means adhering to the path of cultural development with Chinese characteristics, promoting the creative transformation and innovative development of outstanding traditional Chinese culture, inheriting revolutionary culture, developing advanced socialist culture, stimulating the cultural innovation and creativity of the entire nation, and building a strong socialist cultural country.

69.中华优秀传统文化是中华民族的文化根脉,其蕴含的思想观念、人文精神、道德规范,不仅是我们中国人思想和精神的内核,对解决人类问题也有重要价值。

A. China's finest traditional culture is the cultural lifeline of the Chinese nation. Its visions, concepts, values and moral norms are the core of Chinese thinking, and they also hold invaluable references to resolving problems of humanity.

B. Excellent traditional Chinese culture is the cultural root of the Chinese nation, and its ideological concepts, humanistic spirit and moral norms are not only the core of our Chinese ideology and spirit, but also of great value in solving human problems.

C. Chinese excellent traditional culture is the cultural root of the Chinese nation. The ideas, humanistic spirit, and moral norms it contains are not only the core of our Chinese people's thoughts and spirit, but also have significant value in solving human problems.

70.生态文明是人民群众共同参与共同建设共同享有的事业,要把建设美丽中国转化为全体人民自觉行动。

A. Eco-environmental progress is a common cause that requires the participation and contribution of the general public. Its results will also be shared by the people. To build a beautiful China, we should transform our efforts into conscientious action on the part of all.

B. Ecological civilization is a cause that the people participate in, build and enjoy together, and we should translate the building of a beautiful China into the conscious action of all the people.

C. Ecological civilization is a cause that the people participate in, build together, and share together. We must turn the construction of a beautiful China into the conscious action of all people.

71.现在,生态文明建设已经纳入中国国家发展总体布局,建设美丽中国已经成为中国人民心向往之的奋斗目标。

A. Advancing eco-environmental progress has become part of China's overall plan for national development, and building a beautiful country continues to inspire the Chinese people.

B. Now, the construction of ecological civilization has been incorporated into the overall layout of China's national development, and building a beautiful China has become the goal that the Chinese people yearn for.

C. Now, ecological civilization construction has been incorporated into China's overall national development plan, and building a beautiful China has become the aspiration and goal of the Chinese people.

72.要建立健全市场化、多元化生态补偿机制,在长江流域开展生态产品价值实现机制试点。

A. We need to build a market-oriented, multidimensional mechanism to provide recompense for eco-protection, and introduce a pilot mechanism for realizing the value of eco-environmental undertakings in the Yangtze River Basin.

B. It is necessary to establish and improve a market-oriented and diversified ecological compensation mechanism, and carry out pilot projects on the value realization mechanism of ecological products in the Yangtze River Basin.

C. Establish and improve a market-oriented, diversified ecological compensation mechanism, and carry out pilot projects on the realization of ecological product value in the Yangtze River Basin.

73.转变政府职能,深化简政放权,创新监管方式,增强政府公信力和执行力,建设人民满意的服务型政府。

A. The government needs to transform its functions, further streamline administration and delegate powers, develop new ways of regulation and supervision, and strengthen its credibility and administrative capacity, building itself into a service-oriented government able to satisfy the needs of the people.

B. Transforming government functions, deepening simplification and decentralization of government, innovating supervision methods, enhancing government credibility and execution, and building a service-oriented government that people are satisfied with.

C. Transform government functions, deepen decentralization, innovate regulatory methods, enhance government credibility and execution, and build a service-oriented government that satisfies the people.

74.我们要继续在"上海精神"指引下,同舟共济,精诚合作,齐心协力构建上海合作组织命运共同体,推动建设新型国际关系,携手迈向持久和平、普遍安全、共同繁荣、开放包容、清洁美丽的世界。

A. Guided by the Shanghai Spirit, we should work closely to build an SCO community of shared future, move towards a new model of international relations, and build an open, inclusive, clean and beautiful world that enjoys lasting peace, universal security, and common prosperity.

B. Under the guidance of the "Shanghai Spirit", we should continue to work together and cooperate sincerely to build a community of destiny of the Shanghai Cooperation Organization, promote the construction of a new type of international relations, and work together towards a world of lasting peace, universal security, common prosperity, openness, inclusiveness, cleanliness and beauty.

C. We need to continue under the guidance of the "Shanghai Spirit", work together, cooperate sincerely, and join hands to build a shared destiny community for the Shanghai Cooperation Organization, promote the construction of a new type of international relations, and move towards a world of lasting peace, universal security, common prosperity, openness, inclusiveness, and a clean and beautiful environment.

75.金砖国家要顺应历史大势,把握发展机遇,合力克服挑战,为构建新型国际关系、构建人类命运共同体发挥建设性作用。

A. We BRICS countries need to keep abreast of the historic trend, seize development opportunities, jointly meet challenges, and play a constructive role in building a new model of international relations and a global community of shared future.

B. BRICS countries should conform to the historical trend, seize development opportunities, work together to overcome challenges and play a constructive role in building a new type of international relations and a community of human destiny.

C. BRICS countries should follow the historical trend, seize development opportunities, work together to overcome challenges, and play a constructive role in building a new type of international relations and a community with a shared future for mankind.

76.尽管文明冲突、文明优越等论调不时沉渣泛起,但文明多样性是人类进步的不竭动力,不同文明交流互鉴是各国人民共同愿望。

A. For all that we keep hearing such rhetoric as the clash of civilizations or the superiority of one civilization over another, it is the diversity of civilizations that sustains human progress. Indeed, mutual learning between different cultures is a shared aspiration of all peoples.

B. Despite the arguments of clash of civilizations and superiority of civilizations, diversity of civilizations is an inexhaustible driving force for human progress, and exchanges and mutual learning among civilizations are the common aspirations of all peoples.

C. Although the rhetoric of civilization conflicts and civilization superiority occasionally resurfaces, the diversity of civilizations is an inexhaustible driving force for human progress, and the exchange and mutual learning of different civilizations is the common desire of people from all countries.

77.我们应该以海纳百川的宽广胸怀打破文化交往的壁垒,以兼收并蓄的态度汲取其他文明的养分,促进亚洲文明在交流互鉴中共同前进。

A. We need to be broad-minded and strive to remove all barriers to cultural exchanges. We need to be inclusive and always seek nourishment from other civilizations to promote the common development of Asian civilizations through exchanges and mutual learning.

B. We should break down the barriers of cultural exchanges with a broad mind, absorb the nutrients of other civilizations with an inclusive attitude, and promote the common progress of Asian civilizations in exchanges and mutual learning.

C. "We should break down the barriers of cultural exchange with an inclusive and open-minded attitude, learn from the nourishment of other civilizations with a receptive approach, and promote the common progress of Asian civilizations through mutual learning and exchanges."

78.广大发展中国家是我国在国际事务中的天然同盟军,要坚持正确义利观,做好同发展中国家团结合作的大文章。

A. Other developing countries are China's natural allies in international affairs. We must pursue the greater good and shared interests, and boost solidarity and collaboration between developing nations.

B. The vast number of developing countries are China's natural allies in international affairs, so we should adhere to the correct concept of justice and interests and do a good job of solidarity and cooperation with developing countries.

C. "Developing countries are our natural allies in international affairs. We must adhere to the correct view of righteousness and interests, and do a good job in uniting and cooperating with developing countries."

79.加强军队党的建设,开展"传承红色基因、担当强军重任"主题教育,推进军人荣誉体系建设,培养有灵魂、有本事、有血性、有品德的新时代革命军人,永葆人民军队性质、宗旨、本色。

A. We will strengthen the Party in the military. We will launch activities under the theme of "passing on the traditions of revolution; stepping up to the task of making the military strong". We will move forward with the development of the military honors system. We will train the revolutionary officers and soldiers of a new era with faith, ability, courage, and integrity and see that our forces forever preserve their nature, purpose, and character as the forces of the people.

B. Strengthen the Party building in the army, carry out the theme education of "inheriting the red gene and shouldering the heavy responsibility of strengthening the army", promote the construction of the military honor system, train revolutionary soldiers with soul, ability, blood and moral character in the new era, and always maintain the nature, purpose and nature of the people's army.

C. Strengthen the construction of the Party in the army, carry out the theme education of "Inheriting the Red Gene and Undertaking the Heavy Responsibility of a Strong Army", promote the construction of the military honor system, cultivate revolutionary soldiers of the new era with soul, ability, blood, and morality, and always maintain the nature, purpose, and true colors of the People's Army.

80.中国人民愿同各国人民一道,秉持和平、发展、公平、正义、民主、自由的人类共同价值,维护人的尊严和权利,推动形成更加公正、合理、包容的全球人权治理,共同构建人类命运共同体,开创世界美好未来。

A. Together with the peoples of other countries, and based on the common values of humanity—peace, development, equity, justice, democracy and freedom—China is committed to safeguarding human dignity and rights, and promoting fairer, more equitable and inclusive global governance of human rights, so as to build a global community of shared future and strive for a better world.

B. The Chinese people are willing to work together with people from all countries to uphold the common values of peace, development, fairness, justice, democracy, and freedom for humanity, safeguard human dignity and rights, promote the formation of a more just, reasonable, and inclusive global human rights governance, jointly build a community with a shared future for mankind, and create a better future for the world.

C. The Chinese people are willing to work with the people of other countries to uphold the common human values of peace, development, fairness, justice, democracy and freedom, safeguard human dignity and rights, promote the formation of a more just, reasonable and inclusive global human rights governance, jointly build a community of human destiny and create a better future for the world.

81.实现中华民族伟大复兴,需要各民族手挽着手、肩并着肩,共同努力奋斗。

A. The rejuvenation of the Chinese nation requires all ethnic groups to stand together, to work together with one heart.

B. To achieve the great rejuvenation of the Chinese nation, it is necessary for all ethnic groups to hold hands and work together shoulder to shoulder.

C. To realize the great rejuvenation of the Chinese nation, all ethnic groups need to work hand in hand, shoulder to shoulder and work together.

82.网信事业发展必须贯彻以人民为中心的发展思想,把增进人民福祉作为信息化发展的出发点和落脚点,让人民群众在信息化发展中有更多获得感、幸福感、安全感。

A. We should put people first in the development of cybersecurity and IT application and make the wellbeing of the people its ultimate goal, giving people a stronger sense of gain, happiness, and security;

B. The development of the Internet industry must implement the development concept of putting people at the center, take the improvement of people's well-being as the starting point and foothold of information technology development, and let the people have more sense of gain, happiness, and security in the development of information technology.

C. The development of the Internet and telecommunications industry must implement the people-centered development idea, take the improvement of people's well-being as the starting point and foothold of the development of information technology, so that the people can have more sense of gain, happiness and security in the development of information technology.

83.要以"一带一路"建设等为契机,加强同沿线国家特别是发展中国家在网络基础设施建设、数字经济、网络安全等方面的合作,建设 21 世纪数字丝绸之路。

A. We will take the Belt and Road Initiative as an opportunity to strengthen cooperation with countries along the Belt and Road, particularly developing countries, in internet infrastructure construction, digital economy and cybersecurity as part of our effort to build a digital Silk Road of the 21st century.

B. To take the opportunity of the "Belt and Road" Initiative, strengthen cooperation with countries along the route, especially developing countries, in areas such as network infrastructure construction, digital economy, and cybersecurity, and build the 21st-century Digital Silk Road.

C. We should take the construction of "one belt and one road" as an opportunity to strengthen cooperation with countries along the line, especially developing countries, in the construction of network infrastructure, digital economy and network security, so as to build a digital Silk Road in the 21st century.

84.展形象,就是要推进国际传播能力建设,讲好中国故事、传播好中国声音,向世界展现真实、立体、全面的中国,提高国家文化软实力和中华文化影响力。

A. Building a positive image of China means improving our capacity for international communication, so as to tell better and more accurate stories and make China's voice heard. We should project a true, multi-dimensional and all-round picture of China, and increase China's soft power and the influence of Chinese culture in the world.

B. To build a good image, it is necessary to enhance the capacity for international communication, tell China's story well, spread China's voice, show the world a true, three-dimensional, and comprehensive China, and enhance the country's cultural soft power and the influence of Chinese culture.

C. Exhibition image is to promote the construction of international communication capacity, tell Chinese stories well, disseminate Chinese voice well, show the world a real, three-dimensional and comprehensive China, and enhance the soft power of national culture and the influence of Chinese culture.

85.要加强传播手段和话语方式创新,让党的创新理论"飞入寻常百姓家"。

A. We should improve means of communication and create new means to promote our Party's innovative theories among the people.

B. To strengthen the means of communication and innovate the way of speaking, let the Party's innovative theories "enter the homes of ordinary people".

C. We should strengthen the innovation of communication means and discourse methods so that the Party's innovative theory can "fly into ordinary people's homes".

86.大家读历史都知道,《吕氏春秋》里讲:"尧有欲谏之鼓,舜有诽谤之木。"

A. As we all know from historical records as it is stated in Lü's Spring and Autumn Annals, "Emperor Yao set up a drum for people to beat and offer their advice, and Emperor Shun set up wooden boards for people to write down their criticisms."

B. Everyone who reads history knows that in the "Lüshi Chunqiu", it is said: "Emperor Yao had a drum to encourage advice, and Emperor Shun had a wooden stake to expose slander."

C. Everyone who reads history knows that in Lu's Spring and Autumn Annals, it is said: "Yao has the drum to remonstrate, and Shun has the wood to slander."

87.要把好脉,中国身体怎么样,如果有病是什么病,用什么药来治,对这心里要透亮透亮的。

A. Before prescribing the right solutions for our country, we must first have an idea of its health and then identify the ailments and their causes.

B. To diagnose the condition of the body in China, determine if there is any illness, and use appropriate medication for treatment. It is important to have a clear understanding of this mentally.

C. It is necessary to have a good pulse. How is the Chinese body? If there is a disease, what kind of disease is it? What kind of medicine should be used to treat it? The heart should be bright.

88.除了天赋以外,确实要去积累、去挖掘,很多事情都是在细节,演电影、写小说都是细节,细节感人,细节要真实,而真实要去挖掘。

A. In addition to releasing individual talent, we also need to gather source materials and conduct in-depth and detailed research. Success lies in the details. As screenplays and novels draw on emotive and genuine details, we need to dig deeper into real life to obtain them.

B. Apart from talent, you really need to accumulate and explore. Many things are in the details. Acting in movies and writing novels are all about the details. Details touch people's hearts. Details need to be real, and reality needs to be explored.

C. In addition to talent, really need to accumulate, to dig, a lot of things are in the details, acting in movies, writing novels are details, details moving, details to be true, and true to dig.

89.实现"两个一百年"奋斗目标、实现中华民族伟大复兴的中国梦,需要汇聚全民族的智慧和力量,需要广泛凝聚共识、不断增进团结。

A. To achieve the Two Centenary Goals and the Chinese Dream of national rejuvenation, we need to pool the wisdom and strength of all Chinese people, build broad consensus, and promote unity.

B. To achieve the "Two Centenary Goals" and realize the Chinese Dream of national rejuvenation, it is necessary to gather the wisdom and strength of the entire nation, and to widely consolidate consensus and continuously enhance unity.

C. To achieve the goal of "two hundred years" and realize the Chinese dream of the great rejuvenation of the Chinese nation, we need to pool the wisdom and strength of the whole nation, and we need to build broad consensus and constantly enhance unity.

90.在实现中华民族伟大复兴的新征程上,应对重大挑战、抵御重大风险、克服重大阻力、解决重大矛盾,迫切需要迎难而上、挺身而出的担当精神。

A. In the new journey towards national rejuvenation，we need to respond to major challenges，guard against serious risks，overcome real obstacles，and resolve difficult problems. All these urgently demand the will to step forward in the face of difficulties.

B. In the new journey of realizing the great rejuvenation of the Chinese nation，it is urgent to face major challenges，resist major risks，overcome major obstacles，and resolve major contradictions. It is necessary to have the spirit of taking on difficulties and stepping forward.

C. In the new journey of realizing the great rejuvenation of the Chinese nation，to meet major challenges，resist major risks，overcome major resistance and solve major contradictions，it is urgent to face difficulties and stand up to the spirit of responsibility.

91.我国银行、证券、保险业的抗风险能力和国际竞争力显著提升,为成功应对国际金融危机冲击奠定了坚实基础。

A. China's banking，securities and insurance industries became significantly more resilient to risks and internationally competitive，and they underpinned our successful response to the global financial crisis.

B. The risk resistance and international competitiveness of China's banking，securities，and insurance industries have significantly improved，laying a solid foundation for successfully responding to the impact of the international financial crisis.

C. The anti-risk ability and international competitiveness of China's banking，securities and insurance industries have been significantly improved，laying a solid foundation for successfully coping with the impact of the international financial crisis.

92.绿水青山既是自然财富、生态财富,又是社会财富、经济财富。

A. Clear waters and green mountains are not only natural and ecological wealth，but also social and economic wealth.

B. Green mountains and rivers are not only natural wealth and ecological wealth, but also social wealth and economic wealth.

C. Green water and green hills are not only natural wealth and ecological wealth, but also social wealth and economic wealth.

93.一定要算大账、算长远账、算整体账、算综合账,如果因小失大、顾此失彼,最终必然对生态环境造成系统性、长期性破坏。

A. We should take a broad and long-term view. We must try to avoid earning a little only to lose a lot, or attending to one thing and losing sight of others. Otherwise, our actions are bound to cause systematic and long-lasting damage.

B. Always consider the big picture, the long-term, the overall, and the comprehensive. If you focus on small gains and neglect other aspects, it will inevitably cause systematic and long-term damage to the ecological environment.

C. We must calculate big accounts, long-term accounts, overall accounts and comprehensive accounts. If we are penny-wise and pound-foolish, we will eventually cause systematic and long-term damage to the ecological environment.

94.要推进"一带一路"建设,让生态文明的理念和实践造福沿线各国人民。

A. We will promote the philosophy and practice of eco-environmental progress in the Belt and Road Initiative to benefit the peoples of all countries along the Belt and Road.

B. To promote the construction of the "Belt and Road" and benefit the people of countries along the route with the concept and practice of ecological civilization.

C. We should promote the construction of "one belt and one road" so that the concept and practice of ecological civilization can benefit the people of all countries along the line.

95.山峦层林尽染,平原蓝绿交融,城乡鸟语花香。

A. Lush mountains, vast tracts of forest, blue skies, green fields, singing birds, and blossoming flowers offer more than visual beauty.

B. Mountains and forests are dyed in layers, the plains blend blue and green, and the urban and rural areas are filled with the sounds of birds and the fragrance of flowers.

C. The mountains and forests are dyed, the plains are blue and green, and the urban and rural areas are full of birds and flowers.

96.“取之有度,用之有节”,是生态文明的真谛。

A. Well-measured exploration and use of resources is the key to eco-environmental progress.

B. "Take in moderation, use with restraint" is the essence of ecological civilization.

C. It is the essence of ecological civilization to "take it properly and use it properly".

97.生态治理,道阻且长,行则将至。

A. Although environmental governance is an arduous task, we will ultimately obtain the expected results as long as we take the right steps.

B. Ecological governance, the road is long and difficult, but once we take action, success will be within reach.

C. Ecological governance, the road is blocked and long, the line is coming.

98.中国古人说:“万物得其本者生,百事得其道者成。”

A. An ancient Chinese philosopher observed that "plants with strong roots grow well, and efforts with the right focus ensure success".

B. The ancient Chinese said, "Everything that has its root will grow, and everything that follows its path will succeed."

C. An ancient Chinese said, "All things are born when they have their roots, and all things are accomplished when they have their ways."

99.有的拍脑袋决策,搞家长制、"一言堂",把个人凌驾于组织之上,容不下他人,听不得不同意见。

A. Some make ill-considered or purely arbitrary decisions. They place themselves above the Party organization and allow no dissenting voices.

B. Some make decisions without careful consideration, implement a top-down approach, prioritize individual interests over the organization, and are intolerant of others or different opinions.

C. Some patted their heads to make decisions, engaged in patriarchal system, "one voice", put individuals above the organization, cannot tolerate others, cannot listen to different opinions.

100.苏轼的这份情怀,正是今人所欠缺的,也是最为珍贵的。

A. This sentiment of Su Shi, a great writer of ancient China, as he expressed in these words, is most precious but not seen among us now.

B. The sentiment of Su Shi, is exactly what is lacking in modern people, and also the most precious.

C. This feeling of Su Shi is exactly what people lack today, and it is also the most precious.

101.宋代苏轼在《思治论》中说:"犯其至难而图其至远"。

A. In his article "Proposals on Governance", Su Shi of the Song Dynasty (960—1279) said, "Only by solving the hardest problems can one achieve the loftiest goals."

B. During the Song Dynasty, Su Shi said in his essay "On Governing the Mind": "To challenge the most difficult and aim for the farthest."

C. In the Song Dynasty, Su Shi said in his "Thought on Governance": "It is extremely difficult to make it and try to make it far away."

102.中华文明历来主张天下大同、协和万邦。

A. The Chinese civilization has always valued universal peace and harmony among nations.

B. Chinese civilization has always advocated for a world of unity and harmony among all nations.

C. The Chinese civilization has always advocated universal harmony and universal peace.

103.推进"三去一降一补",着力化解过剩产能,推动市场出清,促进了供求平衡。

A. We have advanced supply-side structural reform, cutting overcapacity, reducing excess inventory, deleveraging, lowering costs, and strengthening areas of weakness. These measures were taken to reduce excess capacity, clear goods from the market, and promote balance between demand and supply.

B. Promoting the "three reductions, one drop, and one supplement" policy, focusing on resolving overcapacity, promoting market clearance, and facilitating supply-demand balance.

C. Promoting "three cuts, one reduction and one subsidy", focusing on resolving excess capacity, promoting market clearance, and promoting the balance of supply and demand.

104.创新从来都是九死一生,但我们必须有"亦余心之所善兮,虽九死其犹未悔"的豪情。

A. In innovation the odds of failure are much higher than those of success, but we should have the determination shown by patriotic poet Qu Yuan, "For the ideal that I hold dear to my heart, I will not regret a thousand deaths to die."

B. Innovation has always been a matter of life and death, but we must have the courage of "even if I have only one breath left to do what I love, I will not regret even if I die nine times".

C. Innovation has always been a lifetime of nine deaths, but we must have the pride of "doing what is good in our hearts, even if we die nine deaths, we still have no regrets".

105.不拒众流,方为江海。

A. Rivers and seas are big because they never reject the small streams that flow in.

B. Do not reject the crowd, then you will become a river or sea.

C. Do not refuse the crowd, just for the river and sea.

106.功以才成，业由才广。

　　A. Feats are accomplished by capable people; undertakings proceed because of capable people.

　　B. Success comes from talent, and achievements come from a wide range of talents.

　　C. Success comes from talent, and career comes from talent.

107.建设海洋强国，必须进一步关心海洋、认识海洋、经略海洋，加快海洋科技创新步伐。

　　A. To build China into a strong maritime nation, we must take good care of, further understand, and manage the ocean, and facilitate innovation in marine science and technology.

　　B. To build a maritime power, we must further care about the ocean, understand the ocean, develop strategies for the ocean, and accelerate the pace of marine scientific and technological innovation.

　　C. To build a powerful marine country, we must pay more attention to the ocean, understand the ocean, manage the ocean and accelerate the pace of marine science and technology innovation.

108.中国将始终是全球共同开放的重要推动者，中国将始终是世界经济增长的稳定动力源，中国将始终是各国拓展商机的活力大市场，中国将始终是全球治理改革的积极贡献者！

　　A. China will remain a strong advocate of openness at the global level, and will continue to act as a stable engine of global growth, a huge market with enormous opportunities, and an active supporter of reform in global governance.

　　B. China will always be an important promoter of global openness, China will always be a stable driving force for world economic growth, China will always be a vibrant major market for countries to expand business opportunities, China will always be an active contributor to global governance reform!

C. China will always be an important promoter of global opening up, a stable driving force for world economic growth, a dynamic market for all countries to expand business opportunities, and an active contributor to global governance reform!

109.人类社会要持续进步,各国就应该坚持要开放不要封闭,要合作不要对抗,要共赢不要独占。

A. The progress of human society requires a continued effort from all countries to further opening up, cooperation and win-win development, and reject isolation, confrontation and monopoly.

B. Human society should continue to progress. All countries should insist on openness instead of closure, cooperation instead of confrontation, and win-win instead of monopoly.

C. If human society is to continue to progress, all countries should adhere to openness rather than isolation, cooperation rather than confrontation, and win-win rather than monopoly.

110."一花独放不是春,百花齐放春满园。"

A. As a Chinese saying goes, "All flowers in full blossom make a beautiful spring."

B. "One flower alone does not make spring, a hundred flowers in full bloom make the garden full of spring."

C. "A single flower does not make spring, but a hundred flowers in full blossom bring spring to the garden."

111.一个时代有一个时代的问题,一代人有一代人的使命。

A. All ages and generations have their own challenges and missions.

B. Every era has its own problems, and every generation has its own mission.

C. An era has its problems, and a generation has its mission.

112."行之力则知愈进,知之深则行愈达。"

A. As an ancient Chinese scholar said, "Practice improves understanding and a deeper understanding guides further practice."

B. "The more you practice, the more you know; the deeper you know, the more you can achieve."

C. "The more powerful the action, the more advanced the knowledge; the deeper the knowledge, the more advanced the action."

113.完成非凡之事,要有非凡之精神和行动。

A. Completing such an extraordinary mission requires exceptional drive and outstanding deeds.

B. To accomplish extraordinary things, one must have an extraordinary spirit and take extraordinary actions.

C. To accomplish extraordinary things, we must have extraordinary spirit and action.

114.中国人民相信,山再高,往上攀,总能登顶;路再长,走下去,定能到达。

A. It is our firm belief that no matter how high a mountain is, if we keep climbing, we will reach the top; no matter how long a road is, if we keep walking, we will reach the destination.

B. The Chinese people believe that no matter how high the mountain is, they can always reach the top by climbing up; no matter how long the road is, they can always reach the destination by keeping on walking.

C. The Chinese people believe that no matter how high the mountain is, if you climb up, you can always reach the top; no matter how long the road is, if you go on, you will surely reach it.

115.路很长,我们肩负的责任很重,这方面不能有一劳永逸、可以歇歇脚的思想。

A. On the long way ahead, we bear heavy responsibility and must not stop or slacken our efforts.

B. The road is long, and the responsibility we bear is heavy. We cannot have the idea of a one-time solution or being able to take a break in this regard.

C. The road is very long，the responsibility that we shoulder is very heavy，this respect cannot have once and for all，the thought that can rest one's feet.

116.我们的目标很宏伟,但也很朴素,归根结底就是让全体中国人都过上更好的日子。

A. We have a grand yet simple goal—a better life for all our people.

B. Our goal is lofty but also simple，ultimately it is to enable all Chinese people to have a better life.

C. Our goal is very ambitious，but also very simple，in the final analysis，is to make all Chinese people live a better life.

117.我们呼吁,各国人民同心协力,构建人类命运共同体,建设持久和平、普遍安全、共同繁荣、开放包容、清洁美丽的世界。

A. We call on the people of all countries to work together to build a global community of shared future，to build an open，inclusive，clean，and beautiful world that enjoys lasting peace，universal security，and common prosperity.

B. We call on people of all countries to work together to build a community with a shared future for mankind，to build a world of lasting peace，universal security，common prosperity，openness，inclusiveness，and clean beauty.

C. We call on the people of all countries to work together to build a community of human destiny and build a world of lasting peace，universal security，common prosperity，openness，inclusiveness，cleanliness and beauty.

118.文化自信是一个国家、一个民族发展中更基本、更深沉、更持久的力量。

A. Cultural confidence represents a fundamental and profound force that sustains the development of a country and a nation.

B. Cultural self-confidence is a more fundamental，profound，and lasting force in the development of a country and a nation.

C. Cultural self-confidence is a more basic, deeper and lasting force in the development of a country and a nation.

119.有的做"老好人"、"太平官"、"墙头草",顾虑"洗碗越多,摔碗越多",信奉"多栽花少种刺,遇到困难不伸手","为了不出事,宁可不干事","只想争功不想揽过,只想出彩不想出力";有的是"庙里的泥菩萨,经不起风雨",遇到矛盾惊慌失措,遇见斗争直打摆子。

A. Some prefer to be risk-averse, avoid confrontation, or sit on the fence. They worry that "the more dishes you wash, the more likely you are to break them". They embrace ideas such as "making friends rather than enemies, and turning a blind eye to indiscretions", "rather do nothing in case something goes wrong", "taking credit for successes but refusing to accept responsibility for mistakes", and "enjoying standing in the limelight rather than working behind the scenes". They panic whenever problems and difficulties arise.

B. Some are "nice guys", "peaceful officials", and "fence-sitters", worried that "the more dishes you wash, the more you drop", believing in "planting more flowers and fewer thorns, not reaching out when encountering difficulties", "preferring to avoid trouble rather than doing things", "only wanting credit without taking responsibility, only wanting to stand out without putting in effort"; some are "mud statues in temples, unable to withstand wind and rain", panicking when faced with conflicts, and getting flustered in the face of struggles.

C. Some do "good old man", "peace officer", "wall grass", worry about "the more dishes washed, the more bowls thrown", believe in "planting more flowers and fewer thorns, do not stretch out their hands when they encounter difficulties", "in order not to have an accident, they would rather not do anything" and "just want to strive for merit and do not want to win, just want to be outstanding and do not want to contribute"; Some of them are "clay Bodhisattvas in temples, unable to withstand the wind and rain", panicking when confronted with contradictions, and swinging when confronted with struggles.

120.不忘初心、牢记使命，必须安不忘危、存不忘亡、乐不忘忧，时刻保持警醒，不断振奋精神，勇于进行具有许多新的历史特点的伟大斗争。

A. We must be mindful of possible dangers in time of peace and possible crisis in time of stability, remain ever-vigilant, boost morale, and be resolved to engage in the great historic struggle with many new features.

B. Never forget the original intention and keep in mind the mission. We must be prepared for danger, be mindful of the possibility of failure, and not forget to be happy or worry-free. Always stay vigilant, continuously uplift our spirits, and bravely engage in the great struggle with many new historical characteristics.

C. To remain true to our original aspiration and keep our mission firmly in mind, we must never forget danger, survival, happiness and worries, keep alert at all times, constantly inspire our spirit and dare to carry out great struggles with many new historical characteristics.

121.古人说："天下之难持者莫如心，天下之易染者莫如欲。"

A. As an ancient Chinese scholar said, "The hardest thing to do under heaven is to keep one's heart under control, and the easiest thing is to be lured by desire."

B. The ancients said："There is nothing more difficult to control in the world than the heart, and there is nothing more easily influenced than desire."

C. The ancients said, "There is nothing so difficult as the heart in the world, and there is nothing so easy as the desire in the world."

122.有的热衷于搞"小圈子"、"拜码头"、"搭天线"；

A. Some have a penchant for forming cliques and factions, cultivating connections or currying favors with higher-ups for personal benefit.

B. Some are enthusiastic about creating "small circles", "paying homage", "building antennas";

C. Some are keen to engage in "small circles", "worship the wharf" and "build antennas";

123.不管是"老虎"还是"苍蝇",无论是大腐败还是"微腐败",都在坚决纠治之列。

> A. "Tigers" and "flies"—major and minor corruption cases—are both to be brought under investigation.
>
> B. Whether it is a "tiger" or a "fly", whether it is a major corruption or "minor corruption", they are all firmly being rectified.
>
> C. Whether it is a "tiger" or a "fly", whether it is a big corruption or a "micro corruption", they are all in the list of resolute rectification.

124.创新就是生产力,企业赖之以强,国家赖之以盛。

> A. Innovation boosts productivity; it makes companies competitive and countries strong.
>
> B. Innovation is productivity, on which companies rely for strength and nations rely for prosperity.
>
> C. Innovation is productivity, on which enterprises depend to be strong and the country depends to be prosperous.

125.当前,世界多极化、经济全球化、文化多样化、社会信息化深入发展,人类社会充满希望。

> A. The world today is moving towards multi-polarity and becoming more economically globalized, culturally diverse, and IT-driven. All this offers hope to humanity.
>
> B. Currently, the world is undergoing deep development in terms of multipolarity, economic globalization, cultural diversity, and social informatization, and human society is filled with hope.
>
> C. At present, with the deepening development of world multi-polarization, economic globalization, cultural diversity and social informatization, human society is full of hope.

126.在这个草木生长的美好季节,来自亚洲47个国家和五大洲的各方嘉宾,为深化文明交流互鉴共聚一堂,共襄盛举。

> A. In this lovely season of thriving green, I am pleased that our friends from 47 Asian countries and five continents are meeting here for a discussion on deeper exchanges and mutual learning among civilizations.

B. In this beautiful season of plant growth, guests from 47 countries in Asia and five continents gather together to deepen cultural exchanges and mutual learning.

C. In this beautiful season of vegetation growth, guests from 47 Asian countries and five continents gathered together to deepen civilized exchanges and mutual learning.

127.国家间要有事多商量、有事好商量,不能动辄就诉诸武力或以武力相威胁。

A. Whenever a problem crops up, countries concerned should always hold deliberations in good faith, rather than resort to the use or threat of force at will.

B. Countries should consult with each other and negotiate when there are issues, rather than resorting to or threatening the use of force.

C. Countries should consult with each other when they have something to discuss, and they should not resort to force or threat of force at every turn.

128.我们人类居住的这个蓝色星球,不是被海洋分割成了各个孤岛,而是被海洋连结成了命运共同体,各国人民安危与共。

A. It does not separate our blue planet into isolated continents; instead, it links the peoples of all countries to form a global community of shared future that remains bound together through thick and thin.

B. The blue planet on which we humans live is not divided into isolated islands by the ocean, but connected by the ocean into a community of shared destiny, where the safety and well-being of people in all countries are intertwined.

C. The blue planet we live on is not divided into isolated islands by the ocean, but is linked by the ocean into a community of destiny, and the people of all countries share safety and danger.

129.变革过程应该体现平等、开放、透明、包容精神,提高发展中国家代表性和发言权,遇到分歧应该通过协商解决,不能搞小圈子,不能强加于人。

A. This reform should be based on the principles of equality, openness, transparency, and inclusiveness. Developing countries should have more say and greater representation in this process. Disagreements should be resolved through consultation. Attempts to form exclusive blocs or impose one's will on others should be rejected.

B. The process of change should reflect the spirit of equality, openness, transparency, and inclusiveness. It should enhance the representation and speaking rights of developing countries. When encountering differences, they should be resolved through consultation and not through exclusive cliques or imposing on others.

C. The process of reform should reflect the spirit of equality, openness, transparency and inclusiveness, increase the representation and voice of developing countries, and resolve differences through consultation, instead of forming a small circle or imposing on others.

130.百舸争流,奋楫者先。

A. In a boat race, those who row the hardest will win.

B. The one who strives first in a hundred boats competing for the flow.

C. Hundreds of competitors are competing with each other, and those who strive for success are the first.

131.一副药方不可能包治百病,一种模式也不可能解决所有国家的问题。

A. Just as one does not expect a single prescription to cure all diseases, one should not expect a particular model of development to fit all countries.

B. A prescription cannot cure all diseases, and one model cannot solve all problems in every country.

C. A prescription cannot cure all diseases, nor can a model solve the problems of all countries.

132."明镜所以照形,古事所以知今。"

A. An ancient Chinese philosopher observed that "one needs to clean the mirror before taking a look at oneself, and should learn the lessons of the past before making the decisions of today".

B. "A clear mirror reflects one's appearance, ancient events help us understand the present."

C. "The mirror reflects the form, and the past knows the present."

133.他山之石，可以攻玉。

A. As a Chinese saying goes, a stone taken from another mountain may serve as a tool to polish the local jade—advice from others may help remedy one's own shortcomings.

B. The stone from another mountain can be used to polish jade.

C. Stones from other hills can be used to polish jade.

134.文明的繁盛、人类的进步，离不开求同存异、开放包容，离不开文明交流、互学互鉴。

A. The flourishing of civilization and the progress of humanity will not be possible without enhancing common ground, openness, inclusiveness, exchanges and mutual learning among civilizations, and agreeing to disagree.

B. The prosperity of civilization and the progress of humanity cannot be separated from seeking common ground while reserving differences, being open and inclusive, and engaging in cultural exchanges and mutual learning.

C. The prosperity of civilization and the progress of mankind are inseparable from seeking common ground while reserving differences, openness and tolerance, and from civilized exchanges and mutual learning.

135.国家的希望、民族的未来在青年。

A. The young are the hope of the country and the future of the nation.

B. The hope of the country and the future of the nation lie in the youth.

C. The hope of the country and the future of the nation lie in the youth.

136.回顾历史，是为了启迪今天、昭示明天。

A. By reviewing the past, we can draw inspiration for both the present and the future.

B. Looking back on history is to enlighten today and illuminate tomorrow.

C. Looking back on history is to enlighten today and show tomorrow.

137.行百里者半九十。

A. As our ancestors said, "On reaching the last leg of a journey, one is only half way there."

B. The journey of a hundred miles begins with the first step.

C. Half of the people who travel a hundred miles are ninety.

138.只有并肩同行,才能让绿色发展理念深入人心、全球生态文明之路行稳致远。

A. Only concerted efforts can drive home the idea of green development and bring about steady progress in building a global eco-civilization.

B. Only by walking side by side can we make the green development concept deeply rooted in people's hearts and the global ecological civilization road stable and far-reaching.

C. Only by walking side by side can the concept of green development be deeply rooted in the hearts of the people and the road of global ecological civilization be stable and far-reaching.

139.奉法者强则国强,奉法者弱则国弱。

A. A country is strong when its law enforcement is strong; it is weak when its law enforcement is weak.

B. Those who abide by the law are strong, and those who do not abide by the law are weak.

C. Those who obey the law are strong and the country is strong; those who obey the law are weak and the country is weak.

140.民之所好好之,民之所恶恶之。

A. We should choose to do the things that win the approval of the people, and avoid doing things that they oppose.

B. People like what is good, and people dislike what is bad.

C. What the people like is good, and what the people hate is bad.

141.人心是最大的政治。

A. The people's support is our top political priority.

B. The people's hearts are the greatest politics.

C. People's hearts are the greatest politics.

142."快递小哥"工作很辛苦,起早贪黑、风雨无阻,越是节假日越忙碌,像勤劳的小蜜蜂,是最辛勤的劳动者,为大家生活带来了便利。

A. Couriers of express delivery services work very hard, rising early and working long into the night, regardless of the weather. They can be particularly busy on weekends and during holidays. Just like bees, they are the hardest-working people, making our lives easier.

B. "Delivery drivers" work very hard, getting up early and working late, rain or shine. They are busiest during holidays, like diligent bees, they are the hardest workers, bringing convenience to everyone's lives.

C. "Courier brother" work very hard, from dawn to dusk, rain or shine, the more holidays the more busy, like hard-working bees, is the most hard-working workers, bringing convenience to everyone's life.

143.要在奋斗中摸爬滚打,体察世间冷暖、民众忧乐、现实矛盾,从中找到人生真谛、生命价值、事业方向。

A. You are expected to go through hardships, understand what life entails, get to know people's concerns and real problems, and identify the true meaning and value of life and work.

B. To struggle and experience the ups and downs of the world, the joys and sorrows of the people, and the contradictions of reality, to find the true meaning of life, the value of life, and the direction of one's career.

C. In the struggle, we should experience the warmth and coldness of the world, the worries and joys of the people, and the contradictions in reality, from which we can find the true meaning of life, the value of life and the direction of our career.

144.面对复杂的世界大变局,要明辨是非、恪守正道,不人云亦云、盲目跟风。

A. Faced with a complex and changing international landscape, young people must differentiate between truth and falsehood and keep to the right path, and never blindly follow what others say or do.

B. In the face of the complex changes in the world，we should discern right from wrong，adhere to the right path，and not follow the crowd or blindly follow trends.

C. In the face of complex changes in the world，we should distinguish right from wrong，abide by the right path，and not blindly follow the trend.

145.人无德不立,品德是为人之本。

A. A person cannot succeed without virtues. This makes morality essential.

B. A man cannot stand without virtue，and moral character is the foundation of being a man.

C. A man cannot stand without virtue，and moral character is the foundation of being a man.

146.鲁迅先生说,青年"所多的是生力,遇见深林,可以辟成平地的,遇见旷野,可以栽种树木的,遇见沙漠,可以开掘井泉的"。

A. As Lu Xun the great writer said，young people "have strength to spare；they can turn a dense forest into flat land，plant trees in the wilderness，and dig wells in the desert".

B. Mr. Lu Xun said，"The youth have abundant vitality. When they encounter deep forests，they can turn them into flat land. When they encounter wilderness，they can plant trees. When they encounter deserts，they can dig wells."

C. Mr. Lu Xun said that young people "have a lot of vitality. When they meet a deep forest，they can open up a flat land. When they meet a wilderness，they can plant trees，and when they meet a desert，they can dig wells and springs".

147.对每一个中国人来说,爱国是本分,也是职责,是心之所系、情之所归。

A. Love of our country，the feeling of devotion and sense of attachment to our motherland is a duty and responsibility for every Chinese.

B. For every Chinese person，loving the country is a duty and responsibility，it is where the heart and emotions belong.

C. For every Chinese，patriotism is a duty，a duty，a heart and a feeling.

148.青年志存高远,就能激发奋进潜力,青春岁月就不会像无舵之舟漂泊不定。

A. High ambitions can stimulate your potential to forge ahead, so that you will not drift aimlessly like a boat without a rudder.

B. Young people with lofty ambitions can unleash their potential for progress, and their youthful years will not be adrift like a rudderless boat.

C. If young people have lofty aspirations, they can stimulate their potential to forge ahead, and their youth will not drift like a rudderless boat.

149.古人讲:"文章合为时而著,歌诗合为事而作。"

A. As an ancient Chinese poet said, "Prose and poetry are composed to reflect the times and reality."

B. The ancients said: "Articles are written according to the times, songs and poems are created according to the events."

C. The ancients said: "Articles are written for the time, songs and poems are written for the matter."

150.正本清源、守正创新,一个国家、一个民族不能没有灵魂,作为精神事业,文化文艺、哲学社会科学当然就是一个灵魂的创作,一是不能没有,一是不能混乱。

A. A nation must have a soul that captures our fine traditions. As cerebral undertakings, literature, art, philosophy and social sciences are creations of the soul; they are indispensable and must never go astray.

B. Returning to the original source and upholding tradition while promoting innovation, a country and a nation cannot be without a soul. As a spiritual endeavor, cultural arts, philosophy, and social sciences are undoubtedly the creation of a soul. They are indispensable and must not be confused or disordered.

C. As a spiritual cause, culture, literature and art, philosophy and social sciences are of course the creation of a soul, one can not be without, the other can not be confused.

附录 2　Python 代码

说明：涉及 txt 的代码，txt 默认为 UTF-8 编码。

(1)docx 文件转 txt 文件

```python
import os
import glob
import docx2txt


# 获取当前目录下所有 doc 和 docx 文件
doc_files= glob.glob("* .doc")+ glob.glob("* .docx")
for doc_file in doc_files:
    # 将 doc 和 docx 文件转换为 txt 文件
    text= docx2txt.process(doc_file)
    # 获取文件名(不带后缀)
    file_name= os.path.splitext(doc_file)[0]
    # 将文件编码转换为 utf-8
    text= text.encode('utf-8')
    # 将 txt 文件保存到同目录下
    with open(file_name + '.txt', 'wb')as f:
        f.write(text)
```

(2)doc 文件转 docx 文件

```python
import os
import win32com.client
from docx import Document


# 获取当前目录下的 doc 文件列表
doc_files= [filename for filename in os.listdir('.')if filename.ends-
with('.doc')]
```

```
# 创建 Word 应用程序对象
word= win32com.client.Dispatch('Word.Application')
# 循环遍历 doc 文件列表
for doc_file in doc_files:
    # 打开 doc 文件
    doc= word.Documents.Open(os.path.abspath(doc_file))
    # 将 doc 文件保存为 docx 文件
    doc.SaveAs(os.path.abspath(doc_file + 'x'), FileFormat= 16)
```

(3)html 文件转 txt 文件

```
import os
import html


# 获取当前目录下所有 html 文件
html_files= [f for f in os.listdir('.')if f.endswith('.html')]
for html_file in html_files:
    # 获取文件名(不带后缀)
    file_name= os.path.splitext(html_file)[0]
    # 读取 html 文件内容
    with open(html_file, 'r', encoding= 'utf-8')as f:
        content= f.read()
    # 将 html 内容转换为 txt
    txt_content= html.unescape(content).replace('< br> ', '\n')
    # 删除 html 标记
    txt_content= txt_content.replace('< html> < body> ', '').replace
('< /body> < /html> ', '')
    # 将 txt 内容写入文件
    txt_file_name= file_name + '.txt'
    with open(txt_file_name, 'w', encoding= 'utf-8')as f:
        f.write(txt_content)
        print(f"Generated {txt_file_name}")
```

(4)txt 文件转 html 文件

```
import os
import html
```

```python
# 获取当前目录下所有 txt 文件
txt_files= [f for f in os.listdir('.')if f.endswith('.txt')]
for txt_file in txt_files:
    # 获取文件名(不带后缀)
    file_name= os.path.splitext(txt_file)[0]
    # 读取 txt 文件内容
    with open(txt_file, 'r', encoding= 'utf-8')as f:
        content= f.read()
    # 将 txt 内容转换为 html
    html_content= "< html> < body> " + html.escape(content).replace
('\n', '< br> ')+ "< /body> < /html> "
    # 将 html 内容写入文件
    html_file_name= file_name.replace(' ', '_')+ '.html'
    # 将空格替换为下划线
    with open(html_file_name, 'w', encoding= 'utf-8')as f:
        f.write(html_content)
        print(f"Generated {html_file_name}")
```

(5)txt 文件转 docx 文件

```python
import os
from docx import Document


# 获取当前目录下的 txt 文件列表
txt_files= [filename for filename in os.listdir('.')if filename.ends-
with('.txt')]
# 循环遍历 txt 文件列表
for txt_file in txt_files:
    # 打开 txt 文件
    with open(txt_file, 'r', encoding= 'utf-8')as f:
        txt_data= f.read()
    # 创建 Document 对象
    document= Document()
    # 添加段落
    document.add_paragraph(txt_data)
    # 保存 docx 文件
    docx_file= txt_file[:-4] + '.docx'
```

```
document.save(docx_file)
```

(6) 合并 docx 文件

```python
import os
import glob
from docx import Document


def combine_docx_files(output_filename):
    combined_document= Document()
    for input_filename in glob.glob('* .docx'):
        if input_filename ! = output_filename:
            # 添加文件名作为新段落
            combined_document.add_paragraph(input_filename)
            # 读取文件内容并添加到合并后的文件
            input_document= Document(input_filename)
            for paragraph in input_document.paragraphs:
                text= paragraph.text
                combined_document.add_paragraph(text)
    # 保存合并后的文件
    combined_document.save(output_filename)
if __name__ = = "__main__":
    combine_docx_files("combined.docx")
```

(7) 合并 xlsx(excel) 文件

```python
import os
import glob
import pandas as pd


def combine_excel_files(output_filename):
    all_data_frames= []
    for input_filename in glob.glob('* .xlsx'):
        if input_filename ! = output_filename:
            # 读取 Excel 文件内容
            input_data_frame= pd.read_excel(input_filename)
            # 将数据添加到列表中
            all_data_frames.append(input_data_frame)
```

```python
    # 合并所有数据,使用 outer join 以保留所有列
    combined_data_frame= pd.concat(all_data_frames, axis= 0, ignore_
index= True, join= 'outer')
    # 保存合并后的文件
    combined_data_frame.to_excel(output_filename, index= False)
if __name__ = = "__main__":
    combine_excel_files("combined.xlsx")
```

(8)合并 txt 文件

```python
import os


# 获取当前目录下的所有文件
files= os.listdir()
# 筛选出所有 txt 文件
txt_files= [file for file in files if file.endswith(".txt")]
# 合并所有 txt 文件并写入 all.txt 文件
with open("all.txt", "w", encoding= "utf-8")as output_file:
    for txt_file in txt_files:
        with open(txt_file, "r", encoding= "utf-8")as input_file:
            content= input_file.read()
            output_file.write(content)
            output_file.write("\n")
# 添加一个换行符,以便区分不同文件的内容
print("所有 txt 文件已合并为 all.txt")
```

(9)删除 txt 文件中的空格

```python
import os
import re


# 获取当前目录中的所有 txt 文件
files= [f for f in os.listdir()if f.endswith('.txt')]
# 遍历文件列表
for file in files:
    # 读取文件内容
    with open(file, 'r', encoding= 'utf-8')as f:
        content= f.read()
```

```
# 删除英文单词之间的多余空格
content= re.sub(r'\s+ ', ' ', content)
# 删除中文字符之间的空格
content= re.sub(r'([\u4e00-\u9fa5])\s+ |(\s+ [\u4e00-\u9fa5])', r
'\1\2', content)
# 将内容写回文件
with open(file, 'w', encoding= 'utf-8')as f:
    f.write(content)
print("All txt files in the current directory have been processed.")
```

(10)txt 文件转 UTF-8 编码

```
import os
import codecs
import chardet


def convert_to_utf8(file_path):
    with open(file_path, 'rb')as f:
        content= f.read()
        detect_result= chardet.detect(content)
        original_encoding= detect_result['encoding']
        if original_encoding ! = 'utf-8':
            try:
                decoded_content= content.decode(original_encoding)
                with open(file_path, 'w', encoding= 'utf-8')as f:
                    f.write(decoded_content)
                    print(f'File {file_path} has been converted from
{original_encoding} to utf-8.')
            except Exception as e:
                print(f'Error encountered: {e}')
        else:
            print(f'File {file_path} is already in utf-8 format. Skipped.')
    if __name__ = = '__main__':
        current_directory= os.path.dirname(os.path.realpath(__file__))
        for root, _, files in os.walk(current_directory):
            for file in files:
                if file.endswith('.txt'):
```

```
    file_path= os.path.join(root, file)
    convert_to_utf8(file_path)
```

(11)txt 文件转 ANSI 编码

```
import os
import chardet


# 获取当前目录中的所有 txt 文件
files= [f for f in os.listdir()if f.endswith('.txt')]
# 遍历文件列表
for file in files:
    # 读取文件内容并检测编码
    with open(file, 'rb')as f:
        content= f.read()
        detected_encoding= chardet.detect(content)['encoding']
    # 如果检测到的编码不是 GBK,则进行转换
    if detected_encoding.lower()! = 'gbk':
        # 转换为 GBK 编码
        content_gbk= content.decode(detected_encoding, errors= 'ignore').encode('gbk')
        # 将内容写回文件
        with open(file, 'wb')as f:
            f.write(content_gbk)
    print("All txt files in the current directory have been converted to ANSI (GBK)encoding.")
```

(12)txt 文件转 Unicode 编码

```
import os
import chardet


# 获取当前目录中的所有 txt 文件
files= [f for f in os.listdir()if f.endswith('.txt')]
# 遍历文件列表
for file in files:
    # 读取文件内容并检测编码
    with open(file, 'rb')as f:
```

```
content= f.read()
detected_encoding= chardet.detect(content)['encoding']
```
如果检测到的编码不是 UTF-16,则进行转换
```
if detected_encoding.lower()! = 'utf-16':
```
    # 转换为 UTF-16 编码
```
     content_utf16= content.decode(detected_encoding).encode('utf-16')
```
    # 将内容写回文件
```
    with open(file, 'wb')as f:
        f.write(content_utf16)
print("All txt files in the current directory have been converted to
UTF-16 encoding.")
```

(13)左右对齐双语单文件转为单语双文件

说明:将同目录下的双语单文件(格式为原文制表符译文)拆分为原文及译文两个文件。支持批量操作。

```
import os

def split_txt_files():
    # 获取当前目录下的所有文件
    files= os.listdir()
    # 遍历所有文件
    for file in files:
        # 判断是否为 txt 文件
        if file.endswith(".txt"):
            # 获取文件名(不含扩展名)
            file_name= os.path.splitext(file)[0]
            # 打开文件,按行读取内容
            with open(file, "r", encoding= "utf-8")as f:
                lines= f.readlines()
            # 分别保存原文和译文的内容
            original_text= []
            translated_text= []
            # 按行处理原文与译文
            for line in lines:
                if "\t" in line:
```

```
                original, translated= line.split("\t", 1)
                original_text.append(original.strip())
                translated_text.append(translated.strip())
            # 将原文和译文写入新的文件
            with open(f"{file_name}_原文.txt", "w", encoding= "utf-8")
as f:
                f.write("\n".join(original_text))
            with open(f"{file_name}_译文.txt", "w", encoding= "utf-8")
as f:
                f.write("\n".join(translated_text))
    # 调用函数进行拆分
    split_txt_files()
```

(14)上下对齐双语单文件转为单语双文件

```
import os
def split_txt_files():
    # 获取当前目录下的所有文件
    files= os.listdir()
    # 遍历所有文件
    for file in files:
        # 判断是否为 txt 文件
        if file.endswith(".txt"):
            # 获取文件名(不含扩展名)
            file_name= os.path.splitext(file)[0]
            # 打开文件,按行读取内容
            with open(file, "r", encoding= "utf-8")as f:
                lines= f.readlines()
            # 分别保存原文和译文的内容
            original_text= []
            translated_text= []
            # 按行处理原文与译文
            for index, line in enumerate(lines):
                if index % 2 = = 0:
                    original_text.append(line.strip())
                else:
                    translated_text.append(line.strip())
```

```
        # 将原文和译文写入新的文件
        with open(f"{file_name}_原文.txt", "w", encoding= "utf-8")as f:
            f.write("\n".join(original_text))
        with open(f"{file_name}_译文.txt", "w", encoding= "utf-8")as f:
            f.write("\n".join(translated_text))
# 调用函数进行拆分
split_txt_files()
```

(15)原文及译文位置互换

说明:文本行的格式为原文制表符译文。

```
import os


def swap_text_in_files():
    # 获取当前目录下的所有文件
    files= os.listdir()
    # 遍历所有文件
    for file in files:
        # 判断是否为 txt 文件
        if file.endswith(".txt"):
            # 打开文件,按行读取内容
            with open(file, "r", encoding= "utf-8")as f:
                lines= f.readlines()
            # 保存互换位置后的文本内容
            swapped_text= []
            # 按行处理原文与译文
            for line in lines:
                if "\t" in line:
                    original, translated= line.split("\t", 1)
                    swapped_text.append(f"{translated.strip()}\t{original.strip()}")
            # 将互换位置后的文本写回原文件
            with open(file, "w", encoding= "utf-8")as f:
                f.write("\n".join(swapped_text))
    # 调用函数进行位置互换
    swap_text_in_files()
```

(16)左右对齐转为上下对齐

```python
import os

def split_text_in_files():
    # 获取当前目录下的所有文件
    files= os.listdir()
    # 遍历所有文件
    for file in files:
        # 判断是否为 txt 文件
        if file.endswith(".txt"):
            # 打开文件,按行读取内容
            with open(file, "r", encoding= "utf-8")as f:
                lines= f.readlines()
            # 保存拆分后的文本内容
            split_text= []
            # 按行处理原文与译文
            for line in lines:
                if "\t" in line:
                    original, translated= line.split("\t", 1)
                    split_text.append(original.strip())
                    split_text.append(translated.strip())
            # 将拆分后的文本写回原文件
            with open(file, "w", encoding= "utf-8")as f:
                f.write("\n".join(split_text))
# 调用函数进行拆分
split_text_in_files()
```

(17)上下对齐转为左右对齐

```python
def merge_text_in_files():
    # 获取当前目录下的所有文件
    files= os.listdir()
    # 遍历所有文件
    for file in files:
        # 判断是否为 txt 文件
        if file.endswith(".txt"):
```

```
# 打开文件,按行读取内容
with open(file, "r", encoding= "utf-8")as f:
    lines= f.readlines()
# 保存合并后的文本内容
merged_text= []
# 按行处理文本
for i in range(0, len(lines)-1, 2):
    line1= lines[i].strip()
    line2= lines[i + 1].strip()
    merged_text.append(f"{line1}\t{line2}")
# 若原文件有奇数行,将最后一行单独添加
if len(lines)% 2 ! = 0:
    merged_text.append(lines[-1].strip())
# 将合并后的文本写回原文件
with open(file, "w", encoding= "utf-8")as f:
    f.write("\n".join(merged_text))
# 调用函数进行合并
merge_text_in_files()
```

(18)词语批量查询

说明:将一个词表文件(expressions.txt)与 py 文件放在同一目录下,将待检索的 txt 文件(支持多个)也放在该目录下。运行 py 文件,则可将词表文件中的全部词条逐一在全部待检索的 txt 中查询,匹配结果会输出到一个 html 表格中。表格分四列,第一列为序号,第二列为词条,第三列为词条匹配的行的全文,第四列为匹配行所在文件。该代码可用于检测学习者译文的术语使用情况,也可查询译文中成语或其他特定词语的使用情况,也可查询原文中特定词语的出现情况,均视乎词表文件而定。

```
import os

def search_expressions_in_files():
    # 获取当前目录下的所有文件
    files= os.listdir()
    # 读取 expressions.txt 中的词语
    with open("expressions.txt", "r", encoding= "utf-8")as f:
        expressions= [line.strip()for line in f.readlines()]
```

```python
    # 初始化结果列表
    results= []
    # 遍历所有文件
    for file in files:
        # 判断是否为 txt 文件,且排除 expressions.txt
        if file.endswith(".txt") and file ! = "expressions.txt":
            # 打开文件,按行读取内容
            with open(file, "r", encoding= "utf-8") as f:
                lines= f.readlines()
            # 在每个文件中搜索词语
            for idiom in expressions:
                for index, line in enumerate(lines):
                    if idiom in line.strip():
                        results.append((idiom, index + 1, line.strip
(), file))
    # 输出结果到 html 表格中
    with open("expressions_in_files.html", "w", encoding= "utf-8")
as f:
        f.write("< html> < head> < meta charset= 'utf-8'> < style> ta-
ble, th, td {border: 1px solid black; border-collapse: collapse;} th, td
{padding: 15px;text-align: left;}< /style> < /head> < body> < table> ")
        f.write("< tr> < th> 序号< /th> < th> 词语< /th> < th> 所在行
< /th> < th> 文件名< /th> < /tr> ")

        for index, result in enumerate(results, start= 1):
            f.write(f"< tr> < td> {index}< /td> < td> {result[0] }< /
td> < td> {result[2] }< /td> < td> {result[3] }< /td> < /tr> ")

        f.write("< /table> < /body> < /html> ")
    # 调用函数进行搜索和输出
    search_expressions_in_files()
```

附录 3　个案原文、参考译文及机器译文

说明： 此附录包括第 5～8 章个案原文、参考译文及机器译文。机器译文除小牛机译外，还提供了两种 AIGC 译文（以 360 智脑及讯飞星火为主，个别为 WPS AI）作为参照。

第五章

个案 1

原文：

> 杨铁心转头去看骑在马后的李氏，要瞧她在战斗之中有无受伤，突然间树丛中射出一枝冷箭，杨铁心不及闪避，这一箭直透后心。
>
> 李氏大惊，叫道："叔叔，箭！箭！"
>
> 杨铁心心中一凉："不料我今日死在这里！但我死前先得把贼兵杀散，好让大嫂逃生。"当时包惜弱被丈夫推开，心中痛如刀割，转眼间官兵追了上来，待要闪躲，早被几名兵士拥上一匹坐骑。
>
> 包惜弱吞声饮泣，心中只是挂念丈夫，不知他性命如何。
>
> 这时天色已明，路上渐有行人，百姓见到官兵队伍，都远远躲了开去。

参考译文：

> Ironheart turned to check that Lily Li was unhurt. At that moment, an arrow whistled through the air towards him and buried itself in his back.
>
> "Brother!" Lily Li cried.
>
> It felt like ice piercing his heart. So this is it, Ironheart said to himself. But I must defeat these men first, so Lily can escape.
>
> The moment her Ironheart had pushed her away, Charity felt as if her

heart had been sliced in two by her husband's own blade. The soldiers were upon her within seconds. There was no escape.

Charity tried to swallow her tears. What had happened to her husband?

The sun had now risen. People started to appear on the road, but they slipped away again at the sight of the soldiers.

360 智脑译文：

Yang Tiexin turned to look at Li Li who was riding behind the horse. He wanted to see if she had been injured in the fight. Suddenly, a cold arrow shot out from the tree 丛 and hit him in the back without his being able to avoid it.

Li Li was surprised and called out, "Uncle, an arrow! An arrow!"

Yang Tiexin felt sorry for himself: "I'm going to die today! But I must kill all of these bandits first so that my wife can escape." At that moment, Bao Xiulan was pushed aside by her husband, and she felt terrible pain.

In no time, the government forces came up, and Bao Xiulan was carried on a horse. She wept silently, only worrying about her husband's safety.

It was already daybreak, and there were more and more people on the road. The citizens saw the government forces and ran away as far as they could.

小牛机译：

Yang Tiexin turned to see Lee riding behind the horse to see if she was injured in the battle. Suddenly, a cold arrow was shot from the trees. Yang Tiexin couldn't dodge, and the arrow went straight through the back heart.

Lee was frightened and cried, "Uncle, arrow! Arrow!"

Yang Tiexin's heart cooled: "Unexpectedly, I died here today! But before I die, I have to kill the thieves so that my eldest sister-in-law can escape." At that time, Bao Xiruo was pushed away by her husband, and her heart was as painful as a knife. In a twinkling of an eye, officers and men caught up, waiting to dodge, and several soldiers had already held a mount.

Bao Xiwei swallowed his voice and wept, but he just missed his husband and didn't know how his life was.

At this time, it was already bright, and there were pedestrians on the road. When the people saw the officers and men, they all hid far away.

讯飞星火译文：

Yang Tiexin turned his head to look at Li Shi, who was riding behind him, to see if she had been injured in the battle. Suddenly, a cold arrow shot from the bushes and Yang Tiexin could not dodge in time. The arrow went straight through his heart.

Li Shi was shocked and shouted, "Uncle, arrow! Arrow!"

Yang Tiexin felt a chill in his heart: "I didn't expect to die here today! But before I die, I need to kill off the bandits and let my wife escape." At that moment, Bao Xueluo was pushed away by her husband, feeling as painful as a knife cutting her heart. In an instant, the soldiers chased them up and before they could dodge, several soldiers grabbed onto one of their horses.

Bao Xueluo choked back tears and only thought about her husband, not knowing what happened to him.

By this time, it was already morning and there were people on the road. When the common people saw the army of officers and soldiers, they all hid far away.

个案 2

原文：

愚公移山①

北山愚公者,年且九十,面山而居。

惩山北之塞,出入之迂也,聚室而谋曰:"吾与汝毕力平险,指通豫南,达于汉阴,可乎?"

杂然相许。

其妻献疑曰:"以君之力,曾不能损魁父之丘,如太形、王屋何?且焉置土石?"

———————————

① 有删减。

杂曰："投诸渤海之尾,隐土之北。"

遂率子孙,荷担者三夫,叩石垦壤,箕畚运于渤海之尾。

河曲智叟笑而止之,曰："甚矣,汝之不惠!

以残年余力,曾不能毁山之一毛,其如土石何?"

操蛇之神闻之,惧其不已也,告之于帝。

帝感其诚,命夸蛾氏二子负二山,一厝朔东,一厝雍南。

参考译文:

The Foolish Old Man Removes the Mountains

The Foolish Old Man of the North Mountain, nearly ninety years of age, lived behind these mountains.

He was unhappy about the fact that the mountains blocked his way to the south and he had to walk round them whenever he went out or came back, so he called the whole family together to talk about the matter. "What would you say," he said to them, "if I suggest that all of us work hard to level the two mountains, so as to open a way to places south of Yu Prefecture and the Han River?"

Many voices said that they agreed to the idea.

But his wife had her doubts. "With your strength," she said, "you could hardly remove a small hill like Kuifu. What could you do with the Taihang and Wangwu Mountains?

"Carry them to the shores of the Bohai Sea and north of Yintu," said several people.

The old man, helped by his son and grandson who could carry things, began to break rocks and dig earth, which they carried in baskets and dustbins to the shores of the Bohai Sea.

The Wise Old Man at the River Bend stopped the old man. He laughed and said, "How unwise you are!

At your age, old and feeble as you are, you cannot remove one hair on the mountain, let alone so much earth and so many rocks!"

The old man's words were heard by a god with snakes in his hands. He was afraid that the old man would really level the two mountains, and reported the whole things to the Heavenly God.

Moved by the old man's determination, the Heavenly God ordered the two sons of Kua'eshi to carry the two mountains on their backs and put one east of Shuo and the other south of Yong.

360 智脑译文：

The Old Man of the North Mountain

The old man of the north mountain, who was nearly ninety years old and faced the mountain, lived there.

He felt frustrated at the blocked access from the north and decided to clear the obstacles by uniting with his family. They discussed the plan and agreed unanimously.

His wife, however, had doubts, asking if they could really destroy Mount Chives or Mount Tai, let alone dispose of the earth and stones.

They decided to throw the earth and stones into the Bohai Sea at the tail end of the Shandong Peninsula.

The river-bank wise old man laughed at them, saying, "You are too foolish! You cannot damage an inch of the mountain with your remaining strength. How will you deal with the earth and stones?"

A snake handler heard about this and feared that the old man would continue to cause trouble, so she informed the emperor of heaven.

The emperor was impressed by the old man's sincerity and ordered two sons of the goddess Kāimu to carry two mountains to places in the North, one at the Shandong Peninsula and the other at the Yangtze River Delta.

小牛机译：

Yugong Yishan

The North Mountain Yugong, who was 90 years old, was living in the mountain.

He was punished for the blockage of the northern part of the mountain and the circuitous access to it, so he gathered in his room and said, "I will work with you to level the danger, and point to the south of Yu and reach Hanyin.

He agreed to do so.

His wife offered doubt: "with the power of the gentleman, had not been able to damage the mound of Kui father, such as too shape, Wang House what? And how to put earth and stone?"

He said, "I will throw it at the end of the Bohai Sea, the north of the hidden earth."

So he led his sons and grandsons, three people with a load, knocking on the stone to reclaim the soil, dustpan transport in the end of the Bohai Sea.

Hequ wise man laughed and stopped him, said: "very much, you do not benefit!

With the remaining strength of the remaining years, had not been able to destroy one of the hairs of the mountain, which is like the earth and stone?"

When the god of the snake heard this, he was afraid that it would not stop and told the emperor.

The emperor felt his sincerity and ordered the two sons of Kua Moth to bear two mountains, one in Shuo East and one in Yong South.

讯飞星火译文：

The Foolish Old Man Who Removed the Mountains

There was an old man living in the north of a mountain called Yugong. He was ninety years old and lived facing the mountain. He complained about the inconvenience of having to go through the mountains when going to and from his home, so he gathered his family and said, "Can we work together to level the mountain and connect Yunan to Hanyin?" His family agreed.

His wife had doubts and asked, "With your strength, can you really move a mountain as big as Qiufu or Wangwu? How will you transport all the soil and rocks?" Others chimed in, saying, "We'll throw them into the ocean at the end of the Bohai Sea and dig up the earth on the northern side of the mountains."

So they started working with three men carrying burdens, digging and carrying soil and stones to the end of the Bohai Sea, where an old man named Zhisou laughed at them and said, "You are so foolish! With your remaining remaining strength in your old age, how can you even move a single grain of sand from that mountain? What use will it be for you?"

The god of snakes heard their story and feared that they would never stop, so he told the emperor. The emperor was moved by their sincerity and ordered two sons of Kua'o to carry the two mountains one to SE Dongyang and one to SE Yongnan.

第六章

个案 1

原文:

The Chinese are comparatively a temperate people.

This is owing principally to the universal use of tea, but also to taking their arrack very warm and at their meals, rather than to any notions of sobriety or dislike of spirits.

Chinese moralists have always inveighed against the use of spirits, and the name of I-tih, the reputed inventor of the deleterious drink, more than two thousand years before Christ, has been handed down with opprobrium, as he was himself banished by the great Yu for his discovery.

The "Shu King" contains a discourse by the Lord of Chau on the abuse of spirits.

His speech to his brother Fung, B.C. 1120, is the oldest temperance address on record, even earlier than the words of Solomon in the Proverbs.

参考译文:

中国人是比较温和的民族。

这主要由于普遍饮茶,也由于吃饭时喝很热的烧酒,而不是由于节制的观念或不喜欢烈性酒。

中国道德家一贯猛烈抨击饮酒,这种有害饮料的发明人是早于基督 2000 多年的著名的仪狄,一直受到责骂,他自己因这一发明而被大禹放逐。

《书经》有一篇周公谴责饮酒的训话。

他于公元前 1120 年对弟弟封的讲话是最古老的关于戒酒训词的记录，早于《箴言》中所罗门说的话。

360 智脑译文：

中国人相对节制。

这主要是因为茶的普遍使用，但还因为喝他们的酒很热，而且在吃饭时，而不是任何关于清醒或讨厌酒精的概念。

中国的伦理家一直反对饮酒，而据称是有害饮料的发明者伊提（I-tih）的名字在基督两千年前就被流传下来，因为他自己被伟大的禹驱逐了。

《尚书》中包含一篇由周公之弟所发表的有关酗酒的演讲。他对他的兄弟丰说的公元前 1120 年的讲话是历史上最早的禁酒讲话之一，甚至比《箴言》中的话更早。

小牛机译：

中国人是一个比较温和的民族。

这主要是由于茶的普遍使用，但也是因为他们的 arrack 非常温暖，在他们吃饭时，而不是任何清醒的概念或不喜欢精神。

中国的道德家一直猛烈抨击烈酒的使用，而在公元前两千多年，这种有害饮料的著名发明者伊提的名字一直受到谴责，因为他自己也因为他的发现而被伟大的余放逐。

《蜀王》包含了周主关于虐灵的论述。

公元前 1120 年，他对哥哥冯的演讲是有记录以来最古老的禁酒演讲，甚至比《箴言》中所罗门的话还要早。

讯飞星火译文：

中国人相对来说是一个温和的民族。这主要是因为普遍使用茶叶，而且在用餐时喝温热的酒，而不是出于任何节制或厌恶烈性饮料的想法。中国的道德家一直反对饮酒，而据说发明有害饮料的伊提希（I-tih）的名字在基督诞生之前两千多年就已经传下来了，因为他本人因发现而被大禹流放。《书经》中记载了周公对烈性饮料的滥用进行的谴责。公元前 1120 年周公对他的兄弟冯（Fung）发表的演讲是现存最古老的节制言论，甚至早于所罗门在《箴言》中的话语。

第七章

个案 1

原文：

屠呦呦秉持的，不是好事者争论的

随着诺贝尔奖颁奖典礼的临近，持续 2 个月的"屠呦呦热"正在渐入高潮。

当地时间 7 日下午，屠呦呦在瑞典卡罗林斯卡学院发表题为"青蒿素——中医药给世界的一份礼物"的演讲，详细回顾了青蒿素的发现过程，并援引毛泽东的话称，中医药学"是一个伟大的宝库"。

对中医药而言，无论是自然科学"圣殿"中的这次演讲，还是即将颁发到屠呦呦手中的诺奖，自然都提供了极好的"正名"。

参考译文：

Dispersing the Shroud over Tu Youyou's Achievement

As the Nobel Prize Award Ceremony draws near, Tu Youyou's two months in the spotlight is reaching its crescendo.

On the afternoon of December 7, Tu delivered a speech entitled "Artemisinin—A Gift from Traditional Chinese Medicine to the World" at the Karolinska Institute in Sweden. Quoting Mao Zedong's saying that Chinese medicine and pharmacology is "a great treasure-house", Tu walked the audience through her breakthrough discovery of the anti-malarial compound artemisinin.

Both speeches, delivered in the Mecca of natural sciences, and the awarding of the Nobel Prize to Tu are celebrated as a vindication of traditional Chinese medicine (TCM).

360 智脑译文：

Tu Youyou upholds, not good for the dispute of those who are in favor.

With the Nobel Prize award ceremony approaching, the "Tu Youyou fever" has gradually entered its climax after two months.

On the afternoon of July 7th，Tu Youyou gave a speech titled "A Gift from Traditional Chinese Medicine to the World-Green Tea Extract" at the Karolinska Academy in Sweden，which detailed the discovery process of green tea extract and quoted Mao Zedong's words that traditional Chinese medicine is "a great treasure chest."

For traditional Chinese medicine，both the natural science "temple" this speech，as well as the Nobel Prize about to be awarded to Tu Youyou，naturally provide excellent "prominence."

小牛机译：

What Tu Youyou upholds is not debated by good people

With the Nobel Prize awarding ceremony approaching，the "Tu Youyou fever"，which lasted for two months，is gradually reaching a climax.

On the afternoon of 7th local time，Tu Youyou delivered a speech entitled "Artemisinin—A Gift of Chinese Medicine to the World" in Karolinska Institute，Sweden，reviewing the discovery process of artemisinin in detail，and quoting Mao Zedong as saying that Chinese medicine is "a great treasure house".

For Chinese medicine，both this speech in the "Temple" of natural science and the Nobel Prize to be awarded to Tu Youyou naturally provide an excellent "correct name".

讯飞星火译文：

What Tu Youyou upholds is not what the skeptics argue about.

As the Nobel Prize ceremony approaches，the two-month-long "Tu Youyou fever" is reaching its climax. On the afternoon of July 7th，Tu Youyou delivered a speech at the Karolinska Institute in Sweden titled "Artemisinin—a Gift from Traditional Chinese Medicine to the World"，which detailed the discovery process of artemisinin and quoted Mao Zedong as saying that traditional Chinese medicine is "a great treasure house".

For traditional Chinese medicine，whether it is this speech in the "sacred hall" of natural science or the upcoming Nobel Prize that will be awarded to Tu Youyou，nature has provided excellent "justification".

第八章

个案 1

原文：

Aesthetic Education and National Progress

The diminution of emphasis on the arts and the humanities and the corresponding increased emphasis on business and STEM disciplines (Science，Technology，Engineering，and Math) has resulted in a normative conception of national progress that excludes aesthetic education.

In this essay，I argue that aesthetic educators should challenge the normative understanding of national progress. (In the humanities，aesthetic educators typically are educators of English，foreign languages and literature，philosophy，art history and film studies.)

To this end，I call attention to the writings of the French philosopher Germaine de Staël (1766-1817) because in the adaptation of her notion of progress lies possible hope for the future of the humanities and the arts.

参考译文：

审美教育与国家进步

人文艺术渐受冷落，而商科和理工学科（STEM，指科学、技术、工程、数学等）却愈发受到重视，形成了一种将审美教育排除在外的国家进步观。

本文认为审美教育者应当对国家进步的这一习惯性理解提出挑战。（在人文领域，审美教育者通常指英文、外国语言文学、哲学、艺术史和影视研究等学科工作者。）

为此，本文呼吁关注法国哲学家斯达尔夫人（1766—1817）的著作，因为借鉴她的进步观或许可以找到人文艺术学科未来的希望。

WPS AI 译文：

美学教育与国家进步

减少对艺术和人文学科的重视，相应地增加了对商业和 STEM 学科（科学、技术、工程和数学）的重视，这导致了一种规范性的国家进步概念，排除了美学教育。

　　在这篇论文中,我认为美学教育者应该挑战对国家进步的规范性理解。(在人文学科中,美学教育者通常是英语、外语、文学、哲学、艺术史和电影研究的教育者。)

　　为此,我呼吁关注法国哲学家吉尔·德勒兹(1766—1817)的作品,因为在她的进步概念的适应中,可能存在着对人文学科和艺术未来的希望。

小牛机译:

美育与民族进步

　　对艺术和人文学科的重视减少,而对商业和 STEM 学科(科学、技术、工程和数学)的重视相应增加,导致了一种排斥美育的国家进步的规范性概念。

　　在这篇文章中,我认为审美教育者应该挑战对国家进步的规范性理解。(在人文学科中,审美教育者通常是英语、外国语言和文学、哲学、艺术史和电影研究的教育者。)

　　为此,我提请注意法国哲学家杰曼·德·斯塔尔(1766—1817)的著作,因为在她对进步概念的改编中,蕴含着人文和艺术未来的可能希望。

讯飞星火译文:

美学教育与国家进步

　　对艺术和人文学科的重视程度下降,相应地,商业和 STEM 学科(科学、技术、工程和数学)的强调增加,这导致了一种将美学教育排除在外的国家进步的规范概念。

　　在本文中,我主张美学教育者应该挑战国家进步的规范理解。(在人文学科中,美学教育者通常是英语、外语和文学、哲学、艺术史和电影研究的教育者。)

　　为此,我呼吁大家关注法国哲学家杰曼·德斯特尔(1766—1817)的著作,因为在她对进步的理解中的转化可能为人文学科和艺术的未来带来希望。

附录4　学习者译文样例

说明:此样例为一次汉译英训练的部分学习者译文。均保留原样,未修改。

原文:

愚公移山

北山愚公者,年且九十,面山而居。

惩山北之塞,出入之迂也,聚室而谋曰:"吾与汝毕力平险,指通豫南,达于汉阴,可乎?"

杂然相许。

其妻献疑曰:"以君之力,曾不能损魁父之丘,如太形、王屋何?

且焉置土石?"

杂曰:"投诸渤海之尾,隐土之北。"

遂率子孙,荷担者三夫,叩石垦壤,箕畚运于渤海之尾。

河曲智叟笑而止之,曰:"甚矣,汝之不惠!

以残年余力,曾不能毁山之一毛,其如土石何?"

操蛇之神闻之,惧其不已也,告之于帝。

帝感其诚,命夸蛾氏二子负二山,一厝朔东,一厝雍南。

学习者译文 1:

[1] Mr. Fool Wants to Move Away the Mountain

[2] Just to the north of the mountains lived an old man called Mr. Fool who was nearly 90 years old.

[3] He suffered from the obstruction of the mountain and had to take a detour to get out and go in, so he gathered the whole family to said, "Let's do our best to eradicate the treacherous mountains, so that the

road will go all the way to the southern part of Yuzhou and reach the southern bank of the Han River, okay?"

[4] Almost everyone agrees.

[5] His wife questioned: "With your strength, you can't even level the
small Kuifu mountain, what can you do to Taixing mountain and Wangwu mountain?

[6] and where will the excavated soil and stones be placed?"

[7] People said, "Throw them to the edge of the Bohai Sea, or north of the
Yintu."

[8] So Mr. Fool led three of his descendants to carry a load to the mountain, cut the stones, dug the earth, and carried it to the edge of the Bohai Sea with a dustpan.

[9] The wise old man on the river bank ridiculed Mr. Fool and stopped him
from doing this, saying, "You are really too stupid!

[10] With your remaining years and strength can not even move a blade of
grass on the mountain, and how about the soil and stones?

[11] The mountain god with the snake in his hand heard about this and,
fearing that Mr. Fool would not stop doing it, so he reported it to the
god of heaven.

[12] Moved by Mr. Fool's sincerity, the god of heaven ordered Hercules'
two sons to carry away the two mountains-one to the east of Shuo
Fang and one to the south of Yong Zhou

学习者译文 2：

[1] The Foolish Old Man Yu's Attempt to Removed the Mountains

[2] North of the mountains lived an old man called Yugong, who is nearly
ninety years old. His house is directly opposite the mountains.

[3] The inconvenience and detour of the mountain worried him a lot, so the
old man summoned his families one day and said, "Can we spare no efforts and work together to level the Taihang and Wangwu Mountain?
In this way, we can build a road from the south bank of Huai River to the

south of Han River."

[4] Almost every member in his family agreed,

[5] except his wife. She questioned, "You can not even remove the small hills like Quifu Hill, how could you remove the two big mountains?

[6] Besides, where can you dispose the rocks and soil moved from the mountain?"

[7] The family offered an answer- to dump them in the Bohai Sea, or on the Yintu District.

[8] The old man Yugong then set out with his son and grandson. They reclaimed the ground on the mountain, burdened with basketful of stones and earth every day, and carried them to Bohai Sea.

[9] A wise man called Zhisou, who lived at the river bend, thought they were so ridiculous and tried his best to stop them. He said, "It's extremely unwise!

[10]Old as you are, you can not even do any harm to the mountains, how can you remove the rocks and earth?"

[11] After hearing the whole thing, the Zunshen Immortal reported it to the Jade Emperor for fear that they will never give up.

[12] Moved by their persistency, the Jade Emperor ordered the two sons of Kuaeshi to carry the mountain and put them in Shuodong and Xiangnan respectively.

学习者译文 3：

[1] Yu Gong Moved the Mountain

[2] To the north of the mountains lived an old man called Yu Gong who was nearly 90 years old. Their house is surrounded by mountains.

[3] His house was stuck inside the two mountains, and he found it isn't convenient to make a detour each time when he went out and came back. So one day he gathered his family together and said, "Why don't we move the mountains so that we can open a road to the bank of the Han River."

[4] Then they all agreed.

[5] "Even a small hill like Kuifu is too immense for our strength, much less a mountain like Taihang or Wangwu."

[6] Besides, how to deal with the earth and rocks.

[7] "I can throw these stones into the Baha'i Sea.

[8] Therefore, he led his descendants, three men who took the burden, knocked on the stone to reclaim the soil, and transported it to the end of Bohai Sea.

[9] A man named Zhi Sou saw them and laugh, and tried to stop him "you are too weak to move it."

[10] With the strength of the remaining years, one of the mountains could not be destroyed. What is it like earth and stone?"

[11] The god of snakes, fearing it, told the emperor.

[12] The emperor was moved by their faith, ordering two sons of Kuae's to carry the two mountains, one to east Shuo, another to south Yong.

学习者译文 4：

[1] Yu Gong, the Foolish Old Man Removes the Mountains.

[2] In the Bei Mountain, there was a foolish old man, Yu Gong, who was nearly ninety years old, lived in front of the mountain.

[3] As a result of the blocking of the Bei Mountain, it took a long detour to get in and out. Yu Gong gathered his family and expected: "Could we try our best to deal with the mountain, making the road lead to the north of Yuzhou and reaching the south bank of the Han River.

[4] Most of his family members agreed with him.

[5] His wife questioned: "With your strength, you can't even cut down the hill like Kuifu, moreover the Taihang Mountain and Wangwu Mountain?

[6] Besides, where can we put the soil and stones?"

[7] Family members said: "Throwing the soil and stones to the edge of the Bohai Sea and the north of Yintu"

[8] So Yu Gong led his three sons and grandsons, three of them who could bear the carrying pole, gouging stones, digging soil and using the dustpan to send the soil to the edge of Bohai Sea.

[9] The wise old man at the river bend laugh at him and discourage:"How unwise you are!"

[10] With the strength of your remaining years, you can't even destroy one of the hairs of the mountain, not to mention the soil and stones?"

[11] The god of mountain heard about it, fearing that Yu Gong would not stop and really move the mountains, so he told the god of the heaven about this.

[12] The god was moved about his sincerity and ordered two sons of Kua'eshi to take the two mountains away, than put one mountain on the east of Shuofang, another on the north of Yongzhou.

学习者译文 5:

[1] The Foolish Old Man Yugong Removed the Mountains

[2] There was a foolish man nearly ninety years old, living in the foot of northern mountain which was directly opposite two big mountains.

[3] He was distressed that the road to the north of the mountain was blocked and he had to take a long way out and in. He called his families together and said, "Shall we try our best to dig up the two mountains so that we can reach the southern part of Yuzhou and Han River?"

[4] Most of them agreed to it.

[5] His wife questioned and asked, "With your power, you are not able to do something with a small mountain like Kui-Fu, what can you do with Taihang mountains?"

[6] Besides, where to put the soil and rocks?

[7] Everyone said, "Throw them to the edge of the Bohai Sea and the north of Yintu."

[8] Yugong then led three of his children and grandchildren who could carry a load. They cut rocks, dug soil, and transported them to the edge of

the Bohai Sea with a skip and dustpan.

[9] An wise man named Hequ laughed and stopped the foolish man, saying, "You are too unwise."

[10] With your remaining strength for the rest of your life, you can't destroy a small part of the mountain, and what can you do with the big mountains?

[11] The god of mountain holding the snake heard about this. He worried that the foolish man would keep digging, so he reported the incident to the emperor of heaven.

[12] Moved by his sincerity, the emperor of heaven ordered two Herculean gods of Kua'e clan, to carry the two mountains on their backs, one to the east of Shuo Fang and one to the south of Yong Zhou.

学习者译文 6:

[1] The Foolish Old Man Yugong Removes the Mountains

[2] Just to the north of the mountains lived an old man called YuGong who was nearly 90 years old.

[3] With the two high mountains just in front of his house, his family and he had to walk a long way around the mountains whenever they had something to do on the other side of the mountains. Yu Gong said to the whole amily, "These two mountains block the doorway of our house. It is very inconvenient for us to come and go. Let our whole family make every effot to remove away these two mountains. How about it?"

[4] Many voices said that they agreed to the idea.

[5] But his wife had her doubt and said, "Do you know how high these two mountains are? How can you move such big mountains?

[6] Where can you put all the stones and earth?"

[7] Everybody said, "So long as we work hard together, we can certainly move away these two mountains. We can carry the stones and earth of the mountains to the sea."

[8] The following day，YuGong led the Whole family and started to remove the mountains.

[9] When a shrewd old man named Zhi Sou saw YuGong's family removing the mountains. He said，"how unwise you are！"

[10] "You are so old that you can hardly walk. Can you remove the mountains?"

[11] Mountain Celestials heard the thing and worried that YuGong and his family won't stop to remove the mountains. Then he told the God about the thing.

[12] They finally touched the God who sent two celestials to the world to move away these two mountains，one in east，another one in south.

学习者译文 7:

[1] Yu Gong moved the mountain

[2] Just to the north of the mountains lived an old man called Yu Gong who was nearly 90 years old. With the mountains just in front of his house.

[3] His family and he had to walk a long way around the mountains whenever they had something to do on the other side of the mountains. One day, Yu Gong called all his family together to talk about how to move the two mountains to other places.

[4] They all agreed.

[5] His wife said, "An old man like you cannot even move a small hill, not to mention the two high mountains.

[6] Even if you can, where can you throw that much stone and dirt?"

[7] Yu Gong said："the end of Bohai Sea is big enough to contain all the stone and dirt."

[8] So he led his childrens，started to dig the mountains，and throw the stones and dirt to the end of Bohai.

[9] A man named Zhi Sou saw them working and tried to stop them，saying that："you are so silly, it's not good for you."

[10] You're so old and weak that you can't even take away the trees. How can you move the high mountain?"

[11] The god of the mountain heard about this, afraid he would keep digging, so he told to the god upon the sky.

[12] The god upon the sky heard YuGong's story, was greatly moved. He ordered another two god to come down and take the two high mountains away. One to the Shuodong, the other one to the Yongnan.

学习者译文 8：

[1] The Foolish Old Man (Yugong) Removes the Mountains

[2] The Foolish Old Man (Yugong) of the North Mountain, nearly ninety years of age, lived behind these mountains.

[3] Yugong found it was very inconvenient to go out. So he gathered his family members in a room to discuss the matter. "We should exert ourselves to remove two mountains out of our way to the south of Yu and the southern bank of Han River. What's your opinion?" said Yugong.

[4] Most of them agreed with him.

[5] But his wife was skeptical of his solution. She said "you are too weak to remove the hill of Kuifu. Not to mention the mountains like Taihang and Wangwu.

[6] Supposing you are strong enough to do it, where can you place the earth and stone?"

[7] Someone said "Throw it to the end of Bo Sea and the north of Ying area."

[8] The old man, helped by his son and grandson who could carry things, began to break rocks and dig earth, which they carried in baskets and dustbins to the shores of the Bohai Sea.

[9] The wise old man Zhisou at the River Bend laughed at Yugong and tried to prevent him from removing the mountains. "It is unwise to remove it." He said.

[10] With your weak body, you can't eliminate the grass in the mountains. How can you remove the earth and stone of the mountains?"

[11] When the God of mountains knew the thing that Yugong wanted to do, he was afraid that Yugong would not stop digging the mountains. So he told the king of the God that Yugong's planning of removing the mountains.

[12] The king of the God was touched by Yugong's sincerity. The king ordered two sons of Kua'eshi (a mighty God like Hercules) to take the mountains away. One took a mountain to the east of Shuozhou. The other took it to the south of Yongzhou.

学习者译文 9:

[1] Yugong Moves Mountains.

[2] The Yugong was ninety years old and lived in front of the mountain in the north of the mountain.

[3] For the fortress in the north of the mountain, and the roundabout way to get in and out, they gathered in the room and said: "I and you have done everything to pacify the danger, and access to the south of Henan to reach Hanyin, is it possible?"

[4] They make an agreement.

[5] His wife doubted on it and said, "With your power, you could never damage the hill of Kuifu, what about the mountain of Taixing and Wangwu.?

[6] And where to put earth and stones?"

[7] they said: "To put the end of the Bohai Sea, and hide them in the north of the land.

[8] Then he led his descendants, the three men who were carrying the load, to knock on the rocks and reclaim the soil, then transported the earth and stons to the end of the Bohai Sea.

[9] A smart elder in Hequ stopped laughing and said, "It's not good for you!"

[10] With the remaining years and energy, you could not destroy a little of the mountain, what about earth and stone?"

[11] The god who control snakes heard about it with fear, so he told the emperor.

[12] The emperor felt his sincerity, and ordered the two sons of the Kuwa clan to carry two mountains putting one in Shuodong and the other in Yongnan.

学习者译文 10：

[1] Yu Gong move mountains

[2] Yu Gong, aged ninety, lived in Bei mountain.

[3] Because of the difficult of entry, Yu Gong discussed with his wife, "How about we making effort to dig a road from Yu Nan to Han Yin?"

[4] They agreed.

[5] His wife put forward, "You can not move a small hill, how can you move the mountains?

[6] And even those soils and rocks?"

[7] He said, "We can rely on the end of Zhu Sea and move those soil to the north."

[8] Then he set off with grandsons and three stick men. They broke rocks and convey it to the end of Bo Sea.

[9] A man near the river laugh at them and said, "You guys are beat the air!

[10] Depending on you old people even can not broke one piece of the mountain, not to speak of those rocks!"

[11] After God of snake knowing that, he told it to the God of king out of afraid Yu Gong defeated.

[12] God of king was touched by Yu Gong's sincerity and then ask two son of E' to help them, which move one mountain to east and another to south.

学习者译文 11：

[1] Foolish Yugong Removes the Mountains

[2] North of these mountains lived an old man named Foolish Yugong, who was nearly ninety years old, and his house faced these mountains.

[3] He found it very inconvenient to make a detour, so one day he summoned his family to discuss the matter: "How about we work together to remove these mountains and open a road to the south of Yuzhou province and the south bank of the Han River?"

[4] Most of his family agreed.

[5] But his wife was dubious: "You have no strength to remove a small hill, how can you remove Tai-hang Mountain and Wangwu Mountain?

[6] Besides, where will you dump all the earth and rocks?"

[7] They replied: "We'll dump them into the edge of the Bohai Sea and the north of Yintu province."

[8] Then Foolish Yugong set out with three men of his sons and grandsons who can carry poles. They dug up stones and earth and carried them in baskets to the sea.

[9] A man living at the river bend called Wise Zhisou laughed at them: "How unwise you are!

[10] Old and weak as you are, you won't be able to remove even a small part of the mountains. How can you deal with so much earth and stones?"

[11] The mountain god heard it and so afraid of it, telling it to the Emperor of the Heaven.

[12] The Emperor of the Heaven was moved by his sincerity and ordered two sons of Kua'eshi, who is like Hercules, to remove two mountains. One was put in the east of Shuozhou province, and the other was put in the south of Yongzhou province.

学习者译文 12：

[1] Yugong removed the mountains

[2] Yu Gong, who is a ninety year old foolish man, lives on the north side and faces the mountain.

[3] It is necessary to detour when people want to go in and out of the mountain because the mountains block the road. So Yu Gong called the people together to discuss. He says: "We bulldoze the mountains together, make the road can straight to South Henan and south bank of Han River, can't we?"

[4] Most of them agree with this idea.

[5] His wife ask, "It is imposible to bulldoze the small hill like kuifu, how can you bulldoze The Taihang and Wangwu mountain?

[6] And how to deal with the stone?"

[7] He says, "I will throw it at the end of the Bohai Sea, the north of the Yintu."

[8] So he leads his three children, who are strong, digging the stone to reclaim the soil, using dustpan to transport the rock to the end of the Bohai Sea.

[9] The wise man on the bay mocked the foolish man and stopped him from doing this, saying, "It is not a wise method."

[10] Your weak strength can not even move a blade of grass on the mountain, and what can the soil and stones?

[11] The mountain god holding the snake heard about this and, fearing that he would dig on endlessly, reported it to the emperor

[12] Moved by Yugong's sincerity, the Emperor of Heaven ordered the two sons of Kua'e, the God of Power, to carry away the two mountains, one to the North East and one to the south of Yongzhou.

学习者译文 13：

[1] How the Fool moved the mountains

[2] There was an old man nearly ninety called the Fool lived in the face of the north of mountains.

[3] Founding very inconvenient to go out and back because of the complex terrain of the north mountain, one day the Fool gathered his family and suggested that they level the mountain and open a road to south of Henan,

reaches the Han River.

[4] They all agreed.

[5] Only his wife asked in doubt: "You can't even level the small hill Kuifu, how could you move Taihang and Wangwu mountains?

[6] Besides, where to place the stones?"

[7] They replied: "We can dump them in the Bohai sea and throw them in the north of the Yintu."

[8] Then the Fool together with his descendants, some of them carried the burden and then excavated the earth and stones, used dustpan to transport them to the Bohai sea.

[9] The wise man lived in Hequ laughted at them and tried to stop them: "How stupid you are!

[10] With your remaining years and weak body, you can't even remove a piece of the mountain, how can you deal with the earth and stone?"

[11] The Mountain soul with snakes heard of it, fearing of his constant digging, he told it to the God.

[12] God was moved by his sincerity, ordered two sons of Kua to move the mountains to the east of the Shuo and south of Yong.

学习者译文 14:

[1] The Mountain Removed by the Old Foolish Man-You Gong.

[2] A 90-year-old foolish man of the north mountain, Yu Gong, who lived facing the mountain.

[3] Fretting about the obstruction of the north mountain that made them detour, Yu Gong gathered his family members for solving it. He said, if I suggest that all of us to work hard together for razing the moutain to the ground from the south of Henan to the north bank of the Yellow River with you. Do you agree with me?

[4] Most of them agreed with him.

[5] However, his wife questioned the idea that, "You might not raze the mound to the ground with your weak power, could you really raze the

Taihang Mountain and Wang wu Mountain to the ground?

[6] Additionally, where do you put the rock and soil?

[7] Some people of them said that, "we can throw them into Bohai sea or the north of the state of Bo-Yin Tu."

[8] Later, Yu Gong, with the help of his son and grandson who can do heavy work, drilled rock, dug earth, and moved the rock and soil into the edge of Bohai sea by dustpan.

[9] An old wise man laughs and exhorts him, "You are so unwise!

[10] Even if you spare no effort to remove it in your whole life, you may neither move a part of the mountain, nor the whole mountain.

[11] The mountain god with snakes in his hands feared that he would stick to removing the mountain, so reported it to the emperor.

[12] The emperor was touched by his relentless spirit. Therefore, he commanded two sons of Kua'ershi, Hercules, to help them. One was placed in the east of Shuo and the other in the south of Yongzhou.

学习者译文 15：

[1] The Foolish Old Man Yugong Removes the Mountain.

[2] Yugong, who was nearly 90 years old, lived at the north of the mountains, and the mountains just in front of his house.

[3] Yugong was unhappy about the fact that the north of mountains blocked their way, and it took extra miles to take detour to another side of the mountains. Therefore, one day Yugong called all his family to discuss: "Can we work together to move the mountains, so that the road can go all the way to the south of Yuzhou and reach the southern bank of the Han River.

[4] Most of his families agreed with him.

[5] His wife doubted: "An old man like you cannot even remove a small hill like Kuifu. How can you remove the two high mountains Taihang and Wangwu?

[6] Even if you can, where can you throw so much earth and stones?

[7] His families said："We can throw the earth and stones to the edge of the Bohai Sea，north of Yintu.

[8] So Yugong led three of his children and grandchildren who could carry a load to the mountain，cut rocks and dug earth，and carried it to the edge of the Bohai Sea with a dustpan.

[9] Zhisou，a wise old man who lived on the edge of a winding river，saw them working an tried to stop them，laughing："You are so unwise!

[10] "With your strength in the remaining years，you can't even remove a small part of the mountain. What can you do with earth and stones?"

[11] The mountain god was frightened after hearing his story an reported to the emperor of heaven.

[12] Moved by Yugong's sincere，the emperor of heaven ordered the two sons of the god of great strength Kua'eshi to carry away the two mountains，one to the east of Shuo Fang and one to the south of Yong Zhou.

学习者译文 16：

[1] The Foolish Old Man Who Removed the Mountains

[2] North of these mountains lived an old man of nearly ninety，who was called the Fool and faced mountains.

[3] He found it is inconvenient to have to make a detour each time he went out and came back；so one day he summoned his family to discuss the matter. "Suppose we work together to level the mountains?"he suggested. "Then we can open a road southward to the bank of the Han River."

[4] To this they almost all agreed.

[5] Only his wife was dubious. "You haven't the strength to level even a small hill," she objected. "How can you move these two mountains?

[6] Besides，where will you dump all the mud and rocks?"

[7] "We'll dump them in the the end of the Bohai Sea，it's somewhere to the north" was the reply.

[8] Then the Fool set out with his son and grandson，the three of them carrying

poles. They dug up stones and earth, and carried them in baskets to the sea.

[9] A man living at the river bend, who was called the Wise Man, laughed at their efforts and did his best to stop them. "Enough of this folly!"

[10] "How stupid this is! Old and weak as you are, you even won't be able to remove even a fraction of the mountains. How can you dispose of so much earth and stones?"

[11] The gods who ruled heaven and earth heard the story of them. Fear that the spirit is willing but the flesh is weak. He warned the Jade Emperor in heaven about it.

[12] The Jade Emperor was moved by his perseverance and then ordered another gods to come down and take the two high mountains away which one to the east and one to the south.

学习者译文 17：

[1] Yu Gong moved the mountain

[2] There was a Yu Gong in the north of the mountains, who was nearly 90 years old and lived directly opposite the two mountains.

[3] Yu Gong suffered from the obstruction of the road in the north of the mountain. He had to go around the long way when he went out and came in. Summon the whole family to discuss and say, "I'll try my best to dig down two mountains with you to make it all the way to the south of Yuzhou and the South Bank of Han River, okay?"

[4] Almost everyone agreed.

[5] His wife asked, "with your strength, you can't cut down the hills like Kui Fu. What can you do to Taihang and Wangwu? Besides.

[6] Where can you put the earth and rock?"

[7] Everyone said one after another: "We can throw the earth and rock to the edge of the Bohai Sea, to the north of the hidden soil."

[8] So Yu Gong took three of his sons and grandchildren who could carry the burden, chiseled stones, dug soil, and transported them to the edge of the Bohai Sea with dustpans.

[9] The wise old man on the bend laughed at Yu Gong and stopped him from doing it, saying, "you are really stupid!

[10] With your remaining years and strength, you can't even move a grass on the mountain. What can you do with the earth and rock?"

[11] The mountain god with a snake in his hand heard about it and was afraid that he would keep doing it, so he reported it to the emperor of heaven.

[12] Moved by Yu Gong's sincerity, the emperor of heaven ordered the two sons of the Hercules Kwae to carry away the two mountains, one in the east of Shuofang and the other in the south of Yongzhou.

学习者译文 18：

[1] the foodlish old man move the mountains

[2] the foolish old man who live in the North mountain is ninety years old and his house faced the mountain.

[3] punishing hill north of the plug, and the winding road. Together in the room and consulted: you and I will do our best to clear the decks, make the road to the south of Henan and the north of the Yellow River.

[4] All of people agreed the things.

[5] His wife questioningly said: "By virtue of your strength, you can't cut down the hill like Kuifu, but what about Taihang and Wangwu?

[6] and how to settle down the soil and stones.

[7] one people said: "To place it to the end of the Bohai Sea, and the north of the Hidden soil.

[8] Then he led the descendants who can carry three loads to chiseling stones and reclaim the soil, and use the dustpan to transit to the end of the Bohai.

[9] Zhi Sou in Hequ stopped the foolish old man with a smile and said: "You are not smart."

[10] Rely on the residual force, you had not destroyed one part of the mountains, much less earth and stone.

[11] Hold the snake god smell it, fear its unceasingly also, tell it to the emperor.

[12] Emperor sense its sincere, kua moth life two sons negative two mountains, a cuo Shuo East, a cuo Yongnan.

学习者译文 19:

[1] The Foolish Man-Yugong Removes the Mountain

[2] Just north to the mountain there lived an old man called Yu Gong, who was nearly ninety years old.

[3] lived just in front of two mountains made them hard to get out. Therefore, they gather together and talked about: "Let us work together to dig the two mountains flat, so we can access easily. Is it ok?"

[4] Almost everyone was agree with him.

[5] However, his wife said doubtfully: "You could not move the small mountain like Kui Fu with your strengthen, how could you deal with the great mountains Tai Xing and Wang Wu?"

[6] And where are you going to throw these excavated earth and stones?'

[7] Somebody: "Throw them away to the side of Bohai Sea and the north of the Yin Tu Plain."

[8] So Yu Gong lead his children began to dig the mountain. Then they carried the earth and stones to the Bo Hai Sea with dustpan.

[9] An old man called Zhi Sou laughed at Yu Gong did and tried to prevent him from moving the mountains: "It is too inadvisable to move this mountain.

[10] With your weak and old body, you even could not remove a piece of the mountain. How could you remove the two high mountains?"

[11] The mountain deity who hold a snake was afraid that Yugong wouldn't give up digging the mountains when he heard Yugong's story. So he reported this to the Emperor of Heaven.

[12] The Emperor of Heaven was greatly touched when hearing Yugong's story. He commanded the sons of Er Shi-hercule to take away the two mountains, putting one to the east of Shuofang and another to the south of Yongzhou.

学习者译文 20：

[1] Yu Gong wanted to move two mountains

[2] At the foot of the mountain in the north, there was a man named Yu Gong, who was nearly 90 years old and lived directly opposite the two mountains.

[3] Because the road on the north side of the mountain was blocked, he had to take a long detour to get in and out. So Yu Gong call a family meeting to discuss: "Let our whole family exert efforts to move away these two mountains, and build a road leading to the south of Henan Province and the south Bank of Han River. How about it?"

[4] Almost everyone was in favor.

[5] His wife questioned, "With your strength, you can't cut down a hill like Kuifu, but what can you do with Taihang and Wangwu?

[6] And where can you put all the earth and stones?"

[7] Everybody said: "We can carry the stones and earth of the mountains to the around of Bohai Sea and the north of Yintu."

[8] And then Yu Gong took three of his sons and grandchildren who could pick the burden chiseled tones, dug soil, and transported them to the around of the Bohai Sea.

[9] The Wise Old Man in the river laughed at Yu Gong and stopped him: "You are too stupid!

[10] With whatever remains of your waning strength, you won't be able to remove even a corner of the mountain. What can you do with the earth and stones?"

[11] When the guardian gods heard the story of Yu Gong, they were struck with fear and reported the incident to the Emperor of Heavens.

[12] Filled with admiration for Yu Gong, the Emperor of Heavens oreded two mighty gods to carry the two mountains away. One in the east of Shanxi Province and one in the south of Yongzhou.

学习者译文 21：

［1］The Foolish Old Man Remove the Mountains

［2］The Foolish Old Man of the North Mountain, nearly ninety years of age, lived behind these mounta

［3］He gathered his family together and discussed with them we will do our best to eradicate the steep mountains. Can we reach the south of Yuzhou and the south bank of the Han River?

［4］There was a chorus of approval.

［5］His wife asked, "With your strength, you can't even level the hill of Father Kai, but what can you do with Taihang and Wangwu.

［6］Besides, where can I put the earth and Stones."

［7］Everyone said, "throw them to the edge of bohai Sea, north of Yintu.

［8］So he led his sons and grandchildren, who could carry the burden, to chisel stones, dig up the earth and carry it with a dustpan to the edge of the Bohai Sea.

［9］The wise Old Man at the River Bend stopped the old man. He laughed and said, "How unwise you are!"

［10］At your age, old and feeble as you are, you can't remove one hair on the mountain, let alone so much earth and so many rocks!"

［11］When the mountain god heard of Yu Gong's removal of the mountain, fearing that he would not stop digging, he reported the matter to the emperor of Heaven.

［12］Moved by the old man's determination, the Heavenly God ordered the two sons of Kua'ershi to carry the two mountains on their backs and put one east of Shuo and the other south of Yong.

学习者译文 22：

［1］The Foolish Old Man Who Removed the Mountains

［2］North of these mountains lived an old man of nearly ninety, who was called the Fool.

[3] His house faced these mountains, and he found it very inconvenient to get out and come back; so one day he gathered his family to discuss the matter. "Suppose we work together to move the mountains?" he suggested. "Then we can open a road to the south of Yuzhou, and to the south bank of the Han River."

[4] They all agreed to this suggestion.

[5] His wife put forward doubt to say: "with your strength, we could not damage the small hills like Kuifu. How can you move these two mountains?"

[6] Besides, where will you dump all the earth and rocks?"

[7] People have replied: "throw it to the edge of the Bohai sea, north of Yintu."

[8] Then the Foolish Old man set out with his son and grandson, the three of them carrying poles. They dug up stones and earth, and carried them in baskets to the sea.

[9] A man living at the river bend, who was called the Wise Man, laughed at their efforts and did his best to stop them. "Enough of this folly!" he cried. "How stupid this is!

[10] Old and weak as you are, you won't be able to remove even a fraction of the mountains. How can you dispose of so much earth and stones?"

[11] The god, who was holding the snack, heard about this matter, afraid of his endless digging down to the emperor of heaven, report.

[12] The emperor of heaven was moved by the sincere of the Foolish Old man, ordered Hercules's two sons went back the two mountain, a place in the North East, a seat placed in the south of Yong Zhou.

学习者译文 23:

[1] Mr. Fool Wants to Move the Mountain

[2] Just to the north of the mountains lived an old man called Mr. Fool who was nearly 90 years old.

[3] With the two high mountains just in front of his house, his family and he had to walk a long way around the mountains whenever they had something to do on the other side of the mountains.

[4] People all agreed with his plan.

[5] His wife said, "An old man like you cannot even move a small hill, not to mention the two high mountains.

[6] Even if you can, where can you throw so much earth and stone?"

[7] "The Bohai Sea is big enough to contain all the earth and stone," said the people.

[8] So it was decided. His children started to dig the mountains, led by the old man Mr. Fool.

[9] A man named Smart saw them working and tried to stop them, saying, "You are so silly!

[10] You're so old and weak that you can't even take away the grass and trees. How can you move the high mountains?"

[11] The god of mountains heard of his story and was afraid of his determinations, reporting his doings to the Jade Emperor.

[12] Later the Jade Emperor, upon learning of Mr. Fool's story, was greatly moved. He then ordered another god to come down and take the two high mountains away.

学习者译文 24：

[1] Yu Gong Moves Away the Mountains

[2] There is a people named Yugong on the North mountain, he is almost ninty years old, living in front of the mountain.

[3] These two mountains block the doorway of our house. It is very inconvenient for us to come and go. So he calls his family to discuss about it. "Let our whole family exert efforts to move away these two mountains, to make the path can go through Yunan and reached Hanyin. How about it?"

[4] They were all agree about it.

[5] His wife doubted: "you cannot move the small mount like kuifu, how can you handle with Taixing and Wangwu?

[6] And where will you to put those soil and rocket moved form the mountain?"

[7] Everybody said: "we can put rockets to the end of Bohai, to transport soil to the north side."

[8] And he go with his grandchildren, there are three people who carry the burden, knock off the rocket from the mountain and dig soil, use dustpan to transpoart it to the end of Bohai.

[9] There is a people called Heso who livw in the corner of a river, laughing and stoping their actions, said, "This is too much, all of you arae so stupid to move those mountain."

[10] With a merely energy of rest of your life, cannot even touch the mount a little bit, and how can you do to deal with rocks and soil?"

[11] The fairy who manipulated snake was so afriad after heard about it that she present it to the god.

[12] The god was touched by the resilisence of Yugong, and called the Ershi's two sons to bear the two mountains, one was placed in the Soudong, the another one was placed in Yongnan.

学习者译文 25：

[1] Yugong (means foolish old man) moving mountains

[2] There is a man named Yugong under the north mountain. He is nearly 90 years old and lives facing the mountain.

[3] He was suffered from the obstruction in the north of the mountain, it's inconvenient to pass through. So he gathered his whole family to discuss and said, "I'll try my best to eradicate the mountains with you, make the road lead to the south of Yuzhou and the south of Han River, okay?"

[4] Almost everyone agreed.

[5] But his wife said in doubt, "With your strength, even the Mt. Kuifu

can't be leveled. What about the Mt. Taihang and the Mt. Wangwu?

[6] Besides, where can you excavated soil and stone be placed?"

[7] Someone answered, "These can be thrown away the Bohai Sea, north of the Yintu."

[8] So Yugong led three of his children and grandchildren who could carry the burden, knocking stones, dugging soil, and transporting them to the Bohai Sea with dustpan.

[9] A wise old man by the river laughed at him and stopped him, "you are really stupid!

[10] With the rest of your time and strength, even if you can't pull up a grass on the mountain, what can you do with the soil and stones?"

[11] A mountain god with a snake in his hand heard about it and was afraid that he would keep doing it, so he reported it to the Tiandi (equivalent to the Christian "God")

[12] Moved by Yugong's sincerity, the Tiandi ordered the two sons of the Hercules kwae to carry away the two mountains, one in the east of Shuofang and the other in the south of Yongzhou.

学习者译文 26:

[1] How Yukong Moved The Mountains

[2] Yukong who lived in the north mountain was about 90.

[3] The obstruction in the northern part of the mountains made them inconvenient to communicate with the outside world. So he gathered his family and discussed with them, "Shall we move the steep mountains and create a road which directly leads to the southern part of Yuzhou and the southern bank of the Han River?"

[4] They all agreed with him.

[5] His wife asked, "you can't even lift this hill named Father Kui, what can you do with Taihang mountain and the mountain of Wangwu?

[6] Where do you put the stones which were digged.

[7] People all said, we can throw them into the sea.

[8] Thus, Yu Gong and his family began to dig the mountain and transferred the stones into the sea.

[9] There was an old man named Zhi Sou, living in Hequ. When he saw what Yu Gong and his family were doing, he couldn't help laughing at them and said you are so stupid!

[10] Yu Gong-you are too old to move the mountain.

[11] The fairy, who held a snake in his hand, heard of this and reported it to the emperor of Heaven in case that Yu Gong would not stop moving the mountain.

[12] Moved by Yu Gong's sincerity, the emperor of Heaven ordered the two sons of Kua'eshi-Titan to move away the two mountains, one mountain was placed to the east of Shuofang and the other was to the south of Yongzhou.

学习者译文 27：

[1] Yu Gong removes the mountain

[2] North of the mountains lived an old man called Yu Gong who was nearly 90 years old and habitat face to the mountains.

[3] Yu Gong is tiresome of the long and hard routine to go out because of the block of the north mountain. He call his family together and said, we try our best to dig the mountains to be flat, which can through the South Henan and reach the south bank of the Han River. Is it OK?

[4] None people have dissenting voice.

[5] His wife questioned, however, "You are too weak to undermine hillock, and how do you deal with Taihang, wangwu mountains?

[6] and where can we put the earth stone?"

[7] They said, "We can throw it on the side of the bohai sea, hidden to the north of soil."

[8] So he lead grandsons three people who can shoulder heavy things, gouging stone, digging soil, using Chinese dustpan in the side of bohai Sea.

[9] The wise old man in the river bend stopped him and laughed, "You are so

unwise!
[10] You are so old now that you can't destroy any parts of the mountains, and how can you deal with these earth stone stuff?"
[11] Mountain God who holds snake was so scared of him that he would do it endless when he heard that, and told it to the Emperor of Heaven.
[12] The Emperor was touched by his perseverance, appoint Kuae'shi two sons back the mountains, puting one in the east of Shuofang, another in the soth of Yongzhou.

学习者译文 28：

[1] The Foolish Old Man Who Removed the Mountains
[2] The foolish old man of the North Mountain was nearly 90 years old, and lived facing the mountain.
[3] The family of the foolish old man got together to plan because the mountain impeded the inlet and outlet, "Could we spare all our efforts to even out the mountain so that we could go straight to the south of Yuzhou and the south side of Hanshui?"
[4] Most of the families agreed with it.
[5] The wife of the old man queried "You couldn't even out the small hill of Kuifu. Not to say the great mountains of Taixing and Wangwu.
[6] Moreover, where could you lay the earth and stone?"
[7] Other families answered together, "Put them on the shore of Bohai Sea and the north of Yintu.
[8] Then, the old man selected three people who could use the shoulder pole from their family and led them to cut stones and dig the earth and delivered them with dustpans to the shore of Bohai Sea.
[9] The clever old man of the river bend laughed at and prevented the foolish old man, "You are so stupid!
[10] you couldn't ruin the grass of the mountain not to speak the earth and stone just with your old and weak body in your remaining years."
[11] The god of mountains who handed with snakes was so afraid that the full

old man wouldn't stop that he reported to God.

[12] God was moved by the sincerity of the full old man, and oredered two children of Kua'eshi-Titan to remove the two mountains to the east of Shuofang and the south of Yongzhou.

学习者译文 29：

[1] Yugong moved mountains

[2] In the north of the mountain, there lived an old man named Yugong, who is ninety years old.

[3] For the mountain blocks the way to the north, it is troublesome to go out of the mountain. He gathers his family and discusses："What about you and me work together, get rid of the mountain, pave a road to south of yuzhou and the south of Han river. Is that alright?"

[4] Almost everyone shows their agreements.

[5] His wife proposed a question："Only by your strength, you can not even move the Kui fu hill, not to mention the Mountain Taihang and Wangwu."

[6] And how do we deal with the rocks and soil?

[7] Someone suggests："we can throw them on the edge of the Bohai Ocean."

[8] Then Yugong leads his children, and three of them can burden the heavy. So they begin digging the stone and the soil, and using dustpan to remove them to the edge of Bohai Ocean.

[9] An old man who lives in Hequ named Zhisou laughs at him："Unbelievable, you are so unwise."

[10] "By your strength, you can not even destroy a tree on the mountain, not to mention the rocks and the soil."

[11] The God with snake heard about it, afraid that they won't stop, and convey the information to the God.

[12] God is moved by Yugong's determination, orders two sons of Kuaershi to remove the mountain. One in to the east and the other one to the south.

学习者译文 30：

[1] Mr. Fool Wants to Move the Mountain

[2] The northern mountain has a foolish old man who age is 90 and lived directly opposite the mountain.

[3] He suffered from the blockage in the northern part of the mountains and had to make detours to get in and out. So he called his family together and discussed with them, "Shall i dig as far as we can to level the steep mountain so that the road will reach the southern part of Henan and the southern bank of the Han River?"

[4] Most of the family agrees.

[5] His wife asked, "With your strength, you can't even level the hill of Father Kui. What can you do with Taihang and King's House?

[6] Where to put the earth and stones?

[7] The people said, "Throw it to the edge of the Bohai Sea, north of Yintu."

[8] As a result, the foolish old man led three people who could bear the burden of his sons and grandsons on the mountains, gouging stones and digging soil, and bring to the Bohai Sea.

[9] A wise old man on the river laughed at the foolish old man and stopped him from doing so, saying: "You are stupid! You are too stupid!"

[10] With your remaining years and strength, you can't even move a single grass on the mountain. What can you do with the earth and stones.

[11] The mountain god who was holding the snake heard of this and reported it to the emperor of Heaven for fear that the snake would dig forever.

[12] Moved by the foolish old man's sincerity, the emperor of Heaven ordered the two sons of Kua e, the god of Hercules, to carry away the two mountains, placing one in the east of Shuo Fang and the other in the south of Yongzhou.

学习者译文 31：

[1] How Mr. Fool removed the mountain.

[2] There is a man of nearly 90 called Mr. Fool living in the North Mountain, whose residence was obstructed by Mountain Taihang and Wuxing.

[3] Being palgued by more devious and larboursome route resulted from the two great mountains for ages, hence, Mr. Fool assembled his family and said: what about exerting ourselves and sparing no effort to gouge out the mountains whereby a path will make it accessible to go straight to the south bank of River Han, southern Yuzhou.

[4] Some of his family approved of his thought.

[5] "There is nothing you can do even in the face of small hills like Kui, so what can you do with these two great mountains?" his wife asked,

[6] "let alone mention where to place the rubbles."

[7] While others answered, "we can cast them into the Bohai sea or dump them in the north of Yitu."

[8] Then he chose three strong men out of his descendents, began to excavate the mountains and transported the rubbles and dirts to the Bohai Sea with dustpans.

[9] Hequ, a wise old man, laughed at him, "You're not wise for doing this." trying to prevent.

[10] "I don't think you can even remove a blade of grass, not to mention the massive stones and earth in your wreckage years."

[11] The god of Caoshe, a mountain god who grabs a snake, was afraid that Yugong will stick to this and reported it to the Emperor of Heaven.

[12] The Emperor of Heaven was impressed by the persistence and determination of Yugong and ordered the two sons of the Hercules Kua'e clan to carry away the two mountains, one to the east of Shuofang and the other to the south of Yongzhou.

学习者译文 32：

[1] How Yugong Removed Away Two High Mountains (Yugong means an unwise man in Chinese culture)

[2] In the North Mountain where Yugong, whose age approaches ninety, lived is in the central area of two opposite mountains.

[3] Road to the north was blocked by the mountain, Mr. fool and his family had to trek a long way in and out. With dissatisfaction to this, Yugong gathered families and discussed that, "How about digging as far as we can to remove the two mountains so as we can reach the south of Yuzhou and the Han River directly?

[4] Most of them agreed.

[5] His wife doubted, "you can't even damage the Mount Kuifu, not even saying to remove mount Taihang and mount Wangwu, How likely if you can't achieve this?

[6] And where the earth and stone should we place?"

[7] His families said in succession: "we can put them into the mouth of Bohai Sea, north to the Yinshi. (Yinshi is a place located in the mouth of Baha'i Sea.)

[8] Thus, with three powerful of his sons and grandsons, Yugong led them bear on burdens on the mountains, gouge stones, dig up soil, and removed it to Bohai Sea.

[9] After seeing this, a wise old man in Hequ laughed and tried to prevent Yugong from removing, "what a unwise man you are!

[10] Upon your remaining years and strength, hardly can you take a piece of mountains, let lone removing soil and stones."

[11] The God who manipulates the snake heard it, being afraid of their continuous movements, told to the heavenly Gods. (The God manipulating the snake is Mountain God in Chinese culture.)

[12] Moved by Yugong's sincerity, the Heavenly God commanded the two sons of Kua'eshi, a god with great strength, to carry away the two

mountains on their backs: one was put east of Shuozhou and the other south of Yongzhou.

学习者译文 33:

[1] Yugong Removes the Mountains

[2] Yugong, living in the foot of the northern Taihang Mountain and Wangwu Mountain, was around 90 years old, facing the mountains.

[3] Owing to the block of mountains and detour of road, Yu's family was going to discuss the solution, "May we exert our utmost to remove the mountains, leading the road through the south of Henan province to the south bank of Hanjiang River?", said Yu.

[4] Many voices said that they agreed with him.

[5] While his wife questioned, "You can't make the Kuifu hill flat yourself. How about Taihang Mountain and Wangwu Mountain?

[6] Besides, where to put the rocks and stones?"

[7] Many voices said that, "We can throw them into the edge of Bohai River, the north of Yintu."

[8] Thus, the descendants with the ability to bear the burden kept carving and digging, using the dustpan to convey.

[9] Nearly bay was a wise old man, stopped him and said that, "You are unwise.

[10] You were even not able to damage a blade of grass with the rest of your strength as going senile. How about that?"

[11] Yugong's words were heard by the mountain god with snakes in his hand. He was afraid that Yugong and others would really level the two mountains, and reported the whole things to the Heavenly God.

[12] Moved by Yugong's determination, the Heavenly God ordered the two sons of Kua'ershi, Hercules to carry the two mountains on their backs and put one east of Shuo and the other south of Yong.

学习者译文 34：

[1] The determination to win victory and courage to surmount every difficulty

[2] North of these mountains lived an old man Yu Gong, who was nearly ninety.

[3] He was troubled by the blockage of the road to the north of the mountain, so he had to take a long way to get in and out. So one day he summoned his family to discuss the matter. "Would you like to work together with me to dig the mountains so as to reach the southern part of Yuzhou and the southern bank of the Hands River."

[4] Almost everyone agreed.

[5] His wife expressed her doubts that your were unable to cut down a hill like Knifu. What could you do with Taihang and Wangwu mountains?

[6] Besides, where could you put the earth and stones?

[7] Everyone said, "We could throw the earth and stones to the edge of the Bohai Sea and to the north of Yitu."

[8] Yu Gong then led three of his family who could bear the burder, gouging stones, digging soil and delivered them to the edge of the Bohai Sea by dustpan.

[9] A man living at the River bend, who was called the Wise Man, laughed at their efforts.

[10] "Enough of this folly!" he said, "How stupid this was! Old and weak as you are, you would not be able to remove even a fraction of the mountains. How could you dispose of so much earth and stones?"

[11] Holding the snake mountain heard about it, for sake he kept digging mountains forever, the Association reported on the matter.

[12] The emperor of the Heaven was touched by his sincerity, and then ordered Kua E's two sons to carry two moynuntai on their backs, one to the east of Shuo Fang and the other to the east of Yongzhou.

学习者译文 35：

[1] The foolish old man who removed the mountain

[2] At the age of nearly 90，Yukong lives in the North，facing the mountain.

[3] He was so confused by the blocked and circuitous mountain roads that he discussed with his family，"We need to try our best to eradicate steep mountains and make the road lead the south of Henan，up to Han River south bank，don't we?"

[4] Most of them gave their support.

[5] But his wife offered doubt and said，"You can't even damage the Kuifu mountain with your own power. So how to damage the Taixing and Wangwu Mountain?

[6] Needless to say，how to dispose the soil and stones excavated."

[7] Most people say，"Throw on the side of the Bohai Sea and the north of the hidden land."

[8] Then Yukong led three of his strong offsprings to the mountain，hitting on the stone，reclaiming the soil，and transporting them to the side of Bohai Sea.

[9] A old wise man standing on the river bend laughed and stopped them.

[10] "At your age，you maybe cannot remove a small part of the mountain，how to remove the soil and the whole mountain?"

[11] The person who takes the snake hearing this thing is afraid of his action and told it to the emperor.

[12] Moved by his sincerity，the God asked two sons of Hercules Quays to remove two mountains，one in the east of Shuofang and one in the south of Yongzhou.

学习者译文 36：

[1] The Foolish Old Man（Yugong）Who Moved the Mountains

[2] The foolish old man of the North Mountain was almost ninety years old who lived in front of the two huge mountains directly.

[3] He had to take a long detour whenever he went out because two mountains blocked the way. To get rid of the inconvenience, he gathered whole family and proposed to chip away two mountains so that they can reach Yunan (South Henan) and Hanyin (a county in Shaanxi).

[4] Most of them agreed.

[5] His wife questioned, "With your strength, you can't chip away a small hill like Kuifu, what can you do toward huge mountains like Taihang and Wangwu?

[6] Besides, where do you put the soil and stones from the mountains?"

[7] Some people said: "We can throw soil and stones to the edge of the Bohai Sea, and the north side of yintu (bozhou in the ancient time)."

[8] The foolish old man then lead his sons and grandsons who could pick up the burden, chiseled stones, dug up the dirt and transported them to the edge of the Bohai Sea with a straw.

[9] The wise old man at the River Bend stopped the old man. He laughed and said, "How unintelligent you are!"

[10] At your age, old and feeable as you are you can't destroy a piece of wood on the mountain, but what about the dirt and stones?

[11] The mountain god holding the snake heard about this incident, afraid that he would keep digging down and reporting the incident to the Heavenly Emperor.

[12] Moved by the old man's determination, the Heavenly God ordered the two sons of Kua! ershi to carry away two mountains and put one east of Shuo, the other south of Yong.

学习者译文 37：

[1] The Foolish Old Man (Yugong) who Removes the Mountains

[2] The Foolish Old Man (Yugong) of the North Mountain, experiencing nearly nine decades of life, lived behind the Taihang and Wangwu Mountains.

[3] Suffering from the fact that the mountains blocked people's way to the south and they had to walk around them whenever they went out or came back, so Yugong called the whole family together to talk about the issue. He said, "If I suggest that all of us work together to remove the two mountains, so as to open a way to places south of Yu Prefecture and the Han River?"

[4] Most members agreed to the idea.

[5] But his wife doubted, "You are too weak to remove a small hill like Kuifu, let alone the great mounatins of Taihang and Wangwu?

[6] Besides, where could you deal with the earth and rocks?"

[7] "Carry them to the shores of the Bohai Sea and north of Yintu," said other people.

[8] With the help of his sons and grandsons who could carry things, Yugong began to break rocks and dig earth, which they carried in baskets and dustbins to the shores of the Bohai Sea.

[9] The Wise Old Man at the River Bend stopped him and said, "How unwise you are!

[10] You are too old and feeble to remove a piece of the mountain, let alone so much earth and so many rocks!"

[11] Hearing Yugong words, the Mountain God was afraid that the man would really remove the two mountains, so he reported the whole thing to the Heavenly God.

[12] Moved by the Foolish Old Man's determination, the Heavenly God ordered the two sons of Kua'ershi, a mighty God like Hercules, to carry the two mountains on their backs and put one east of Shuo and the other south of Yong.

学习者译文 38：

[1] Mr. Fool Movies The Mountain

[2] North of the mountains lived an old man called the Fool. He was about ninety years old, and his house faced the mountains.

[3] He suffered from the traffic trouble in the mountain road, so he called together the whole family to look for a solution. "How about we do our best to clear the steep mountains and make the road from the south of Yuzhou to the south of Han river?"

[4] They all agreed.

[5] His wifi dubious and asked "Your strength can't level the hill Kui Fu let alone these teo mountains.

[6] Where will you dump all the earth and rocks?"

[7] "We will dump them in the Bohai Sea, the north of the Yintu." they replyed.

[8] So the fool set out with his sons and grandsons, threee of them carrying dustpan. They dug up stones and earth and carried them in baskets to the tail of the Bohai Sea.

[9] An old man living at the river bend called Wise man, laughed at the Fool, "How stupid it is!

[10] OLd and weak as you are, you can not even move a single grass on the mountain. How can you dispose of so much earth and stones?"

[11] The mountain god, who was holding the snake in his hand, heard of this, reported it to the emperoe of Heaven for fear that the Fool would not stop doing.

[12] Moved by the Fool's sincerity, the emperor of Heaven ordered the two sons of Kuaeshi-Titan, to carry away the two mountains. One to the east of Shoufang and the other to the south of Yongzhou.

学习者译文 39：

[1] The Foolish Old Man Yugong Who Removed the Mountains.

[2] On the north of the mountains lived an old man called Yugong who was nearly 90 years old.

[3] Suffering from the two mountains in front of his house, he and his family had to walk a long way around the mountains when they went out. Then he gathered the whole family, discussing the solution. He said: "Will

you and I try our best to remove the steep mountains, making the road to the south of Yuzhou and the south shore of the Han River?"

[4] Most of them agreed the proposal.

[5] But his wife asked: "You cannot even remove a small hill with your strength. What can you do with Taihang Mountain and Wangwu Mountain?"

[6] Even if you can, where can you put all the earth and stone from the mountains?"

[7] People said: "Throw them to the seaside of Bohai Sea and the north of Yin Tu."

[8] Therefore, he led three of his sons and grandsons, who could carry the burden, to climb up the mountain, removing earth and stone and carrying them with dustpan to the Bohai Sea.

[9] The Wise Old Man "How unwise you are!"

[10] "With your remaining years and strength, you cannot even remove a small part of the mountain. How can you remove the earth and stones?"

[11] God of mountains heard of Yugong's story and reported it to the emperor of heaven for fear that he would not stop removing the mountains.

[12] Moved by Yugong's sincerity, the emperor of heaven ordered the two sons of Kua'ershi, a mighty God like Hercules, to carry away the two mountains. One to the east of Shoufang and the other to the south of Yongzhou.

学习者译文 40：

[1] Yugong Removes the Mountains.

[2] Yugong is nearly 90 years old, living in the north of mountain.

[3] With the two high mountains in front of his house, they had to walk a long way around the mountains whenever they had something to do on the other side of the mountains. So one day, Yugong gethered his family to talk about how to remove the two mountains to other places and said: "I want to remove the two mountains so that the villagers can have a direct path to town."

[4] Many people agreed with him.

[5] "You don't have the strength to cut even a small mound,"muttered his wife. "How on earth do you suppose you can level Mount Taihang and Mount Wanwu?

[6] Even if you can, where can you place so much earth and stone?"

[7] Others answered, "the Bohai Sea is big enough to contain all the earth and stone."

[8] Then Yugong led his descendants, three of them took the burden, knocked on the stone to reclaim the soil, and transported it to the end of Bohai Sea.

[9] On the bank of the Yellow River dwelled an old man much respected for his wisdom. When he saw their back-breaking labour, he ridiculed Yugong saying, "You are unwise!

[10] You're so old and weak that you can't even take away the grass and trees. How can you move the large mountains?"

[11] Mountain god was frightened by it and reported to the supreme god of all gods, Jade Emperor.

[12] Jade Emperor was stick by his the determination, Jade Emperor order Kua Moth's two sons to take two mountains, one was moved to the east side and the other one was moved to the west side.

学习者译文 41：

[1] How the Fool Moved Mountains

[2] On the north side of the mountain lived a the foolish old man, who was 90 years old, with a mountain in front of his house.

[3] He suffers from the blockage in the northern part of the mountainous area, and he has to turn around in and out. He gathered his family to discuss, "Let's remove these two mountains together and let this place go directly to Henan and Hanyin, okay?"

[4] Everyone agreed in unison.

[5] His wife told him her doubts, "With your strength, even an ordinary mountain

can't be calmed down, how dare you say that the two mountains, Taixing and Wangwu, can be removed?"

[6] Besides, where do you put the excavated soil?

[7] They all said, "Throw them all into the Bohai Sea and the North of the Hidden Land."

[8] So with the descendants, three people carried the burden, knocked on the rocks and reclaimed the soil, and transported the dustpan at the end of the Bohai Sea.

[9] A wise old man smiled and stopped him and said, "You are too unwise.

[10] With the remaining strength of your age, you can't destroy a grass on the mountain, so how can you remove the soil and stones?"

[11] The god who can manipulate snakes heard about this, and was afraid that he would keep digging, and reported it to the Emperor of Heaven.

[12] The Emperor of Heaven was moved by his sincerity and ordered the two sons of Kua'e to carry two mountains on their backs, one in the east of Shuofang and the other in the south of Yongzhou.

学习者译文 42：

[1] Yu Gong Moves a Mountain

[2] Yu Gong was a ninety-year-old man who lives at the north and faces the mountain.

[3] It was difficult to pass through due to the mountains. So Yu Gong gathered his family and said:"Shall we try our best to remove the obstacles and construct a road that leads to South Henan and south bank of Han Shui?"

[4] Everyone was in favor of him except his wife.

[5] However, his wife doubted: "You could not flatten even a small mound and how could you move the Mount Taixin and Mount Wangwu.

[6] Besides, where will we set all the earth and rubblr?"

[7] "Throw them into the edge of Bohai sea and the north of Bozhou."

[8] He, immediately started to break up rocks and carried them to Bohai by dustpan with his son and grandson.

[9] A wise old man, who lived on the bank of the Yellow River ridiculed Yu Gong and said: "You are so foolish.

[10] You are too old to remove even a wood in the mountain, let alone earth and rock."

[11] After the mountain deity with snake in hand hearing this movement, he was fearful and told the Jade Emperor.

[12] The emperor was moved by Yu Gong's sincerity. Then he asked.

学习者译文 43：

[1] Yu Gong Moves Away the Mountains?

[2] In the north of mountain, there was a man called Yu Gong (literally "Foolish Old Man"), who is nearly 90-year-old, facing the mountain to live.

[3] Suffering from the blockage in the northern part of the mountain area, he had to make a detour when he came out and went in, so he gathered the whole family to discuss and said, "I will try my best to eradicate the steep mountains with you, so that the road will lead to the southern part of Yuzhou and reach the south bank of Hanshui River, what do you think?"

[4] Everyone agreed.

[5] His wife questioned, "You can not even flatten the hill of Kuiu only resort to your strength, how can you move the mountains of Taihang and Wang-wu?

[6] and where are the dug soil and stone placed?"

[7] The other family members said, "Throw it to the edge of Bohai Sea, hide the soil in the north."

[8] Then Yu Gong led three of his children and grandchildren who could carry the burden up the mountain, chiseled Stone, dug the earth, and transported it to the edge of Bohai Sea with a dustpan.

[9] Zhi Sou (literally "Wise Old Man") who lived beside the river band laughed at Yu Gong and stopped him from doing this, said, "You are really foolish!

[10] With you remaining years of life and little power, you can't even move a grass away on the mountain. What can you do with dirt and stone?"

[11] The mountain god, who was holding the snake in his hand, heard about it and was afraid that he would keep doing it, so he reported it to the Jade Emperor from heaven.

[12] Moved by Yugong's determination, the Jade Emperor from heaven ordered the two sons to carry away the two mountains, one on the east side of the north and the other on the south side of Yongzhou.

学习者译文 44:

[1] Yugong moves mountains.

[2] There is an old man called Yugong, almost 90 years old and living by the mountain.

[3] Suffered from the remote location, there are two high mountains just in front of the door. Yugong and his family had to walk a long way around the mountain whenever they went out. One day, they gathered together to talk about how to remove these two mountains and make their way straightly toward the south of Yu and Hanyin. Considered if it is possible.

[4] All the family members are in compatible with him.

[5] Yu's wife asked: "By force of your own power, you are unable to remove the mount of KUIFU, not to mention both the mount of TAIXING and WANGWU?"

[6] Besides, where did you find the place for sand and stones?

[7] People says: "Put them into shore of Bohai Sea, or the north of Yintu."

[8] Then, Yugong leads three of his children who can shoulder the load and go to the mountain. They digged up the rock, the earth, packed them up and send it to the shore of Bohai Sea.

[9] An wise old man stay by the riverside and sneered at the Yugong said: "What a fool man!"

[10] In the rest of you life, it's impossible for you to remove all the plants, let alone the mountains."

[11] The god of mountain who hold the snakes was so afraid of him and told everything to the emperor.

[12] Later, the god was moved by Yugong's spirit, to order another two gods come down the heaven and take two mountains away. One is moved to the east, the other is towards the south.

学习者译文 45：

[1] YuGong who moved the mountain.

[2] There is a man named Yugong under the north mountain. He is nearly 90 years old and lives facing the mountain.

[3] Suffering from the obstruction in the north of the mountain area, he had to take a detour when he came out and went in, so he gathered the whole family to discuss and said, "I'll try my best to eradicate the steep mountains with you and make the road lead to the south of Yuzhou and the south bank of Han River, okay?"

[4] Everyone agreed.

[5] His wife asked, "with your strength, even the hill of Kui Fu can't be leveled. What can you do to Taihang and the king's house? Besides, where are the excavated soil and stones?"

[6] They said, "throw it to the edge of the Bohai Sea, to the north of Yintu."

[7] They said, "throw it to the edge of the Bohai Sea, to the north of Yintu."

[8] So Yugong led three of his children and grandchildren who could carry the burden up the mountain, chiseled stones, dug earth, and transported them to the Bohai Sea with dustpan.

[9] The wise old man on the bend of the river laughed at Yu Gong and stopped him from doing it. He said, "you are really stupid!

[10] With your remaining years and strength, you can't even move a grass on the mountain. What can you do with the earth and stone?"

[11] The mountain god with a snake in his hand heard about it and was afraid that he would keep doing it, so he reported it to the emperor of heaven.

[12] Moved by Yugong's sincerity, the emperor of heaven ordered the two sons of the Hercules kwae to carry away the two mountains, one in the east of Shuofang and the other in the south of Yongzhou.